Ecological Key

Editors
E. Christopher Mare
and
Max Lindegger

Designing Ecological Habitats

creating a sense
of place

D1710207

Permanent Publications

GE
196
.D47
2011

Published by
Permanent Publications
Hyden House Ltd
The Sustainability Centre
East Meon
Hampshire GU32 1HR
United Kingdom
Tel: 01730 823 311
Fax: 01730 823 322
Overseas: (international code +44 - 1730)
info@permanentpublications.co.uk
www.permanentpublications.co.uk

Distributed in the USA by
Chelsea Green Publishing Company
PO Box 428, White River Junction, VT 05001
www.chelseagreen.com

First edition © 2011 Gaia Education, reprinted 2013

Edited by E. Christopher Mare and Max Lindegger

Designed by Two Plus George Limited, www.TwoPlusGeorge.co.uk

Printed in the UK by
CPI Antony Rowe, Chippenham, Wiltshire

Printed on paper from mixed sources certified by the
Forest Stewardship Council

The Forest Stewardship Council (FSC) is a non-profit international
organisation established to promote the responsible management of
the world's forests. Products carrying the FSC label are independently
certified to assure consumers that they come from forests that are
managed to meet the social, economic and ecological needs of
present and future generations.

British Library Cataloguing-in-Publication Data
A catalogue record for this book is available from the British Library

ISBN 978 1 85623 061 2

Contents

Introduction

1 Green Building

2 Local Food

3 Appropriate Technology – Energy & Infrastructure

4 Restoring Nature

5 Integrated Ecological Design

The Editors

In the midst of a spiritual awakening, E. Christopher Mare discovered a Permaculture Design Course in 1993 and has been a full time student ever since. A self-designed B.A. was the world's first effort at organizing the emerging discipline of Ecovillage Design into a formal degree. Two Master's degrees later, he is currently preparing for his doctoral dissertation through Fielding Graduate University in Santa Barbara. Mare was selected to be the Curriculum Coordinator during the production of the EDE curriculum and later went on to edit the GEDS curriculum offered through UOC Barcelona. During four appearances at the EDE Wongsanit, Mare introduced the Design Studio format as the climax of the course; and during the EDE Albuquerque, the Design Studio was applied to urban retrofit. A big highlight of this career was being funded by Gaia Trust to participate in residency at the 2008 Oxford Round Table. In 2002, Mare set up an educational non-profit – Village Design Institute – which will one day secure a land base for the establishment of 1) a research, training, and demonstration site; 2) an Academy of Village Design; and 3) a community of contemplative scholars. This project most likely will be called an 'ecovillage.'

Max O. Lindegger is a respected and sought-after teacher in the disciplines of sustainable systems. His dynamic teaching style is born of 30 years of hands-on experience and leadership in the design and implementation of practical, workable solutions to the challenges of sustainability. The value of this knowledge-from-experience is recognised in frequent invitations to present lectures at international symposia and conferences on themes such as Environment, Ecology, Sustainability, Permaculture and Ecovillage Design. Max has taught Ecovillage Design and Permaculture courses in over 24 countries. He was the creator, and for many years a Director, of the Oceania/Asia secretariat of the Global Ecovillage Network, and continues to participate in and contribute to the international flow of current thinking and best practice in the fields of sustainable systems design and education. As a designer, Max was a primary partner in the design and development of the Habitat Award winning Crystal Waters Permaculture village, Queensland. He has designed and consulted on numerous community developments including the Spiers Project (S. Africa), Gqnubie Green (S. Africa), Living & Learning Centre (Sri Lanka), Vatukarasa Village (Fiji), and Garopaba Project (Brazil) Malt Farm (Australia).

Foreword

The UN Decade of Education for Sustainable Development (DESD, 2005-2014), for which UNESCO is the lead agency, has moved into its second half and continues to seek to integrate the principles, values and practices of sustainable development into all aspects of education and learning. The DESD, as a global educational movement and effort, has been encouraging changes in behaviour worldwide to create a more sustainable future in terms of environmental integrity, economic viability, cultural diversity and a more just society for present and future generations.

Designing Ecological Habitats – Creating a Sense of Place is an important and eloquent exploration of humanity's limits to growth and addresses the problems arising from climate change, habitat destruction, population growth and resource depletion. This is not a book of theoretical ideas but an anthology of solutions, of experience, tried and tested, from experts all over the world. The designs and practices included in this book present a vision for the future, already tested out in ecovillages, sustainable communities and projects in many countries. These are practical low carbon solutions which provide significant improvements in the quality of life.

By understanding the process of creating integrated ecological designs, we also make explicit the process of creating integrated social and economic systems. We reconnect with the true meaning of ecology that comes from the Greek word *oikos*, meaning 'home' or 'a place to live'. Humanity's greatest challenge is to ensure that planet Earth can support human life far into future centuries by not only by adapting to climate change but also by mitigating it. We must start to do this at home and in our personal lives, our communities, our bio-regions, our nations and ultimately on our planet. *Designing Ecological Habitats* offers us human-scale solutions to do just this.

The DESD Secretariat at UNESCO is thus pleased to be partnering with Gaia Education in launching the 4 Keys for Sustainability Book series and in particular the Ecological Key: *Designing Ecological Habitats – Creating a Sense of Place*. The 4 Keys are reference books for anyone seeking solutions to the complexly interwoven, transdisciplinary issues pertaining to the transition to low carbon societies.

The DESD concerns all stakeholders, who can contribute to the success of the Decade and be agents of change at their own level, in their own communities and nations. Gaia Education is actively engaged in actions in support of the DESD in 23 countries in different stages of development, in both urban and rural settings. UNESCO is committed to continue mobilizing stakeholders around ESD and to lead the global movement to a successful completion of the Decade. It sees the 4 Keys as a meaningful contribution to the wide range of books and publications generated within the framework of the Decade.

MARK RICHMOND
Director, Division of Education for Peace and Sustainable Development
UNESCO Education Sector

Welcome!

Welcome to the Ecological Key of the Ecovillage Design Education! The Ecovillage Design Education (EDE) is a four-week introductory course to the complexities of Ecovillage Design brought to you by the international consortium of educators at Gaia Education. The course has been implemented on six continents since its introduction in 2005 and has introduced hundreds of enthusiasts, from many different cultural backgrounds, to this vital way of perceiving and conceiving the emerging theme of sustainable community design.

The Ecological Key is intended to be used as a textbook to accompany the course – or may be utilized as a valuable resource in its own right. Early conceptions of Ecovillage Design tended to regard ecological concerns as the overriding essence of sustainable community. The EDE, however, situates the 'Ecological' as just one of four dimensions to consider equally in any comprehensive Ecovillage Design scenario – the other dimensions being Social, Economic, and Worldview. Each of these other dimensions has a textbook Key of its own, so serious students may wish to get the whole series to stay fully informed.

The Ecological Key itself is a 'whole systems design' of a nested holarchy of comprehension required for the ecological dimension of ecovillage designing. It has rhythm and symmetry, form and purpose, at multiple levels of understanding. An Introduction is provided to address some of the important over-arching issues facing designers today, while introducing some fundamental vocabulary that will be used throughout the book. Following are five sections with titles corresponding to the five Modules of the Ecological dimension of the EDE curriculum: Green Building, Local Food, Appropriate Technology, Restoring Nature, and Integrated Ecological Design – the summation chapter where all the previous sections are brought together in integrated design theories.

The book is overflowing with valuable perspectives, information, and experience, with many ideas being presented for the first time in this type of forum. Yet as full as it is, each article itself is only a cursory introduction to what may be considered an entire field of its own – indeed, each article could grow into an entire separate book! This organization makes the Ecological Key fractals within a fractal of the EDE curriculum as a whole. The articles

are of the size that one-a-day could be read comfortably during breakfast
so that by the end of a month-and-a-half one will have been introduced to
the full range of considerations for the Ecological dimension of ecovillage
designing. Students may be expected to take those presentations they
particularly resonate with and follow up with more thorough study.

I'm exceedingly jubilant about the assembly of authors that have been
gathered in this volume – some being published for the very first time.
Each is a world-class teacher; each has offered a professional treatment of
the material they have become familiar with. There are both Ph.D.s and
grassroots activists, long-time permaculture educators and sustainability
entrepreneurs, NGO administrators and ecovillage pioneers. What they
all have in common is a lifetime of giving their heart and soul to a vision
whose fruition is still to come. I believe there is something in this book for
everybody. I hope you will enjoy reading it as much as I have putting it
together. Thanks to all.

E. Christopher Mare
Editor

Introduction

Contents

World-renowned ecovillage designer Max O. Lindegger leads off this volume with a well-researched introduction to our favorite subject: Ecovillage Design. Max uses a wealth of available data to make the claim that fundamental changes are coming our way, whether we want them or not. According to the analysis presented here, the sustainable, full-featured ecovillage is the obvious solution to any challenge that may arise: the ecovillage is the context where all the sustainable practices and technologies can come together, in one place. A key assertion in this presentation is that we all must learn to get along with less; and this, according to Max's estimation, will lead to greater quality of life.

Introduction to Ecovillage Design

Max Lindegger – Crystal Waters, Australia

Introduction

There is, at this time, no generally agreed upon definition of an ecovillage. For the purposes of this article, we will define an ecovillage as follows:

- Human scale
- Full-featured settlement
- In which human activities are harmlessly integrated into the natural world
- In a way that is supportive of healthy human development, and
- Can be successfully continued into the indefinite future

Diane and Robert Gilman (1991)

Ted Trainer (University of New South Wales, Australia) says

> Would it be an exaggeration to claim that the emergence of the ecovillage movement is the most significant event in the 20th Century? I don't think so.

We have serious issues to deal with: climate change and its impact, potential energy shortages, loss of biodiversity and arable land, depletion of fresh water sources, just to mention a few. Our extremely resource-rich lifestyles are taken for granted by most in the West. There is very little doubt that within the lifetime of many of us we will have to make major changes – or change will be forced upon us. The ecovillage movement represents a recognition that change needs to come and that some of these changes will be considered quite radical – what has been called elsewhere a 'paradigm shift' (Kuhn, 1970).

As I have tried to illustrate previously, some communities, including my own, the ecovillage of Crystal Waters, have made moves towards a greater level of sustainability. Ted Trainer suggests that we need to be careful about the meaning of 'sustainability'. Basically, existing ecovillages have not gone far enough. Often the easy changes have been implemented while the difficult ones are left for later. The fact is that the hard ones are those which will make the big needed difference. We could look at the needed changes on a scale from easy to difficult, or as Peter Harper (Centre for Alternative Technology, Wales) calls them 'Light Green to Dark Green'.

The Easy Light-Green End:

- Households are more self-reliant: vegetable growing, composting, recycling, repairing, solar hot water, insulation
- Solar passive architecture, energy conservation, energy efficient technologies – lights, refrigeration, washing, use of bicycles
- Renewable energy (sun/wind), building using earth and recycled materials
- Rainwater collection, bio-remediated sewage treatment, water recycling, sustainable agriculture, permaculture

The Light-Green Urban Level:

- Greening cities – planting to improve air, climate and aesthetics
- Traffic calming
- Wild-life corridors
- Better public transport
- Water catchment and conservation
- Waste treatment, sorting garbage, recycling centres, composting, grey and black water recycling
- Organic agriculture, community supported agriculture
- Urban layout – narrowing roads, cul-de-sacs, bike paths, urban agriculture, roof gardens, commons, limiting the number of through roads

Many governments are taking action in this direction. We need to encourage this transition by applying pressure where it will be most effective. When possible we need to take the lead. As Margaret Mead pointed out long ago, real change comes from the bottom up – rarely from top down.

Sadly, even these sorts of changes will leave us short of where we need to go. Let's look at the 'limits to growth' analysis (Meadows, Meadows, Randers, 1992). If we tried to increase fuel and mineral production to the point where the 9 billion people expected by about 2040 (U.N. median projection) could have present developed-world living standards, all fuels and one-third of mineral items would be totally exhausted by about 2060.

The latest reports estimate that world oil supply will peak very soon, that prices will rise steeply thereafter, and that supply will be down to one half of the present volume by 2025. (Petroconsultants, 1995; Ivanhoe, 1996; Fleay, 1995). The scientists are saying that if we are to prevent the greenhouse problem from getting any worse we must cut fossil fuel use by 60 to 80 percent. If we cut it by 60%, and shared energy equally with the 9 billion people expected, everyone would have to get by on only about 1/18th the amount Australians average today.

Many agricultural and biological indices of productivity or fertility seem to be tapering to a peak, or to have fallen. It seems that we are reaching limits to biological production; yet we are only providing high living standards for about 1 billion people and we will soon have 9 billion (Brown, 1991, 1996).

In our view, considerations like this leave no doubt that if we are to achieve a sustainable and just world order we must design and develop settlements in which we can live well on levels of resource use that are far lower than they are in rich countries today, possibly of the order of one-tenth to one-twentieth lower, and we must reduce many environmental impacts to zero. Thus we must add the following much more difficult and far-reaching elements – 'Dark Green' in Harper's terminology – to our checklist of features and requirements to reach the potential for a real, full-featured, fully sustainable ecovillage.

Developing Highly Self-sufficient Ecovillages

In the coming era of serious resource scarcity, especially of petroleum, it is essential that we develop highly self-sufficient nations, regions, and especially towns, suburbs and neighbourhoods. The essential element in the new economy must be the 'ecovillage' – highly self-sufficient in its capacity to provide goods and services. We need to use our land efficiently and sustainably. We must pool our talents, skills, labour, resources and capital. One of the main reasons for this is that transport will not be available at today's easy level for moving people to and from work and leisure, or for the transport of goods. Local production will have the added benefits of improved quality and freshness, and reduction in storage and packaging.

The greenhouse problem indicates that fossil fuel energy needs to be drastically reduced. Only the development of such self-reliant communities will find lasting solutions to issues such as unemployment and deteriorating communities on the social level. There will always be a need to import those few essential goods which cannot easily be produced in small communities. Small manufacturing processes, modest sized water storages, and careful use of resources like clay, wood and stone can contribute to bioregional self-sufficiency.

We must take control of our finances. There are many examples which show that local money can help support local development. Voluntary taxes, LETS and related systems, working bees – all can enable us to build our own futures with our own money and energy. We must take control of our economy at the local community level.

A highly sustainable society must also involve a high degree of self-sufficiency in government. We must discuss, debate, and decide our own local affairs. Central governments cannot make all our local decisions. Only we who understand our local conditions can make the right decisions. A sustainable society must evolve a high level of participatory democracy. Issues of love, gender and sexuality will form part of the discussion; so will care of the old and the young, and those in need of healing or on the verge of death and dying.

Barry Goodman's ecological homestead at Crystal Waters.

Much more Communal, Cooperative Ways

Only if we cooperate can we all live well. Therefore we need to learn to share, to distribute surpluses. We need to work towards a gift economy. Individuals and groups need to take care of libraries, windmills, orchards, ponds, wood lots. Entertainment will be local, as will be markets and festivals. We will develop a New Village culture with New Village traditions.

These points connect with the above notion of self-reliance in governance. Most of the executive functions in a village could and should be in the hands of villagers. We need to wean ourselves off grants and reduce our dependence on subsidies. Authority and responsibility must go hand in hand. Ordinary citizens must again become aware of the requirements of the community and the land. We need to learn how to take responsibility for our own situation and local affairs. Self-governing communities would have mechanisms for ensuring that no one is unemployed, or poor, or lonely. In a sustainable community there must be cohesion but also a consciousness of the fact that we are taking control of our own fate.

Is that all? I'm afraid not.

We must live more simply so that others can simply live

There is no possibility that the growing world population can exist at a 'living standard' of the typical present-day Westerner. We must establish lifestyles which are frugal. We need to reduce our demand on most resources. This need not be a threat to our quality of life; indeed, such a lifestyle can lead to a lot more satisfaction and achievement.

Many people in the permaculture, ecovillage, urban ecology, new economics, peace and similar movements fail to grasp this need for simplicity. Many of the lifestyles in settlements which have otherwise excellent designs are much too affluent, in my opinion.

The key is to focus on 'need'. *What is sufficient* for comfort, health and hygiene, and a high quality of life? The difference between wants and needs can be enormous. Focusing on what is sufficient does not necessarily jeopardise the pursuit of social wealth, rich life experience, or personal and spiritual wealth. Indeed, excess accumulation of goods could be a hindrance to health and happiness.

The Need for a New Economy

A long-term sustainable economy must have a 'zero-growth' policy. Current levels of output are already unsustainable – compounding growth will only make matters worse. Consumer society has this manic obsession with economic growth, an obsession with obtaining and possessing more goods that we don't really need.

Consider the multiples of present levels of production and consumption that further growth implies. If the world averages only 3% per annum growth, then by 2060 total world output will be 8 times what it is today. But our recent history shows that 3% is not enough to make our economy 'healthy'.

One of the 13 large strategically placed ponds at Crystal Waters. Each pond is an element with many functions.

Do you realise that if we had 4% growth, if world population rises to the expected 9 billion, and if all those people were to come up to the 'living standards' of present-day Westerners, total world economic output would be *180 times* what it is today! Yet *the present level* is unsustainable. How do you explain the fact that no conventional politician or economist seems to recognize any problem with this enthusiastic commitment to increasing the GNP as the supreme and sacred goal?

At present, the richest one-fifth of the world's people is consuming four-fifths of the world's resource production. As a result, billions of people are so seriously deprived of necessities that one child dies every three seconds; yet we insist on increasing our rich-world living standards, output and consumption on a linear trajectory that is rapidly heading for overshoot. Rather than increasing output in terms of *quantity*, we should aim at improving the *quality* of goods and services. Better tools, high level care, more efficient use of land – examples exist already.

In the new economy, the cash sector will be rather small. Home and community based production will be emphasized. Swapping, gifts, barter, working bees, shramadamas[1], will increase. Indeed, there is no shortage of examples in the North and the South presently being practiced right now, at this very moment – so what are you waiting for?

Conclusion

Is this Utopian dreaming? If the 'limits to growth' analysis is correct, then we will have no choice but to move toward these kinds of ways of living; otherwise, we will not be able to make the necessary vast reductions in our present global resource consumption and resulting environmental impacts. However, paradoxically, these simpler, more down-to-earth ways of living will at the same time actually improve the quality of life for all.

Notes

1 The term 'shramadama' comes from the Sarvodaya network in Sri Lanka, and means 'to work together for the common good'.

References

Brown, Jeffrey, retrieved March 2009: "Jeffrey Brown and the Net Oil Exports Crisis." www.citizen. com/future-energies

Fleay, Brian, retrieved June 2009: "On the Coming Australian Hubbert Peak." www.oilcrisis.com/ Fleay

Gilman, Diane and Robert Gilman, et al. (1991) "Ecovillages and Sustainable Communities." A Report for Gaia Trust by Context Institute; Bainbridge Island, Washington

Ivanhoe, Buz, retrieved May 2009: "The Coming Global Oil Crisis." www.oilcrisis.com/Ivanhoe

Kuhn, Thomas (1970) *The Structure of Scientific Revolutions.* University of Chicago Press

Meadows, Donella, Dennis Meadows and Jorgen Randers (1992) *Beyond the Limits: Confronting Global Collapse: Envisioning a Sustainable Future.* Chelsea Green Publishing Company; White River Junction, Vermont

Petroconsultants, retrieved June 2009: "World Oil Reserves: The Problem of Reliable Data." www.planetforlife.com/oilcrisis

Max O. Lindegger is a respected and sought-after teacher in the disciplines of sustainable systems. His dynamic teaching style is born of 30 years of hands on experience and leadership in the design and implementation of practical, workable solutions to the challenges of sustainability.

This depth and breadth of knowledge communicates naturally to his audience. The value of this knowledge-from-experience is recognised in frequent invitations to present lectures at international symposia and conferences on themes such as environment, ecology, sustainability, permaculture, and ecovillage design.

With special thanks and acknowledgment to Ted Trainer, School of Social Work, UNSW, Kensington, Australia.

This Introduction section provides some of the meta-issues or global perspectives relevant to ecovillage designing. Ted Trainer, a long time proponent of the ecovillage solution, continues in this vein by offering the rationale for instituting his Simpler Way. Professor Trainer claims that most 'greening' doesn't go far enough, that the transition to any truly 'sustainable' society will require a complete dismantling and replacement of current market economies and social systems based on the uninhibited acquisitiveness of a few. Ted is sharp in his critique of these outworn systems; yet it becomes apparent that his motivation is an underlying compassion. The article closes with an urging for ecovillage designers to apply their 'craft' to the larger scales of societies and political systems.

The Global Significance of the Ecovillage Movement

Ted Trainer – University of New South Wales, Australia

Introduction

The basic argument in this article is that when the nature of the global predicament is understood it is obvious that the alarming problems now threatening to destroy civilization cannot be solved unless we move toward the ideas and practices evident within the global ecovillage and permaculture movements. Thus it would be difficult to exaggerate the importance of these movements and the role they have played over recent decades in the transition to a sustainable and just world.

My argument will be that the alarming global problems we face cannot be solved in a society that is obsessed with affluent consumer lifestyles, production for profit rather than need, letting market forces determine society, and especially with a growth-forever economy. We cannot solve the big problems unless and until we accept the need for vast and radical transition to some very different systems, ways and values. My hope is that this article will persuade permaculture and ecovillage designers that this is the appropriate perspective from which to operate, and that their craft is therefore of far greater importance than is generally realized. Their field is nothing less than the design of not just gardens, homesteads, farms and villages, but of whole satisfactory societies. Sustainability and justice on a global scale cannot be achieved unless we build very different economies, political systems, geographies, and indeed cultures. Hopefully this article will embolden future designers to work with this very big vision in mind.

The Global Situation

The foregoing remarks reveal a quite radical view of our situation, indeed one which goes much further than most 'green' people are willing to go; so here is an indication of the reasons why I think this view is valid. There are two major faults built into the foundations of our society: one to do with 'sustainability' and the other to do with 'justice'.

Fault 1: Sustainability

The way of life we have in rich countries is *grossly* unsustainable. There is no possibility of the 'living standards' of all people on Earth ever rising to rich-world per capita levels of consumption of energy, minerals, timber, water, food, phosphorous, etc. These rates of consumption are the cause of the many alarming global problems now threatening our survival. Yet most people have no idea of the *magnitude* of the overshoot, of how far we are beyond a sustainable level of resource use and environmental impact. Consider: If all the estimated nine billion people likely to be living on Earth after 2050 were to consume resources at the present per capita rate in rich countries, world annual resource production rates would have to be about eight times greater than they are now. There are already worrying signs of shortages of food, water, fish, various minerals, forests, and especially petroleum.

'Footprint analysis' indicates that the amount of productive land required to provide one person in Australia with food, water, energy and settlement area is about eight hectares. The US figure is closer to 12 hectares. If nine billion people were to live as Australians do now, more than 70 billion hectares of productive land would be required. However, the total amount available on the planet is only about eight billion hectares. In other words, *our rich-world per capita footprint is about 10 times as big* as it will ever be possible for all people to have.

The greenhouse problem provides probably the clearest argument. It is increasingly becoming evident that we must completely eliminate all CO_2 emissions by about 2050 if we are to keep global temperature rise below two degrees (Meinschaun, et al., 2009).

Such considerations make glaringly obvious the impossibility of all people having the 'living standards' we have taken for granted in rich countries like Australia. We are not just a little beyond sustainable levels of resource demand and ecological impact – we are *far* beyond them. Yet few people seem to grasp the magnitude of the overshoot. We must face up to dramatic reductions in our present per capita levels of production and consumption, and this cannot be achieved without abandoning the pursuit of affluent 'living standards' and facing up to enormous changes in institutional and system dynamics.

Now Add the Absurd Commitment to Economic Growth

The main worry is not the *present* levels of resource use and ecological impact, it is *the level we will rise to given the obsession with constantly increasing volumes of production.* The supreme goal in all countries is to raise incomes, 'living standards' and the GDP as much as possible, relentlessly, without any notion of limits; that is, the most important social goal is economic growth.

If we assume a) three per cent per annum economic growth, b) a population of nine billion, c) all the world's people rising to the 'living standards' we in the rich world would have in 2070 given three per cent growth, then the total volume of world economic output would be **60 times** as great as it is today. So even though the *present* levels of production and consumption are grossly unsustainable, the determination to have continual increase in income and economic output will multiply these towards absurdly impossible levels in coming decades.

This 'limits to growth' perspective is essential if we are to understand the most serious global problems facing us:

1. **The environmental problem** is basically due to the fact that far too much producing and consuming is going on, taking too many resources from Nature and dumping too many wastes into Nature. It cannot be solved in an economy that is geared to providing ever-rising production, consumption, 'living standards' and GDP.

2. **Third World poverty and underdevelopment** are inevitable if a few living in rich countries insist on taking far more of the world's resources than is their share. The Third World can never develop to rich world ways, because there are far too few resources for that (see Note 1).

3. **Conflict and war** are inevitable if all aspire to rich-world rates of consumption, and if rich countries insist on never-ending growth on a planet with limited resources (see Note 2).

Fault 2: It is a Grossly Unjust Society

We in rich countries could not have anywhere near our present 'living standards' if we were not taking far more than our fair share of world resources. Our per capita consumption of items such as petroleum is around 17 times that of the poorest half of the world's people. The rich 1/5 of the world's people are consuming around 3/4 of the resources produced. Many people get so little that 850 million are hungry and more than that number have dangerously dirty water to drink. Three billion live on $2 per day or less. Conditions for the world's poorest are deteriorating.

This grotesque injustice is primarily due to the fact that the global economy operates on market principles. In a market, need is totally irrelevant and is ignored – things go mostly to those who are richer, because they can offer more to pay for them. Thus we in rich countries get almost all of the scarce oil and other resources traded, while billions of people in desperate need get little or none. This explains why one third of the world's grain is fed to animals in rich countries while tens of thousands of children die every day because they have insufficient food and clean water.

Even more importantly, the market system explains why Third World development is so very *inappropriate* to the needs of Third World people.

What is developed is not what is needed; it is always what will make most profit for the few people with capital to invest. Thus there is development of export plantations and cosmetic factories but not development of farms and firms in which poor people could produce for themselves the things they need using the land, water, talent and labour they have all around them. (On the concept of *Appropriate* Development see Note 1).

These are the reasons why conventional development can be regarded *as a form of plunder*. The Third World has been developed into a state whereby its land and labour benefit the rich, not Third World people. Rich world 'living standards' could not be anywhere near as high as they are if the global economy was just. Rich world governments will not allow poor countries to pursue any other approach to development than one which lets the market determine development, and which therefore gears their economies to our interests.

It should be clear from this that a just and peaceful world cannot be achieved unless we in rich countries move to lifestyles and an economic system which allows us to live well on a small fraction of our present resource consumption, allowing the Third World to have its fair share.

Conclusions on our Situation

These considerations of sustainability and global economic justice show that the big global problems *cannot be solved in consumer-capitalist society*. This society cannot be fixed. The problems are caused by some fundamental structures and processes of our society. Thus reform is ruled out; the faulty systems and structures have to be replaced.

Many good green people do not understand this crucial point. For instance, sustainability is not possible unless we have a zero-growth economy, and you cannot reform a growth economy to be stable while it remains a growth economy. Similarly, Third World development cannot possibly be achieved while development is conceived in terms of rising to the 'living standards' rich countries have. Needs, rights, justice, the environment and future generations cannot possibly be attended to if you allow what happens to be determined by market forces, because markets only attend to those who can pay most. Reforms to a market system cannot mould it into a form that meets needs, etc., while it remains a market system; that's logically impossible because a market is something that by definition does not attend to needs.

The Required Alternative: The Simpler Way

If the foregoing analysis of our situation is valid, then many radical implications follow regarding the form that a sustainable and just society must take. We must move to ways that allow us to live on a small fraction of present resource consumption and ecological impact. The basic principles for an alternative way that would solve the big global problems, would work well, and would be attractive and enjoyable, must be as follows (for details see Note 3):

1. Adopt far simpler material living standards
2. High levels of self-sufficiency within households, nations and especially neighbourhoods and towns, with relatively little travel, transport or trade. There must be mostly small, *local economies* in which most of the things we need are produced by local labour from local resources
3. Basically cooperative and participatory systems, whereby local citizens govern themselves
4. A quite different economic system, one not driven by market forces and profit, and in which there are far less work, production, and consumption, and a large cashless sector, including many free goods from local commons. There must be far lower GDP than at present, and no economic growth at all
5. Most problematic, *a radically different culture*, in which competitive and acquisitive individualism is replaced by frugal, self-sufficient collectivism

The argument here is that these elements are not optional; if our predicament is more or less as has been sketched, we have to move to these kinds of practices whether we like them or not. But this need not be a matter of reluctantly doing what survival requires. Advocates of the Simpler Way believe that its many benefits and sources of satisfaction provide a much higher quality of life than most people experience in consumer society (see Note 4).

As I see it, the principles and designs I have put in terms of the Simpler Way correspond to those advocated by the ecovillage and permaculture movements. If there is any significant difference, it is probably only in focus. I have been most concerned to argue at the whole-system level; for instance, for the need to get rid of a growth economy, to transcend market systems and production for profit, to take local control of local economies, and to move beyond an acquisitive, competitive culture. But when it comes to the *design* and functioning of towns, neighbourhoods and households, it should be obvious that the ecovillage and permaculture movements are pioneering the essential ways.

Transition Issues: How on Earth do we Get There?

The transition cannot be driven or forced on people by government. The new local societies can only be built and made to work by the willing efforts of local people who understand why the Simpler Way is necessary and who want to live that way because they find it rewarding. Only local people know the local conditions and social situations so only they can develop the systems, networks, trust, cooperative climate, etc. that suit them and will generate enthusiastic and energetic contributions.

Thus, the most important task for people concerned about the fate of the planet is to help ordinary people where they live to understand the need for transition from consumer society, and to move toward willing and happy acceptance of alternative ways. By far, the best way for concerned people to do this is to plunge into the actual building of whatever new ways we can initiate where we live; thus the enormously valuable contribution of the Ecovillage movement in providing examples over thirty years is apparent.

But there is an extremely important point here that I fear is not clearly understood by people in these movements. *Simply building here and now more of the practices we want in the new society is not enough,* and if this is all we do it will not result in a sustainable and just society. Nothing of lasting significance will be achieved unless we bring about that huge change in general awareness of the need to transition from consumer society to some kind of Simpler Way. This is the supremely important task for anyone concerned about the fate of the planet. Building new permaculture gardens and even whole ecovillages is not nearly as important as building the collectively-shared vision. If we can do that, people will begin happily remaking their settlements and economies in no time! (For more detailed thoughts on the transition process, see Note 5).

It is, I think, beyond dispute that if we make it through the next fifty years to a sustainable and just world, then this transition will have been led by the ecovillage and permaculture initiatives. As I see it, ecovillage and permaculture designers have a special opportunity and responsibility here. My hope is that they will define their task widely and radically, as going beyond designing gardens, farms and villages to embracing the design of whole sustainable and just social, economic and political systems.

Notes

1 http://ssis.arts.unsw.edu.au/tsw/08b-Third-World-Lng.html
2 http://ssis.arts.unsw.edu.au/tsw/13-Peace-Conflict.html
3 http://ssis.arts.unsw.edu.au/tsw/12b-The-Alt-Sust-Soc-Lng.html
4 http://ssis.arts.unsw.edu.au/tsw/D65TW-Benefits.html
5 http://ssis.arts.unsw.edu.au/tsw/15-Transition.html

References

Meinshausen, M., N. Meinshausen, W. Hare, S. C. B. Raper, K. Frieler, R. Knuitti, D. J. Frame, and M. R. Allen (2009), "Greenhouse gas emission targets for limiting global warming to 2 degrees C". *Nature*, 458, 30 April, 1158 -1162
Trainer, T. (2007) *Renewable Energy Cannot Sustain A Consumer Society*. Dordrecht, Springer; Amsterdam

Ted Trainer is a Lecturer in the School of Social Work, University of New South Wales. He has written numerous books and articles on global problems, sustainability issues, alternative social forms and the transition to them including: *The Conserver Society: Alternatives for Sustainability*, (1995) London; Zed. He is also developing 'Pigface Point', an alternative lifestyle educational site near Sydney, and a website for use by critical global educators: **http://ssis.arts.unsw.edu.au/tsw/**

Albert Bates, founder of the Ecovillage Training Center at The Farm, reveals his store of encyclopedic knowledge in this upbeat and optimistic essay. The essay is upbeat and optimistic because Albert has seen for himself sustainable food growing systems in operation as part of larger ecosystem restoration strategies. What's more, there are historical precedents to choose from. You can tell by the way he uses the word that Albert is proud to be a 'permaculturist'. This group of eco-pioneers already possesses all the tools and knowledge we need to transition into 'sustainability'. What's lacking, in the author's opinion, is the will to move from Civilization 1.0 (Globalization) to Civilization 2.0 (Glocalization).

Civilization 2.0

Albert Bates – The Farm, Tennessee, USA

The Problem

Assume that, all of a sudden, we were to awaken to the existential threat posed by our addiction to exponential growth as an economic prerequisite. What changes in our arrangements might, even at this late hour, offer some prospect of survival? It seems altogether obvious that it would involve some combination of bioregionalism, permaculture, and ecovillage design science. Frankly, I cannot imagine any alternative excluding those strategies that would remain viable for very long.

Fortune has been our constant companion. We enjoy the rare condition of having water in all three states of repose, and lots of it. It took water in liquid form to permit the evolution of our multicellular organisms. Several major extinction events passed before we had the Cambrian explosion, the Chixcalub impact, the die-off of the dinosaurs, and the ascent of the mammals. Only over very long periods of geological and climate stability could we have evolved our elaborate metabolism, our long in-utero gestation, a childhood lasting more than 25 percent of the average life span, and a holographic brain. We have benefited from stable climate and dense biodiversity. That biodiversity has given our linear thought limitations a safe refuge within a non-linear web of life that minds the store when we are out to lunch.

This stability is something we will soon have a lot less of and adjusting to the suddenness of changed circumstances will likely become our greatest challenge. By and large, the scale of the emergency is yet unrecognized. Gaia is infirm, needs time to convalesce, and would improve faster with some healing therapies. If we continue draining her vital essences while we slowly come around to recognizing the situation we risk losing her.

The Potential

As Jared Diamond reminds us, the Fertile Crescent was not always a desert:

> In ancient times, however, much of the Fertile Crescent and eastern
> Mediterranean region, including Greece, was covered with forest ... Its
> woodlands were cleared for agriculture, or cut to obtain construction timber,
> or burned as firewood or for manufacturing plaster. Because of low rainfall
> and hence low primary productivity ... regrowth of vegetation could not
> keep pace with this destruction, especially in the presence of overgrazing by
> abundant goats. With the tree and grass cover removed, erosion proceeded and
> valleys silted up, while irrigation agriculture in the low-rainfall environment
> led to salt accumulation. These processes, which began in the Neolithic era,
> continued into modem times.[1]

The same could be said for the sands of the Mu Us desert in Mongolia,
or the Sahel. And just as farmers helped spread many of the deserts of
Asia, Northern Africa and Southern Europe, so farmers in North America,
encouraged by subsidies to grow grain for World War I, plowed up marginal
land and grasslands and doubled the cropping area of the southern plains
between 1910 and 1920. When the drought years came, as they did in
the 1930s, the dust turned their Capitol on the Potomac dark at midday
and made those farmers environmental refugees, begging for bread on the
Capitol Mall.

At a site called Santa Catarina, in modern Brazil, anthropologist Lilian
Rebellato uncovered a mound of oyster shells that is overlain by a dark band
of rich *terra preta*, the 'dark earths' of the Amazon. This was the 'ah ha!'
moment, she theorized. Below the oysters were a more random series of
strata showing haphazard development of the soils. Above the oyster shells
was the methodical production of *terra preta* for agriculture. This was the
point at which agriculture in the Americas became sustainable, in contrast
with the types of agriculture arising from the Fertile Crescent, in Asia and in
Africa, whose common feature is the eventual production of deserts.

Archaeological work at the Açutuba site on a bluff over the Rio Negro
tells us that the recipe for *terra preta* was well understood by the time the
Orellana expedition passed below that village in 1542. It is likely that the
Açutubans had a kiln that they built and operated for making their charcoal,
and they may have used the larger pieces in smokeless stoves inside their
homes while heaping the finer powders onto their compost piles. By doing
this simple exercise, they insured that *the land bequeathed to their successors
would always be richer than their ancestors had bequeathed to them*. While growing
food with greater ease and in greater abundance, they sequestered carbon,
changing the cycling time to the atmosphere from 14 years on average (for
labile carbon) to 1000 years or more (for recalcitrant carbon, now being
called biochar).

When 18th and 19th century settlers reached the Amazon and the
Mississippi, where 15th and 16th century explorers had viewed great shining

megalopoli, vines and moss covered the ruins. Trees had broken through the paving stones in the market plazas and engulfed palaces and temples, swallowing entire their ornate tapestries and gilded dinner services. Rain had rotted the roof timbers and insects had eaten the scientific and literary parchments, leaving only a remnant to the bonfires of priests. Seed stocks that had been hybridized and improved for 5,000 years had vanished, their last kernels eaten by rodents.

So great was the burst of vegetation over open fields and elevated ramparts that the carbon drawn from the air to feed this greening upset atmospheric chemistry in an almost mirror image of the way the felling of forests to build and clad those cities in bright-colored lime-washes and murals had altered it before. The reforestation of land following collapse drew so much carbon out of the atmosphere so rapidly that Europe literally froze.[2]

And that's a good thing.

The significance was not that Louis XIV had to put parquet floors in the Palace of Versailles to keep his feet warm, but rather, to the climate observers now parsing our frightening future, that humans can alter the atmosphere to take us back to pre-industrial carbon levels without risky, short-lived and costly geo-engineering gambits like space mirrors, sulfur aerosols and fish-suffocating plankton blooms. All we have to do is plant trees, build *terra preta* soils, and organically store carbon in our planet's terrasphere instead of in its atmosphere.

At the Ecovillage Training Center at The Farm in Tennessee, USA. Even children are prototyping architectures using simple, inexpensive and carbon-negative materials like straw, mud, sand and stone in the place of cement and steel.

The Method

Suppose everyone in the world planted one tree every day. How long would it take to restore the carbon balance? My co-workers and I at the Global Village Institute for Appropriate Technology[3] have done this calculation a number of different ways. The simple answer is that if everyone in the world planted one tree each day, by the end of the second year, the sequestered carbon would exceed current global industrial emissions. Atmospheric concentrations would begin to decline and return to normal. The principal obstacle is not lack of manpower, however, it's the availability of land. Seven billion planters could plant the equivalent of global CO_2 emissions in two years, but they would use up all the fallow arable land in the world.

Where do we send those treeplanters after all the unused arable land is planted? Deserts cover a third of the earth's surface. Climate change is causing deserts to expand at an accelerating pace; and yet, what is true about desertification affecting climate is also true about de-desertification. By greening barren lands the hydrological cycle is restored, ecosystems are re-invigorated, and carbon is steadily removed from the atmosphere.

"Here's where we have to be thinking deeply", Kansas farmer Wes Jackson says. "Agriculture had its beginning 10,000 years ago. What were the ecosystems like 10,000 years ago, after the retreat of the ice? Those ecosystems featured material recycling and they ran on contemporary sunlight. Humans have yet to build societies like that. Is it possible that embedded in nature's economy are suggestions for a human economy in which conservation is a consequence of production?"[4]

Jackson was mistaken. Humans *have* built societies in which conservation is a consequence of production. Ronald Nigh discovered one when he went into the Peten to study the Lakandon milpas.[5] There, agroforestry combines trees and shrubs with annual crops and livestock in ways that amplify and integrate the yields and benefits beyond what each component offers separately. Like other methods of sustainable agriculture, the Lakandon's is based on observing productive natural ecosystems and mimicking the processes and relationships that make them more resilient and regenerative.

Nigh observed that under Lakandon management, through the propagation of fast-growing pioneer trees, canopy closure is achieved in two to three years rather than up to ten as described by ecologists. Bats and birds are attracted to these pioneer species and bring the seeds of more shade-tolerant trees. Though most Lakandon farmers would probably prefer to prolong the forest-growth stage for a few more years, the field is ready to be reconverted to milpa at around 12 to 15 years.

Why would the Lakandon farmers prefer to prolong the forest-growth stage? It is because that is the most productive part of the cycle when it comes to food, fiber, and animal products. The corn and beans are needed, but compared to the yields that come from mature trees, those corn crops are a lot more work. Their energy return on investment (ERoI) might be only 1.2:1 to 1.4:1, not nearly enough to create monumental architecture and elegant public arts and sciences.

Parts of the traditional milpa practice are techniques that add to soil

The archaeological site at Açutuba, Brazil. While growing food with greater ease and in greater abundance, the ancient Amazonians sequestered carbon, changing the cycling time to the atmosphere from 14 years on average (for labile carbon) to 1,000 years or more (for recalcitrant carbon, now being called biochar).

fertility. Small fires of moist weed piles build up char in the soil and prevent hotter forest fires that would leave only ash. Besides planting legumes, which contribute nitrogen and beneficial nematodes, the Lakandon are fond of the balsa tree, which drops rich leaf clutter favored by soil microorganisms and whose star-shaped, aromatic blossoms attract birds, bees and bats. These pollinators transfer the seeds of food trees. Selective burning is a tool in the food-sustainability-kit that the last remaining 800 Lakandon Maya forest farmers in the Petén have saved from cultural extinction.

Near the town of San Pedro, Columbia, in Southern Belize, Christopher Nesbitt has been growing food crops in the ancient style at his Mayan Mountain Research Farm for over 20 years. He mixes some fast-growing native tree species, some annual crops, and some intermediate and long-term tree crops to build soil and produce continuous harvests. Some of his trees are leguminous and hold nitrogen by the microbial attraction of their roots. Some are pollinator-friendly and attract bees and hummingbirds to transfer the fertile pollen of important food plants. Understory trees like coffee, cacao, cassava, allspice, noni, ginger, neem and papaya benefit from intercropping with high canopy trees like breadfruit, açai and coconut palm, cashew, and mango. Fast-yielding crops like avocado, citrus, banana, bamboo, yams, vanilla, and climbing squashes provide an income for the farm while waiting for the slower harvest of samwood, cedar, teak, chestnut and mahogany to mature.[6]

The World Agroforestry Centre reports that farming methods like Nesbitt's can double or triple food yields per acre while reducing the need for commercial fertilizers. If best management practices were widely used, by 2030 up to six gigatons of CO_2e (Carbon Dioxide Equivalent) could be sequestered each year using agroforestry, an amount equal to the current emissions from global agriculture as a whole.[7]

Geoff Lawton got a chance to try that in 2001 when the government of Jordan approved a proposal for a test farm in one of the least hospitable places on Earth for farming. In the Kafrin area of the Jordan valley, 10 kilometers from the Dead Sea, the nearly flat desert receives only two or three light rainfalls in winter. The fine-grained silt is salty, and even the wells in the area are too saline to be used for irrigation.

Lawton and his team of permaculturists set up a small, 5-hectare farm and began digging swales – 2 meter-wide mounds and shallow trenches that crossed the farm in wavy lines on contour. They planted leguminous forest trees in the mounds to fix nitrogen and make leaf fodder. Each tree was given a drip-node from an irrigation line coming from a water dam built to capture road runoff; the water behind the dam was stocked with tilapia and geese, which contributed organic fertilizers for the trees.

In the moist trenches, they planted olive, fig, guava, date palm, pomegranate, grape, citrus, carob, mulberry, cactus, and a wide range of vegetables. Barley and alfalfa were planted as legumes and forages for farm animals between the swales. Tree and vegetable plantings were mulched with old newspapers and cotton rags, and animal manure was added before and after planting. Chickens, pigeons, turkey, geese, ducks, rabbits, sheep, and a dairy cow all contributed droppings. They were fed from the farm once there were enough trees and plants growing to harvest regularly without overtaxing the system.

Within the first year the soil and well water began showing a marked decline in salinity and the garden areas had significant increases in growth. Pests were minor and largely controlled by the farm animals. The combining of plants and animals brought about the integration of farm inputs and outputs into a managed ecosystem of continuous production, water conservation, and soil improvement. In less than a decade a permacultural balance had been achieved, with lessening inputs and improving outputs.

Chris Nesbitt and Geoff Lawton are permaculturists. They are concerned for the fate of the Earth and they are trying to do something about it. The greatest challenge for them, however, is not growing food. That is the easy part.

The Challenge

Geoff Lawton is fond of saying that all of the world's problems can be solved in the garden. His obstacle is not gardening; it's not even switching broadscale agriculture from 'conventional' (using chemical salts, herbicides, pesticides and machinery to derive the greatest dollar profit) to organic (marking 'profits' not in dollars but in the health and continued productivity of the soil food web). The greatest challenge is in changing the growth paradigm away from Civilization 1.0 – Fossil-fueled Industrial Globalization – to Civilization 2.0 – 'Glocalization'; a steady state economy characterized by stable (and in the near term rapidly declining) population size.

Col. Edwin Drake's remarkable discovery of a way to pump rock oil in the Seneca Nation permitted *homo* to dramatically accelerate Civilization 1.0 because of the sudden cheap supply of both energy and industrial chemicals. That innovation arrived precisely at the moment when coal smoke and horse manure were imposing severe constraints on both city size and war mechanization. With an ERoI of 30:1 to 100:1, petroleum allowed human eco-niche expansion to assume an exponential trajectory. Heck, we even aimed for the stars.

Mathis Wackernagel, Donella Meadows and others have calculated that Earth has been in deficit ecological spending ever since 1989-1990, adding stress and diminishing resilience with every passing year, so that by 2050, at present rates, we will be 34 planet years in debt (see graph).

Looking ahead on the exponential economic decline curve, we can see that a seven percent decline rate would mean halving every 10 years. A decline in our liquid fuel availability at a seven percent rate would halve what is available to automobiles by 2020, and for that matter, halve production of automobiles. Absent organized rationing, it would likely halve production of tractors and fertilizers, and so, in all likelihood, halve available food production by that year. It would halve heating fuels, halve electricity, and

The Annual Deficit becomes an Ecological Debt.

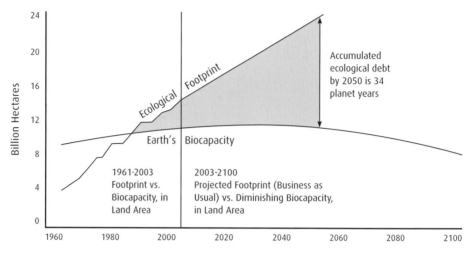

probably halve the First World's standard of living. It would certainly halve the value of many currencies and economies. If the decline were a mere 3.5 percent, the halving time would extend out to 2040, but resource depletion being exponential, the curve inevitably steepens as time goes on. Descent might also be marked by stair-step plateaus, 'green shoots' to use the current parlance, punctuated by more breathtaking drops.

Our collective challenge is not gardening, bioregional reinhabitation or even restoring the climate. We know now that all of those are do-able. The challenge is to reform an economy based on exponential growth so that it functions well in an unrelenting pattern of decline and descent, a pattern that is at odds with our evolutionary experience and perhaps even our biological meta-program.

The Conclusion

All of the necessary changes are not only do-able, they are being done in myriad ecovillages around the globe. A sustainable future, as best we can divine it, provides each requisite for human survival – food, shelter, heating and cooling, cooking, the daily activities of commerce and ennobling pursuits – but with a new, added mandate to separately or in combination sequester more greenhouse gases than we emit.

The suite of village self-audit tools provided by the Global Ecovillage Network offers helpful guidance and monitoring metrics.[8] District heating from a local biomass or waste product, employing pyrolysing kilns that co-generate electricity while producing biochar, are already in prototype, marking a path to renewable, carbon-negative community housing, food and power supplies. Anticipating climate change, ecovillages on six continents are constructing and occupying self-heating and self-cooling buildings, using materials with low embodied energy that absorb carbon from the atmosphere and provide more than mere warmth and shelter, but

Construction at The Farm is a family and community event, just as it was for the Lakandon of the Peten.

also nourish the souls of their inhabitants.

In the case of energy and transportation, we will, by fits and starts, switch to being entirely based on renewables, extracted in ways that are carbon negative when full life-cycle costing is performed and do not impose scandalously inequitable financial and toxic burdens on generations of newborn, millions of years into the future. Lower energy densities and higher distance costs suggest that bioregional re-inhabitation will become the rule, rather than the exception.

We don't know exactly what our future built environments will look like, but we can make some educated guesses. They are unlikely to look like today's Tokyo, Sao Paolo, or Shenzhen. More likely, they will resemble the description Father Gaspar de Carvajal, scribe to Francisco de Orellana, made of the net carbon-sequestering cities of the Amazon in 1542.

> There were many roads here that entered into the interior of the land, very
> fine highways. Inland from the river at a distance of 30 leagues more or less
> there could be seen some very large cities that glistened in white and besides
> this, the land is as fertile and as normal in appearance as our Spain.[9]

That passage could as well describe the vista that stretches now in front of us; the path we can take if we so choose: ecovillages, practicing sustainable, bioregionalist agriculture, in a permacultural landscape of cultivated ecologies, in millennial balance with the orbit and precession of Earth.

Notes

1 Diamond, J., Collapse: How Societies Choose to Fail or Succeed (New York: The Penguin Group, 2005).
2 Dull, Robert A. , Nevle, Richard J. , Woods, William I. , Bird, Dennis K. , Avnery, Shiri and Denevan, William M., "The Columbian Encounter and the Little Ice Age: Abrupt Land Use Change, Fire, and Greenhouse Forcing," Annals of the Association of American Geographers, 100(4):1-17; (2010); and see Ruddiman, W.F., Plows, Plagues and Petroleum: How Humans Took Control of Climate (Princeton and Oxford: Princeton University Press, 2005).
3 www.i4at.org.
4 Robert Jensen, "Sustainability and Politics: An Interview with Wes Jackson," Counterpunch, 10 July 2003; T. X. Cox et al., "Prospects for Developing Perennial Grain Crops," Bioscience, August 2006, pp. 649–59.
5 Nigh, R. Trees, fire and farmers: making woods and soil in the Maya forest, Journal of Ethnobiology 28(2) Fall/Winter 2008; etbi-28-02-06.3d
6 Bates, A., Going Deep in Belize, The Permaculture Activist 71 (Spring 2009).
7 World Agroforestry Centre Communications Unit, "Trees on Farms Key to Climate and Food Security," press release (Nairobi: 24 July 2009); K. Trumper, et al., Natural Fix? The Role of Ecosystems in Climate Mitigation: A UNEP rapid response assessment (Cambridge UK: UNEP-WCMC, 2009).
8 http://ena.ecovillage.org
9 Carvajal, G., Descubrimiento del río de las Amazonas: relación de Fr. Gaspar de Carvajal (1584), exfoliada de la obra de José Toribio Medina (1851), edición de Sevilla por Juan B. Bueno Medina (1895); Biblioteca Virtual Miguel de Cervantes, Madrid; L.A. Clayton, V. Knight and E. Moore, The De Soto Chronicles Volume II: The Expedition of Hernando De Soto to North America 1539-1543 (Birmingham: Univ.of Alabama Press, 1994); G. Menzies, 1421: The Year China Discovered America (New York: Harper Collins, 2006); G. Menzies, 1434: The Year a Magnificent Chinese Fleet Sailed to Italy and Ignited the Renaissance (London: Harper Collins, 2008).

This article first appeared in a publication preceding the conference: 'Study Panel on Localizing Environmental Anthropology: Bioregionalism, Permaculture and Ecovillage Design for a Sustainable Future', Communal Studies Association Annual Meeting, New Harmony, Indiana, October 1, 2010.

Albert Bates is author of *The Biochar Solution: Carbon Farming and Climate Change*, *The Post Petroleum Survival Guide and Cookbook* and numerous books, films and new media on energy, environment and history. A former environmental rights lawyer, paramedic, brick mason, flour miller, and horse trainer, he received the Right Livelihood Award in 1980 as part of the Steering Committee of Plenty, working to preserve the cultures of indigenous peoples, and board of directors of The Farm, a pioneering intentional community in Tennessee for the past 35 years. A co-founder and past president of the Global Ecovillage Network, he is presently GEN's representative to the UN climate talks. When not tinkering with fuel wringers for algae, hemp cheeses, or pyrolizing cookstoves, he teaches permaculture, ecovillage design and natural building and is a frequent guest on the ETC Podcast. He tweets at **@peaksurfer** and blogs at **peaksurfer.blogspot.com**

"We are facing not just a climate crisis, an oil crisis, a food crisis, and a population crisis – we are facing a systemic crisis that is due to unsustainable lifestyles." So concludes Kaj Hansen from Hjortshoj ecovillage in Denmark. Kaj bases his conclusion on verifiable facts: In the article he references a study conducted in 2009 of three Danish ecovillages that demonstrated the ecovillage lifestyle produces 60% less CO_2 emissions than the typical Danish lifestyle. Therefore, if the world is really serious about climate change, then the most effective solution would be to adopt ecovillage-type lifestyles. Everyday life in the three ecovillages is then described to get a feel for what an 'ecovillage' lifestyle is like.

Lifestyle Change as Climate Strategy

Kaj Hansen – Hjortshøj Ecovillage, Denmark

Summary

Measurements of CO_2 emissions at three Danish ecovillages by environmental consultants Pöyry A/S in 2009 documented that their average CO_2 emissions are a full 60% below the national average. The study is consistent with foreign studies which have shown that the 'ecological footprints' of three ecovillages in the USA, Great Britain and Hungary were less than half of their respective national averages. The Global Ecovillage Network (GEN), numbering thousands of ecovillages across the world, has long argued that lifestyle change is a key strategy in reducing pressure on the ecosystem without sacrificing quality of life. Now we have additional evidence.

Background

The ecovillage movement started in Denmark in 1991 and is growing steadily. Denmark has more ecovillages per capita than any other industrialized country, and was the first to form a national network, in 1993. Ecovillages are relatively small sustainable communities, both rural and urban, both North and South. Southern members of GEN are mostly traditional villages, e.g. 15,000 in Sri Lanka. The Northern variety are mostly intentional communities built by ecovillage pioneers who, through personal commitment and with little encouragement from governments, are designing and building small sustainable communities and teaching about sustainable living in their regions. The three in this study include two of the oldest, Svanholm and Hjortshøj, and one of the newer, more 'mainstream' ecovillages, Munksøgaard near Roskilde, which is currently the largest in Denmark with about 250 residents.

Pöyry AS was consultant to the Danish Climate Ministry's '1 Ton Less' campaign, and has used the same calculation model in this study. The report calculates only CO_2 emissions; it does not consider other greenhouse gases. In addition, Pöyry looked at the effect of some special ecovillage CO_2 emissions from:

1. Domestic production of organic vegetables, etc. on there own territories.
2. Organic products in general.
3. Water consumption and wastewater treatment.
4. The composting of organic waste from households.

The full report is posted on the website of the Association of Danish Ecovillages (LØS) at www.losnet.dk: "CO_2 Emissions in Ecovillages", Pöyry, July 2009.

Results

Average Emissions

A Dane emits on average 10 tones of CO_2 per year, of which 3.8 tons are due to state and municipal works and the export of various goods. This means that every Dane is individually responsible for the remaining 6.2 tons. Emissions come from heating of homes, transportation, electricity consumption, water consumption and emissions associated with food and other consumables.

Ecovillage Data

The average resident of the three Danish ecovillages emits just 2.5 tons of CO_2 per year – 60% less than the average Dane. See Figure 1 and Table 1. The difference lies primarily in that ecovillages:

- typically use CO_2-neutral heating (e.g. wood chips)
- have reduced transportation costs
- use primarily organic products

70% Less for Heating

The Danish ecovillages' home heating has no effect on CO_2 accounts, since they all use CO_2-neutral heating. It should be noted that the average ecovillage resident uses only 1825 kWh per year for heating – 70% lower than the average Danish consumption of 5967 kWh per year.

37% Less CO_2 from Electricity

A Dane emits on average 0.95 tons CO_2/year due to electricity consumption.

The Danish ecovillages in the study emitted just 0.60 ton CO_2/year –
37% less. Svanholm's CO_2 emissions are zero because Svanholm produces
all its electricity needs from its CO_2-neutral wind turbine.

35% less CO_2 from Transportation

The Danish ecovillages emitted only 35% of the Danish average CO_2 due to
transportation. The lower CO_2 emissions in the ecovillages are due to less
driving in private cars, greater use of public transportation and less air travel
than the average Dane.

29% less CO_2 from General Consumption

On average, the ecovillages emitted 29% less CO_2 from goods consumption,
due to own food production, higher consumption of organic and eco-labeled
products and more recycling than the average Dane.

12% less CO_2 from Water Consumption

On average, the ecovillages emitted 12% less CO_2 due to water use. This is in
spite of the fact that Svanholm – the largest organic farm in Denmark with
over 400 hectares – uses substantial water for its large scale agriculture. The
other two ecovillages emitted 56% less CO_2 than the Danish average.

CO_2 Emissions from Ecovillages are probably even lower

Additional factors, which were not included in this study, would probably
increase the ecovillage deviation from the average Danish household even
more; for example, the importance of organic food production and local
production in general, which saves packaging and transportation. Nor did
the study look at the importance of the materials life-cycle. This means that
some of the activities in the ecovillages are not yet sufficiently clarified, so
here are obvious opportunities for further refinements.

Another topic that has not been studied in this context, and which the
ecovillages would like to have studied, is the difference between conventional
and organic/biodynamic agriculture in Denmark. There are foreign studies

in tons CO_2 per year	Heat	Electricity	Transportation	Goods	Water	Total
Danish average	**1.59**	**0.95**	**2.02**	**1.49**	**0.17**	**6.22**
Munksøgaard	0	0.81	0.55	1.16	0.09	2.61
Hjortshøj	0	0.72	0.52	1.07	0.10	2.41
Svanholm	0	0.00	0.71	0.87	0.26	1.84
Ecovillage average (*weighted*)	0	0.60	0.70	1.06	0.15	2.51

Fig.1 from "CO_2 Emissions in Ecovillages", Pöyry, July 2009.

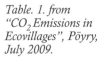

*Table. 1. from
"CO$_2$ Emissions in
Ecovillages", Pöyry,
July 2009.*

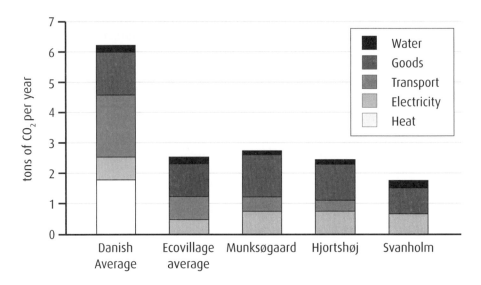

on this issue showing that organic/biodynamic agriculture is more resistant
to climate changes than conventional farming. Moreover, the reports indicate
that there is more stored CO_2 in the soil in organic/biodynamic agriculture
than in conventional.[1,2] There is a great need for incorporating such factors
into the discussions of climate strategies.

The Ecological Footprint

The international focus right now is on greenhouse gasses and the problem
of climate change. But the environmental problem is broader and includes a
general overloading of the ecosystem and irresponsible use of non-renewable
resources. These other aspects must not be forgotten. There are a number
of resource-saving measures in ecovillages, which have no effect on CO_2
emissions, yet reduce pressure on the ecosystem. It is important to point this
out because we can focus so much on CO_2 emissions that we forget about
the use of resources. There is a method for measuring resource consumption
which is broader than estimates of CO_2 emissions – namely the Ecological
Footprint. For example, Findhorn Ecovillage in Scotland,[3] Ecovillage
at Ithaca, USA,[4] and Eco-Valley Ecovillage in Hungary,[5] have all been
measured to have ecological footprints less than half their national averages.

Education in Sustainability

But even the Ecological Footprint is not comprehensive enough. We should
look at the efforts of sustainable development in the context of everything
we deal with, in every part of living. This approach requires an increased
focus on education in thinking sustainably in all aspects of life. For example,

Gaia Education is an educational initiative developed by an international team of ecovillage teachers that has contributed to this concept through the establishment of two educational programs: (1) Gaia Education Design for Sustainability (GEDS) taught over the Internet in conjunction with the Open University of Catalonia in Barcelona, and (2) Ecovillage Design Education (EDE) a 4-week program taught all over the world in cooperation with the Global Ecovillage Network, endorsed by the United Nations Institute for Training and Research (UNITAR), and an official contribution to the United Nations Decade of Education for Sustainable Development 2005-2014.[6]

Lifestyle in the Three Ecovillages as described by the members themselves

Hjortshøj Ecovillage

The Co-operative Community of Hjortshøj (AIH) near Aarhus has over 200 adults and children who have chosen to live in environmentally friendly houses. Hjortshøj is an emerging location for research, training and demonstration of ecology and sustainable development, including construction, power generation, social development, culture, consumption, food, waste and wastewater management, business, economics and agriculture. Our goal is solidarity among fellow human beings, and responsibility in the handling of natural resources.

Initiatives in AIH, which reduce CO_2 emissions include: Approximately half of the houses have one or more walls made of the moraine clay on our site. If you compare with traditional bricks made of clay, we save 99% of the energy normally used. When the houses eventually have to be demolished, the earth walls will return to the local soil – no construction waste involved.

The houses are largely insulated with 'paper wool', which is granulated recycled paper. Energy use for this type of insulation is much lower than the energy used for the traditional melting of glass and minerals. The houses are also very well insulated (including some that are 15 years old), which reduces heat consumption and hence CO_2 emissions.

All heating of homes and water is done either by burning wood chips or through solar heating. Wood chips are burned in our own central wood chip stove, which is coupled to a Stirling engine, which optimizes efficiency by also producing electricity. [Editor's Note: please see Gunnar Olesen's article in Module 3 of this book for more on the Stirling engine].

We have 1.5 hectares of vegetables and fruits. From here, approximately 100 persons have totally fresh, sun-ripened organic food without energy consumption for packaging and transportation. In our organic agriculture program, we also produce fertilizer, animal feed, meat and eggs for our own consumption. The proportion of each person's consumption covered by locally produced commodities is voluntary and quite variable.

Biodynamic cultivation has clearly improved the structure of the soil, now containing a large carbon reservoir. The degree of tillage is very low, whereby both the release of CO_2 and the much stronger greenhouse gas, nitrous oxide, is reduced significantly. Approximately one third of the agricultural land is used for multi-year willow, fruit trees and pastures, all of which build soil carbon.

A portion of the effluent from AIH is used as fertilizer for willow trees, thus binding CO_2 by solar means, saving energy and eliminating the emission of nitrous oxide from basins as in conventional treatment.

We sort our waste into many categories, so a significant part is reused. This is very satisfying, and, once systematized, is no burden.

We have 2 jointly-owned cars at Hjortshøj. For some, it means that they do not need a car. For others it means the chance not to buy car No. 2. In both cases, it becomes clearer what the costs are. This promotes the use of bicycles and public transportation.

There are so many things to do in AIH that there is simply no one with weight problems. How about that for a new angle on lifestyle change!

The Svanholm Collective

In 1978, the 800 year-old Svanholm Estate was acquired by a group of people with a dream to live a sustainable life in community – and the dream is still alive. Today, the 420 hectares are inhabited by 90 adults and 60 children. Together, we operate an organic farm and several businesses. We have a common purse, common meetings and a common kitchen, but no common dogma. We also have apartments and privacy.

Community with a Common Purse

The collective is formally organized as a limited partnership in which all are members. The collective makes all major decisions at the monthly common meeting. Decisions can only be taken by consensus, not by voting.

Svanholm Ecovillage.

Svanholm is based on an economic system whereby the broadest shoulders carry the greatest burden, but where the individual does have some financial flexibility – what we call an 80/20 joint economy. Each member can keep 20% of his/her gross salary for personal use. The remaining 80% goes to cover a range of common and fixed costs: taxes, rent, telephone, all meals, social care, pension contributions and more.

Service Provides Leisure Time

Nearly half of the adult members work outside the collective, as teachers, doctors, TV editors, forest workers, etc. The rest work in various forms of on-site production or in service groups such as: the Kitchen Group, which cooks the meals in the common kitchen, the Construction Group, which maintains the many old buildings, the Accounting Group, which manages finances, the Kindergarten Group, which takes care of the children, and the Cattle Group, which is in charge of the dairy, cows, etc., and of course, the Organic Farming Group, which is responsible for agricultural production, packaging and sales.

The many Service Groups perform tasks which would otherwise be performed by each person or family. This gives more leisure time to members.

Diversified Farming

Svanholm has historically prioritized diversified organic farming with traditional crops, forestry, sheep and dairy cows. In modern times it is more common to have monoculture production, but for Svanholm it has always been important to maintain the cycle between livestock and crop rotation, and also ensure an active life on the farm.

Life on the Estate

Svanholm is a lively estate, unlike many other estates that are currently occupied by a small family or working as a corporate domicile. At Svanholm, people live in the many beautiful buildings, and are here around the clock, because many are working on-site. There are many children who live a free country life in a safe environment.

Sustainability Pioneers

Svanholm was a pioneer in developing sustainable lifestyles and now has considerable experience in organic agriculture, climate-friendly food, organic milk production, wind power, CO_2-neutral heating, sustainable construction, sustainable timber trade, organic vegetable packing and local democracy, governance and community. Svanholm has existed for more than 30 years, and has proved to be a sustainable and viable example of an alternative lifestyle in today's Denmark.

Munksøgaard

150 adults and 100 children live together in the ecological co-housing community of Munksøgaard. The community is built on two fundamental values: environmental sustainability and spirit of community. The 100 living units in Munksøgaard are grouped into five distinct housing blocks, each of which contains 20 housing units. Three of these blocks comprise rental units, one is made up of cooperatively-owned units and in the third, units are privately owned. One of the three rental blocks is reserved for young people and one for senior citizens. Apartments range in size from 30 m^2 to 200 m^2. In addition to these private living spaces, each of the five housing blocks also has a common house. These various ownership arrangements ensure that low, medium and high-income families are all able to live at Munksøgaard. We consider it especially important to the health and happiness of the community that it is open for all kinds of people. The one thing that unites us here at Munksøgaard is the desire to create a sustainable lifestyle: we share the goal of minimizing our ecological footprint on the Earth.

In the planning of the project, we prioritized sustainable technologies. To keep our CO_2 emissions low, we have a central heating system working primarily on wood pellets. The project is located close to public transportation and we utilize a car pool. We also have extensive water saving initiatives, which include urine-separating toilets and a shared laundry that uses rainwater.

But these technological initiatives alone are not sufficient for permanent sustainable reduction in our ecological impact: there is also a need to fundamentally change our lifestyles. We need to fly less, drive less, live in less-heated houses, and use less water. In order to guide us in improving our behaviour, we have decided to undertake ecological audits every year. And now we are taking part in this CO_2 comparative study.

Where appropriate, we encourage the introduction of new technology or a change in lifestyle to facilitate reduction in emissions. By way of example, electricity consumption in our common houses tends to be relatively high, but we do not know which gadgets are responsible for the electricity consumption. We are currently studying this and will make the results available to the community in due course.

Conclusion: Lifestyle Change is the Key

We are facing not just a climate crisis, an oil crisis, a food crisis, and a population crisis – we are facing a systemic crisis that is due to unsustainable lifestyles. We need to reassess the way we live and work. We need to reassess whether ever-increasing growth and consumption is desirable, or even possible. We need to address all these problems in a holistic manner. If we are to avoid destructive climate changes, then our total greenhouse gas emissions (not just CO_2 emissions) must be reduced to between 1 and 2 tons per person per year by 2050.[7]

Ecovillagers have adopted a positive vision of the future based on a lifestyle in keeping with the concept of being an integral part of Nature and having a responsibility to respect the need to live lightly on the Earth. Through personal commitment, they walk their talk. Ecovillages provide living examples of how we can live sustainably without overloading the ecosystem and without sacrificing any quality of life. To the contrary, ecovillagers all across the world claim they have a more satisfying lifestyle than their mainstream colleagues, not least the children. Just ask them! The ecovillage movement is now worldwide and is growing slowly but surely as more and more people become aware of the benefits of a change in lifestyle.

Interested parties wishing to learn more or see for themselves should check out the Global Ecovillage Network and visit an ecovillage in their area.[8]

Notes

1 "Mitigating Climate Change through Localized Organic Agriculture and Food Systems",
   Institute of Science in Society, Report 31/1/08.
   http://www.i-sis.org.uk/mitigatingClimateChange.php
2 "Organic Farming and Climate Change", International Trade Centre, UNCTAD / WTO, 2007.
   http://www.fibl-shop.org/shop/pdf/mb-1500-climate-change.pdf
3 http://www.ecovillagefindhorn.org
4 http://ecovillageithaca.org
5 http://ecovalley.hu
6 www.gaiaeducation.net.
7 Synthesis report, Climate Change, Copenhagen 2009. www.climatecongress.ku.dk
8 gen.ecovillage.org

Kaj Hansen is a trained geologist but has mostly worked with environmental consulting and is now retired. Beside his work he participated in establishing the Hjortshøj ecovillage, has been chairman of the Danish association for ecovillages and has been on the board of GEN-Europe. He is currently on the board of Gaia Trust, and is prioritising his spiritual development in a secluded area of Denmark.

With the inclusion of Declan Kennedy here, we now have in this Introduction section three of the original Four Musketeers who started the Global Ecovillage Network. Declan demonstrates the vastness of his experience with a truly comprehensive vision of Ecological Design – a vision as enticing as it is practical. Since this vision is listed as so many points, it also could be considered a comprehensive checklist of design criteria for sustainable settlements. Declan emphasizes that ecological design is a process, and since the biggest challenge the world over is the 'ecological renewal' of existing places, this process invariably will include multiple stakeholders. The ultimate aim, according to Declan, is to make places that are 'easier to love'.

A Vision of Ecological Design

Declan Kennedy – Lebensgarten, Germany

Design Criteria

When an ecological settlement – and this concept covers both new construction and renewal projects – works well both technically and socially, it is not only the highest quality product that building and conversion can offer at the present time, but also a process of development. It is a process that changes people and their relationships to one another, as well as their relationships to buildings, open spaces and supply and disposal technology. The aim is to make a place easier to live in, easier to love, and consequently more sustainable. My vision of an ecological settlement, whether it is a new or an old one, a section of suburbia or the renewal of an existing area of a town or a city, looks like this:

An Ecovillage of Diversity – where living and working are reconciled and long trips to work are unnecessary; where social and cultural activities, recreation and further training, community and individuality can exist side by side.

An Ecovillage on a Human Scale – with neighbourhoods in which residents can develop a direct relationship or a personal bond, but which have their own character as well.

An Ecovillage of Nature Corridors – with woods, orchards, streams or wetland marshes separating the individual areas and linking them to the surrounding landscape; a place where plants and animals have room to thrive, something which has become all too rare in our current civilisation.

An Ecovillage which Fits – in terms of its own bio-region, its landscape, its climate, its flora and fauna and the local culture; where open spaces and bodies of water typical of the area provide biological enrichment and orientation.

An Ecovillage of Short Distances – the density leaves our ecological settlement not much larger than 1.5 km in diameter, meaning that everyone can walk from one end to the other in less than half an hour, or cycle or drive their solar mobiles across in five minutes; car and minibus sharing is available to the community for all medium distances; public means of transport – buses and trains – are faster and cheaper alternatives for longer journeys; efficient infrastructure planning is facilitated by service centres specialising in different aspects and located at public transport pick-up points.

An Ecovillage which Uses as Little Space as Possible – the size and density of the ecovillage depend on the degree to which the area required for material supply and disposal is within close proximity, without being a burden on the region or the prevalent cultural norms; expansion beyond this size leads to the founding of a new settlement; this creates a network instead of the cancer-like urban sprawl typical of our times.

An Ecovillage Based on Occupant Responsibility – all occupants are involved, to the extent they are able and willing, in local and community self-administration, and in formulating and implementing the ecological settlement design; all decisions are made at the lowest level possible, based on the principle of 'subsidiarity'; as far as possible, everyone uses the local range of services, production and trade, education and leisure, while supporting links and communication with regional, national and international groups and networks.

An Energy-efficient Ecovillage – energy saving options – including the rational use of energy for heating purposes, electricity and transport – cut energy consumption to less than 10% of its current level; energy is primarily generated on a renewable basis through sun, wind, tides, geo-thermal and organic mass sources; buildings are designed for optimum passive solar utility, in both cooling and heating; intelligent design achieves a maximum annual consumption rate of only 20 kWh per square metre of living space, which is amply covered by regenerative energies.

An Emission-free Ecovillage – such practices as reducing energy consumption, treating waste water in nature-based systems, limiting traffic and tree-lining streets, all lower CO_2, SO_2, NO_4 and other toxic gas emissions while simultaneously reducing dust particles; sod roofs and cob facades covered with climbing vines, as well as natural corridors between individual neighbourhoods, improve the air and temper climate extremes.

A Quiet and Beautiful Ecovillage – by limiting traffic and noise pollution from production processes, the ecovillage becomes a place of calm and quiet; the architectural expression and ecovillage design emphasize criteria of beauty, elegance and simplicity, fitting into the existing landscape and cultural heritage of the region.

An Ecovillage which Values Water – on-site rain water collection and seepage and the blanket ban on toxic substances entering the ground water allow the ecovillage to have its own drinking-water supply; water-saving fixtures and the separation of faeces and other organic waste (for composting and fermentation) cut drinking-water consumption to less than 60 litres per person per day; grey water from showers and baths, washbasins and washing machines is purified in nature-based treatment processes, and then seeps back though swales into the ground water.

The Ecovillage Preserves Natural Drainage Conditions – this means that, wherever possible, storage rooms at ground level replace basements; vertical and horizontal filters become an integral component of open spaces, for example in the form of constructed wetland marshes, as moving water is creatively allowed to come to the fore in flow forms, open gutters, streams and ponds.[1]

A Predominantly Waste-free Ecovillage – governed by the principle that 'every item of waste is a resource in the wrong place', the ecovillage belongs to regional, national and international networks specially devoted to this aspect of sustainable husbandry; this practice helps to eliminate the disposal of over 90% of the current volume of waste, be it domestic waste, excavation soil, building materials or waste from commercial or industrial production; the little waste still produced is then sorted on-site, before entering the respective recycling, down-cycling or re-use processes.

Vegetable plots at Lebensgarten ecovillage.

An Ecovillage of Healthy Buildings – building materials and construction systems used in all buildings, whether converted or constructed, are healthy, save primary energy and conserve resources in their production, use and recycling (as per the principle of 'Cradle to Cradle'); they are (re)planned for multi-purpose use, easy conversion and expansion or reduction in size; electrical cables and appliances are installed and connected in accordance with the latest technology to generate as little 'electric smog' as possible; before design commences, zones of geo-pathological interference are detected, and thus locating bedrooms and living spaces on top of them can be avoided.[2]

An Ecovillage of Native Species and Productive Plants – special care is taken with selecting plant types, sizes and growth times; thus, the ecovillage contains fruit-bearing bushes and trees, gardens, lean-to greenhouses, facade espaliers and herbaceous soil coverings that meet a good proportion of the settlement's needs for fresh fruit, vegetables and salad all year round, without much extra effort; the natural corridors, streams, ponds and wetland marshes also produce edible and medicinal plants for human and animal consumption – these products are fresher and cost less in terms of embodied energy, waste and money than imports which have traveled great distances, although these will be imported to ensure added variety at the table; sale of commercial products and exchange of 'surplus' production creates permanent jobs and provides high quality products at reasonable costs for everyone.

A solar array situated amongst skylights: Lebensgarten, Germany.

An Ecovillage trading within its regional exchange system – a complementary currency that works for everybody and protects the earth. It is created decentrally – everyone makes her/his own vouchers – all that is needed to create this exchange medium is a printer or a copying machine – but they can be used internationally. It is legal in almost all countries. The notes are guaranteed by a human value that is known to everyone – trust – and still free from speculation. It is comprehensible to everyone.[3]

An Ecovillage of Creative Conflict Resolution – conflicts are seen and dealt with as creative learning processes; 'using together instead of consuming individually'; sharing jobs, cars, fruit-trees, playgrounds, buildings and open spaces for play, sport, leisure and communication also mean going through learning processes together, leading to perhaps a more challenging but also richer life.

An Ecovillage of Human Values – settlements and cities can be seen as collective artworks; the individual and collective efforts of many generations lend them a special, unmistakable character; nowadays it is possible to simulate and accelerate this historical development while making various alternatives (building anew or renewing existing quarters) understandable to all; thus, the complex process of reaching consensus between the demands and needs of the occupants, the administrative authorities, the economy and the environment can be resolved more easily, until a plan has emerged that

is tailored to the combined needs of all those involved; it takes time to make this shared vision a reality, but the shared vision forms the basis of the settlement's spiritual, intellectual and material character. Many of the ideas expressed here can be found in the concept of 'Transition Towns', as formulated by permaculture designer Rob Hopkins.[5]

In its book, *The First Global Revolution*, the Club of Rome made an appeal to humanity by stating: "We need a vision", because, they argued, "global problems cannot be solved by market mechanisms alone". The vision sees the way ahead as the thousands of small 'smart' decisions that reflect a new awareness, shared by millions of people, which will help ensure the survival of society as a whole. The strategy of ecological design has the advantage of not only being feasible, but also of corresponding to the vision many people share of a world in which they would like to live. Making the vision a reality only requires the will to take calculated risks and shed old prejudices and patterns of behavior. In view of the problems bombarding us from all sides, this can only be seen as a hopeful perspective.

Declan's atrium.
The solar gain
facilitates comfortable
conversation.

Renewal instead of New Construction

The biggest challenge for everyone involved in building all over the world is the ecological renewal of existing buildings, villages and towns. Renewing ecologically means converting and renovating buildings with a view to sustainable use of resources. This involves, for instance, saving non-renewable materials such as copper, aluminum and iron from dismantling operations in cities and reusing them efficiently, rather than mining them anew from the Earth. It also means allowing waste water to flow back into the ground water, or into rivers and lakes, in a state that is just as clean, or cleaner, than it was when we extracted it as drinking-water; keeping the air clean, so that we can once again smell the scent of plants; planning quietness and reducing noise; and providing a diversity of uses in a small area, so that living, working and leisure can be combined to reduce transport distances and improve the quality of life for all. In almost all our cities, but also in many of our ecovillages, we are still very far away from the full implementation of this vision. However, some of the new urban ecovillages indicate that there are ways and means *of getting closer* to these goals. What we need now are examples of ways *of attaining* these goals.

Naturally, renewing older urban areas ecologically requires greater sensitivity, patience and openness to teamwork than developing new urban or green pasture ecovillages. One of the differences compared with new building projects is that it is considerably more difficult to find ground-breaking models and documentation of such projects, probably because urban ecovillages are less spectacular. At first glance, they generally appear to differ very little from completely 'normal' projects, and, with the exception of the Danish project in Kolding with its Bio-works – a glass pyramid, in which all the waste water is purified – they tend toward the conventional, and are almost a little boring from the 'Design' point of view. However, a closer look at the planning processes reveals that they are far more diverse and complicated than new projects.

As with new settlements, the examples of renewal projects range from socially-oriented processes with a very high degree of occupant input, to more hierarchically organized planning processes with low occupant input. People living near a demolition project can even work with architects to develop plans for preserving and converting a complex, and can bring about the funding and implementation of the project with the support of clients and administrative decision-makers. However, they also show the extent to which developers and authorities can block ecological design. In Vienna, it emerged that permission to plant climbing plants in the street area had to pass through at least 14 different administrative offices! As a result, it is less time-consuming to plant the climbers in boxes or planters and attach them to the wall than to plant them in the ground. New urban ecological design can orient itself on something resembling a guiding model of an integrated, multi-faceted re-design of the settlement. Bearing in mind how much more important it is to use the various existing resources and potentials, both physical and social, in the urban renewal process, this is more than understandable. The paradox is that the solutions in these projects are often more diverse, imaginative and better tailored to the needs of the occupants.

With both new construction and renewal, the key to success lies in winning over the support of everyone involved to the goals of environmental quality, and making the planning and building process a joint success despite – or perhaps because of – the many participants, all of whom are pursuing different interests. The Transition Town movement shows that the quality of life and of housing gained through the juxtaposition of old and new ideas, past and future, is well worth the effort in the present.

Notes

1 Efficient Management of Wastewater in Water-Scarce Countries by I. Al Baz, R. Otterpohl & C. Wendland
2 http://www.flipkart.com/whole-building-handbook-varis-bokalders-book-1844075230
3 see www.minuto-zeitgutscheine.de/sprachen.html and then click on: minuto-voucher-english.pdf
4 Creating harmony: conflict resolution in community by Hildur Jackson
5 see: http://en.wikipedia.org/wiki/Transition_Towns

Prof. Declan Kennedy, Irish Architect, Urban Planner, Mediator, Permaculture Designer, and Spiritual Healer; practicing urban design and permaculture, landscape, renewable energy and agricultural planning, coupled with holistic strategies, in Germany since 1972, and teaching in intensive seminars – organized in many countries. 1972 to 1990, Professor of Urban Design and Infrastructure at the Architectural Department of the Technical University of Berlin, Germany, editor and advisory board of the Journal EKISTICS and member of the World Society of Ekistics since 1972; 1975-1978: member of the Permaculture Insitute of Europe, since 1982; 1985 co-founder of ecovillage Lebensgarten Steyerberg, near Hanover, Germany;1995 Founding Chairman: Global Ecovillage Network (GEN); research work on "New and Renewed Ecological Settlements" in five countries of Europe until 1996, supported by the European Academy of the Urban Environment, Berlin; since 2006 Chairman of Advisory Board, Gaia University and 2008 Co-Founder of Gaia Action-Learning Academy for Sustainability (GALA), the European workshop provider for Gaia University.

In the past several years, the term 'Resilience' has surged into the lexicon of sustainable community designers as being a goal of the utmost importance; yet not until I read this exposition by Daniel Wahl did I fully grasp what it meant. Daniel does an excellent job explaining not only the essence but the context of this rapidly spreading meme. In well-versed systems languaging, the author draws on numerous recent studies to make the case that not only is resilience an important goal, it is the way of Nature herself. Dr. Wahl makes accessible these recent scientific findings to our global readership.

Transformative Resilience

Daniel Christian Wahl, Ph.D. – Son Rullan on Mallorca, Spain

Living beyond Planetary Boundaries

We are living in a more and more brittle world. The most pervasive effect of the modern industrial growth society and its expansion via colonialism and later the neo-colonialism of economic globalization has been to erode away the intricate pattern that connected humanity to the unique conditions of the particular places in which communities found themselves. We have severed the hidden connections that were the lifelines of people who lived in intimate reciprocity with the places they called 'home' for thousands of years.

By and large, humanity lived in a locally and bioregionally adapted way until the burning of fossil fuels – first coal, and then oil and gas – made a massive expansion of global trade volume, human population, and over-consumption possible. This is not say that human history is not full of examples of regionalized civilizations overexploiting their available natural resources and eroding resilience to a point that either triggered the collapse of those civilizations or forced them into aggressive expansion and war with their neighbours.

We are living in the age of Resource Wars over access to oil and water. Soon, the localized and dwindling reserves of elements that are critical to the production of information technologies, batteries and catalytic converters, such as iridium, palladium, lithium and platinum, will lead to more power differentials and conflict. The pace and scope of overconsumption is pushing resource availability and ecosystem resilience to a limit. We are beginning to exceed planetary boundaries.

Humanity's collective actions have now reached a scale that we are eroding the health, vitality, and resiliency of biological processes and ecosystems to such an extent that we are interfering with the planetary life-support system itself. The Gaian process of creating conditions conducive to life is the basis of sustainability, resilience, and human as well as planetary health. We utterly rely on the fixing of solar energy into plants and distribution of that energy up the food chain, along with the cleaning of water, the building up of fertile soils, and the regulation of climate.

Every year around mid-August, humanity as a whole has used up the naturally regenerated resources produced in that year. In 2010, World Overshoot Day was August 21st and rising population and overconsumption, along with falling bioproductivity, will ensure that global overshoot will be reached even earlier in 2011 (see www.footprintnetwork.org).

The abundance of renewable resources and ecosystem services generated by life each year is called 'planetary bioproductivity.' The secret of sustaining the human presence on Earth is to stay within the limits of this planetary bioproductivity. On a planet over-populated with humans, our future depends upon our ability to learn how to live off the interest (annual bioproductivity) rather than the ecological capital (the store of abundance accumulated throughout the evolution of Life on Earth). We need to rapidly redesign the human presence on Earth in such a way that all of humanity manages to live within the safe limits of planetary boundaries.

A recent study by an international group of scientists led by the Stockholm Resilience Centre (Rockström, et al., 2009) identified at least eight critical planetary boundaries that we will need to pay close attention to in our quest to create a more sustainable human presence on Earth. At least three of these boundaries have already been breached. We are at the point of triggering dangerous climate change; biodiversity loss has reached a rate unprecedented in the history of life on Earth; and our unsustainable methods of agricultural production have interfered with biogeochemical flow boundaries like the nitrogen cycle and the phosphorous cycle.

Not enough research has been done yet to understand to what extent we may also have breached the planetary boundaries for chemical pollution and atmospheric aerosol loading, but evidence is mounting that endocrine system disrupting chemicals in plastics and cosmetics are interfering with sexual differentiation and fertility in many species, including humans. It is clear that ocean acidification, stratospheric ozone depletion, land system changes, and global freshwater use will have to be monitored closely as they are all rapidly approaching the point where safe planetary boundaries will be breached (see light grey circle in Figure 1). For a more detailed explanation of this research and the concept of planetary boundaries and how they relate to resilience at a local, regional, and planetary scale, please have a look at the link to Johan Rockström's presentation at TED (the link is in the references below).

Many of these boundaries are interrelated. Most of them cause a loss of biodiversity, resilience, and ecosystem health at multiple scales, from local to global. With each species that is lost, we weaken the complex web of interdependencies and connections that support the health of the world's ecosystems. As we lose biodiversity, we unravel the complex pattern of health based on diversity, symbiotic relationships, multiple redundancies, and complex interconnections and feedback loops. The resilience of an ecosystem or a community critically depends on this scale-linking pattern of health that connects individual health to community health, ecosystem health, the health of bioregions and nations, and in due course planetary health.

Ultimately, when we talk about sustainability from a whole systems design perspective, what we are trying to sustain is not just the future of the human species but also the pattern of ecological interdependencies and planetary health upon which the fate of our own and so many other species depends. It is this pattern of health that allows us to stay responsive, adaptable and resilient in the face of change. Improving community resilience and paying close attention to the effect of our actions on multiple, interconnected scales lies at the heart of creating thriving communities and a sustainable culture.

So What Exactly is 'Resilience?'

Almost 40 years ago, Buzz Holling (1973) published research on the complex dynamics of change within ecosystems. He looked at how a mature forest ecosystem can get drastically disturbed by a fire, to the point where it reverts back to grassland and then, via ecological succession, transforms first into shrubland then a young forest and finally much later into a mature forest again. Holling saw that ecosystems could exist in a variety of dynamically stable (dynamic equilibrium) conditions, and that after disturbance ecosystems could either bounce back to their initial state before the disturbance or they could degenerate to less diverse and less vibrant new equilibrium conditions. In some cases, disturbance could also lead to a transformation of the ecosystem into a more diverse and more vibrant dynamic equilibrium condition. These insights led Holling to formulate the foundations of Resilience Theory:

> Resilience is structured around the acceptance of disturbance, even the generation of disturbance, and the production of variability. The whole history of life on this planet has been one of dynamic change and it occurred long before humans appeared, but humans did add something more...by exploiting resources and reducing diversity and in so doing reducing the resilience of these systems. The fluctuations that are normal still occur, but they are more limited. So you can get situations because of human intervention where the diversity has been so compromised that the fluctuation rather than operating within a persistent region flips the system somewhere else.
>
> HOLLING, 1973

Over the last decade it has become evident that understanding ecosystem and community health and resilience lies at the heart of sustainability as a community-based process of learning how to integrate our social systems into unique conditions of local and regional ecosystems, as well as how to stay within safe planetary boundaries. The Resilience Alliance, an international network of researchers and practitioners focussed on understanding the complex dynamics of social-ecological systems, defines resilience as follows:

- Resilience is... the ability to absorb disturbances, to be changed and then to re-organise and still have the same identity (retain the same basic structure and ways of functioning).
- It includes the ability to learn from the disturbance. A resilient system is forgiving of external shocks. As resilience declines the magnitude of a shock from which it cannot recover gets smaller and smaller.
- Resilience shifts attention from purely growth and efficiency to needed recovery and flexibility. Growth and efficiency alone can often lead ecological systems, businesses and societies into fragile rigidities, exposing them to turbulent transformation. Learning, recovery and flexibility open eyes to novelty and new worlds of opportunity (www.resalliance.org).

Fig. 1: Changes in control variables for key planetary boundaries since the Industrial Revolution (reproduced from: Rockström et al., 2009).

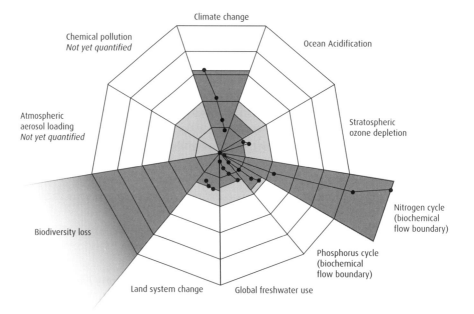

There is an important distinction between ecosystem resilience and resilience in social systems. As human beings and communities, we have the capacity of foresight. We can anticipate and plan for the future, even if we cannot predict it accurately. Since human beings have become the most disruptive species in most of the world's ecosystems, we need to pay attention to the interaction of social and ecological systems and regard them as one interacting social-ecological system (SES). This understanding has to be central to the design of sustainable communities. Resilience in SESs depends on a number of important capacities:

- Persistence – the capacity to withstand drastic disruptions without losing its basic structure and function. One example of persistence is the way a forest or a coastal town manages to recuperate from the effects of a hurricane.

- Adaptive capacity enables a social-ecological system like a community or a bioregion to maintain key functions during periods of change. For example, a sustainable community needs to maintain the ability to produce enough food and generate enough electricity as the effects of climate change and peak oil begin to disrupt harvests and global supply lines.

- Transformability – the capacity to transform in response to change in order to create more appropriate systems when ecological, political, social or economic conditions make the existing systems unsustainable. For example, the series of ever more rapid and severe economic crises is forcing the conclusion that a profound transformation of our economic and monetary system towards a differently structured green economy is now urgently required (Huitric, 2009).

The multiple and converging crises we are facing will increasingly require a transformative resilience response. As these crises progress, we are gradually losing our ability to persist in the face of change and maintain our adaptive capacity. If we wait for these crises to cause widespread disruptions, we run the risk of irreversible deterioration. The International Futures Forum distinguishes Resilience 1.0 (based on adaptive capacity and the 'bounce back' to business as usual) from Resilience 2.0 (based on fundamental systemic transformation that increases the ability to respond creatively to change). Resilience 2.0 is also called transformative resilience.

How Can We Cocreate Transformative Resilience in Social-Ecological Systems?

In social-ecological systems (SESs) the effect of our actions can sometimes only be observed after long-time delay. In such complex dynamic systems, with diverse agents and processes all interacting, cause and effect can be non-linear with feed-back loops leading to sudden escalations, unforeseen consequences and side effects.

What determines change in SESs over time are mainly the underlying, slowly changing variables such as climate, land use, nutrient stocks, human values and policies, as well as systems of governance and interdependencies between local, regional, and global scales. SESs never exist in isolation; they are nested within a holarchical or scalelinking structure of other SESs. Spatial scalelinking connects individuals, communities, ecosystems, bioregions, nations, all the way to the planetary scale (and beyond). *Temporal scale-linking* can be understood as the way slow processes and fast processes

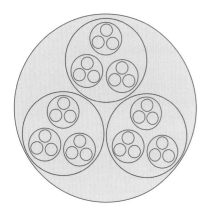

Fig.2: Schematic of a Holarchy of nested Social-Ecological Systems.

interact at and between various spatial scales. Sustainable community design has to take place within such a spatially and temporally scale-linking frame of reference (Wahl, 2007).

Many of the factors that will cause a loss of resilience at one particular scale, say within a community and its ecosystem, will also affect resilience at another scale, say at the national, or planetary level. Localized actions, like the burning of fossil fuel, can accumulate to have global effects like climate change, which in turn can affect local conditions in multiple and unpredictable ways. This is the nature of the fundamentally interconnected nested system (holarchy) in which we live. Within emerging field of resilience research and practice these nested spatial and temporal dynamics have been explored under the concept of panarchy (see: www.resalliance.org for more information).

Among the factors that can degrade resilience at multiple scales are: loss of biodiversity, toxic pollution, interference with the hydrological cycle, degradation of soils and erosion – but also, inflexible institutions, perverse subsidies that incentivise unsustainable patterns of consumption, and inappropriately chosen measures of total value that focus on short-term maximization of production and increased efficiencies at the loss of redundancy and diversity in the system as a whole.

The World System Model of the International Futures Forum (IFF) is structured around 12 critical aspects or components of a resilient system that have to be considered in an interconnected way. The model can be applied at various scales, and has already been used to create more integrated 'transition plans' for community and bioregional resilience (see: www.iffworldmodel. net).

All the aspects (or nodes) of the World Systems Model have to be considered in the creation of a viable and resilient system, whether at the scale of a community, a bioregion, a nation, or the (a) planet. The aim is not to create isolation or self-sufficiency at every scale, since in an interconnected and interdependent holarchically structured system complete isolation is impossible and would lead to the collapse of the system. Rather than self-sufficiency, what we should aim for is greater self-reliance at each scale: an increased ability to meet basic human needs as close to home as possible and within the limits of regional and planetary boundaries. It is time to create import substitution strategies based on regional production!

An example for systemic re-design of our systems of governance that would enable transformative resilience responses at the community and bioregional scale would be the implementation of subsidiarity. The political principle of subsidiarity is the idea that a central authority should have a subsidiary function, performing only those tasks that cannot be performed effectively at a more immediate or local level. Such a governance structure would empower active citizen participation in the transition to a more resilient society, without doing away with political collaboration at the national and international scale.

The Permaculture Design movement, the Global Ecovillage Network and the approach of the Ecovillage Design Education (EDE) of Gaia Education, as well as the recent bloom of the Transition Town movement, are all expressions of participatory, grass-roots or local citizen-based approaches to co-creating resilience at a local and regional scale. Rob Hopkins (2009) identifies three key design principles that resilience at a community scale depend upon:

- Increased diversity: a broader base of livelihoods, land use, enterprise, and energy systems than at present.
- Modularity (scale-linking design): not advocating self-sufficiency, but rather an increased self reliance; with surge protectors for the local economy such as local food production and decentralized energy.
- Tightness of feedback (increased capacity to learn from local successes or failures): bringing the results of our actions closer to home, so that we cannot ignore them.

Transformation Starts with the Individual: Inner and Outer Resilience

Last but not least, it is important to emphasize that there is an inner and outer dimension of resilience, both in individuals and communities. Our ability to stay creative, flexible, collaborative and adaptive in the face of a changing environment or even drastic disruptions of business as usual is affected by our worldview, our value systems, and the quality of our relationships. This is why *worldview* is at the top of the IFF World System Model, as so much of our behaviour is guided and affected by our value system and worldview. Here are three ways of building inner resilience that can lead to personal

Fig.3: The Love & Fear Loop (IFF)

and collective transformation: *Meditation*, in whatever form, as a way of connecting to ourselves and our ability to have intuitive insights; *The Way of Council* as a community communication practice fostering deep listening and deep sharing of feelings and insights which can help us connect to collective wisdom and group intelligence as we are faced with unprecedented and unpredictable change; *Reconnecting with Nature* as a source of insight and strength. This can be done in many ways, but time alone in Nature (solo time or vision quest) has proven a powerful tool for many people aiming to build inner resilience. The diagram to the right emerged out of a conversation on September 12th 2001, as the tutors and students of the MSc in Holistic

Science at Schumacher College tried to make sense of the significance of the attack on the World Trade Centre. It summarizes, in a simplified form, an important aspect of inner resilience at the individual and collective level. The extent to which we are able to respond to change with transformative resilience depends on whether we choose to act out of love (for life in all its manifestations) or out of fear.

References

Hodgson, T. (ed.) 2010 "Transformative Resilience – A Response to the Adaptive Imperative", Report of a workshop on community resilience held in Scotland in December 2009, International Futures Forum

Holling, C. S. 1973 "Resilience and stability of ecological systems". *Annual Review of Ecology and Systematics* 4:1–23.

Hopkins, R. 2009 "Resilience Thinking", *Resurgence*, No. 257, November/December 2009, pp.12-15

Huitric, M. (Ed.) 2009 "Biodiversity, Ecosystem Services and Resilience – Governance for a Future with Global Changes." Background report for the scientific workshop in Tjärnö, Sweden, [online] http://lowres.stockholmresilience.org/download/18.235c0ace124479a1f73800013572/Tjarno_report_final.pdf

Rockström, Johan 2010 "Let the environment guide our development". TED presentation, [online] http://www.ted.com/talks/johan_rockstrom_let_the_environment_guide_our_development.html

Rockström, J., et al. 2009 "Planetary Boundaries: Exploring the Safe Operating Space for Humanity," *Ecology and Society*. 14(2): 32 [online] URL: http://www.ecologyandsociety.org/vol14/iss2/art32/

Wahl, D. C. 2007 "Scale-linking Design for Systemic Health: Sustainable Communities and Cities in Context". *International Journal of Ecodynamics*, Vol.2 No.1, pp.57-72

Daniel Christian Wahl has more than 12 years of experience in sustainability education and consultancy (e.g. for the UK government and UNITAR/CIFAL Findhorn). Originally trained as a biologist (University of Edinburgh, 1996), he also holds an MSc in Holistic Science (Schumacher College, 2002) and a PhD in Natural Design (University of Dundee, 2006). Daniel was the director of Findhorn College between 2007 and 2010 (see Findhorn College). He now works independently with organizations like the Bioneers (**www.bioneers.org**), Gaia Education (**www.gaiaeducation.org**), the CLEAR VILLAGE Foundation (**www.clear-village.org**), and the Open University of Catalunya (UOC). He lives at Son Rullan on Mallorca (**www.sonrullan.es**) and is working on new methods to facilitate and mentor nature-based experiences of deep insight, reconnection, and transformation (**www.creativesustainability.eu**). Daniel writes freelance on sustainability issues (**www.ecohabitar.org**).

Just who is it that's doing the designing? Dr. Guy Burneko takes us to the origins of the universe and back to demonstrate that the answer has been here all the time, and we never had to go anywhere to find it. He suggests that an ecosocial sustainability begins with this contemplative kind of attitude. By referencing the I Ching hexagram #20, what the Cleary (1986) translation titles 'Observing', we are led to believe that functional ecohuman conduct is nothing less than an expression of cosmogenesis, the universe coming to know and understand itself. This essay may stretch your conceptual comfort zone but it will be well worth it: with a poetic flare for sculpting language, Guy reminds us ever so sublimely why we're all here doing this work.

Contemplative Ecology: An Intercultural Story

Guy Burneko, Ph.D. – Institute for Contemporary Ancient Learning, Seattle, USA

This presentation uses ideas and analogies from different cultures to say something about the kind of story or narrative we might tell on behalf of sustainability. The stories we tell about the origins and ongoing life of the universe set up the conditions for the sustainability or damage of the life systems of the Earth, because stories influence how we behave and how we treat the living systems with which we interact. In one kind of story, these systems are expressions of the overall life of the universe – and so are we and our story too.

But if we tell a story that all living things are just machine-like parts of the Earth and not its actual participants or members, this inclines us to look at Earth itself as a big machine and ourselves as controllers and operators detachable from it, something separate. In dividing the universe this way, we keep reaching 'out there' to get things from the Earth that will suit us rather than finding satisfaction in experience not carved up into pieces called me, you, me, the woodlands, waters and the animals. Dividing or dualizing outlooks intensify our drive to make unsustainable demands on the natural environment, turning it and ourselves into marketable commodities.

Suppose the story we tell is the story the universe tells about itself through us. In this case, our values, ideas and behaviors become skilful means (*upaya*) expressing the evolving universe becoming conscious in us and in our relations with it – with our greater Self. Thomas Berry calls this 'the Great Story'. Long ago, the Confucian sage Zhang Zai expressed such integrated understanding as our companionship with all things. And we may say today that mature ecological citizens are sage-like. Their comprehensive responsiveness (Chinese *kanying*) with things is a microcosm of the undivided macrocosmic universe process of interacting Heaven, Earth and Humankind. This would be cosmic evolution experiencing itself without dividing human being from all of being. In this case, our Earth-sustaining ideas and conduct would demonstrate what *Yijing* #20 calls *guan*, (contemplation, view), "a process in which the forms of things and [our] forms of seeing things coincide and in which the object and subject co-determine what look a thing has or how [a] thing presents itself".[1] Here is an integral narrative where ancient wisdom and contemporary ecoscience may join in the human-cosmic process of universe-storying on Earth. This could guide us to sustainable conduct.

The scholar Cheng writes, *guan* is not "biased by any scope or any level or any perspective". Rather, its undivided or holistic quality overcomes the fragmentation of outlooks in optimizing the potentials for *common* well-being. One who *guan*s does this by way of contemplation or meditation. We might think of this as experience that is self-rewarding because it is not divided into subject(s) seeking external gains through object(s). Or to put this idea another way, we can participate with the world in fully attentive interactions that are their own end and not means to some external end or bottom-line. Where our interactions are fully, contemplatively, attentive, there is nothing much left over in the way of a selfishly gain-seeking self – instead, we become full participants in self-rewarding experience; we embody it. The narrative of *guan* offers *intrinsic* accord and satisfaction beyond partial, sectorizing consciousness. Its ecosocial mindfulness is sustainable and sustaining because it makes less of a demand on the natural environment.

Through attentive responsiveness with the Dao of natural processes, the eco-contemplative sage practicing *guan* is alert to and expressive of subtle changes in the environment, even able to anticipate their appearance. S/he thereby spontaneously conducts hirself in a way based on a sincere and serious attentiveness which feels and comprehends nature through responsiveness from overall viewing rather than from fragmented ego-separateness. We may see this as a way of maintaining links and identification with the ever-present origins of being and evolution. Where we form one body with all things, our eco-contemplative mind is the mind of Heaven and Earth; sustainability is sagely.

A story of cosmology that helps us transform from an instrumental, acquisitive and fragmented perspective on Earth to holistic guan-like participation with the universe rhythms and patterns of experience evokes appropriate conduct and thinking. It evokes the experience that there is no privileged, anthropocentric point-of-view. Variants of this narrative have included shamanic ecstasy, discussed by Berry. These point towards a genuinely eco-poetic and celebratory mode of well-being rather than one based in consumerism or power and control. We may thus regard the development of sustainable ecosocial consciousness and conduct as

> [T]he primordial creation of a creative mind based on a vastly comprehensive and profoundly contemplative observation and understanding of a universal reality both outside and inside.[2]

Enacting analogies and interactions among insights and cultures as well as among environments and ourselves, *guan* reveals each event as a fractal, a microcosm, of undivided earth-human 'co-worlding'. Diverse events and species are mutual and reciprocal in their coevolution and with our participant-observation which, in the concepts of quantum science, participates in their expression in space, time and consciousness. Contemplative *guan* comprehensively attends with the processes of worlding so to sustain the interrelations of all its forms in beneficial and optimal, non-anthropocentric, accord. A genuinely 'functional cosmology', as Berry speaks of it, expresses the Earth-human link through 'reinventing the human' as a sustaining 'Being-inspired' dimension and member of ongoing cosmogenesis, not just as its occupant or engineer.[3]

The older Confucian idea of a continuity of being preceded Berry's of a 'functional cosmology' in which the human is not just a part but "a dimension of the Earth and indeed of the universe itself".[4] This suggests that in comprehensively engaging the environment *guan* is sustainably integrating and optimizing self-environment coevolution. *Guan* reveals characteristics of the unfolding patterns of life and universe that are analogous in the inorganic and organic as well as the cultural or mental realms. For instance, thinks Berry, differentiation is seen in the evolutionary variety of forms. Subjectivity or interiority, an inward dimension in the experience of all things, appears with an increase in the psychic unity that arises with the complexification of structures. And communion is the connection of each reality in the universe with every other reality.[5]

Analogously, communion is expressed as Hindu *Mahapurusha*, or cosmic person, *parousia*, the theological presence of God, all pervading *qi* in Chinese lore, the Christian mystical body of Christ or the alchemists' *anima mundi*, and in the collective wavefunction of particle physics, or the quantum zero-point field of self organizing complexity. Such holistic insight and its related numinosity may be attributable to archetypes of the collective unconscious which Jung and interpreters like Laughlin believe are ultimately indistinguishable from cosmic nature itself. In this narrative (of) ecology, attuning with the transformations of archetypal, organic and physical tendencies over evolutionary time is participating in cosmic nature while learning to be human. The astrophysicist Haisch's related notion is that we understand laws of nature because we and they are of the same origin – in mutual resonance and interpenetration.[6]

In "transformational interpenetration," notes Cheng, "there is no static and fixed relationship but always an exchange and interchange against a background of creative unity". Hereby, the contemplative "achieves participation from within rather than an effect from without ... as [s/he] approach[es] perfect congruence with the system", reflect Jones and Culliney. Thus, sages teach us sustainably to balance the ecology of mind and of nature by not overdoing our ego desires or inattentively undoing optimal coevolutionary connectedness. With *Yijing*, for example, *guan* does not completely divide and reduce experience into persons and nature.

Its judgments are not alien to the scientific hypotheses of Jahn and Dunne that "consciousness... can marginally influence its physical reality to a degree dependent on its subjective resonance with the system or process in question" or that symbol systems may even neurognostically 'true' our experience (i.e. the brain may be wired for holistic experience) and teach us "to perceive everyday objects, events and states of affairs as instantiations of the totality".[7]

In the symbolism of the *Yijing*, the all-connected life of the universe presences right here and now; it is not only a matter of remote eons and light-years. And its authenticity coexists in cultural creations expressed within us. In every concrete situation of life, *guan* imparts and receives the "'presencing of Being' which is the Way of [sustaining and sustainable] Transformation".[8]

Analogously, suggests Berry, the universe as the Great Self is fulfilled in the individual self, the individual self is fulfilled in the Great Self; and the universe can only be explained in terms of celebration. Disconnection from the re-source-fullness of a contemporary *guan* is a primary factor in our unsustainable ecosocial deracination.

A fruitfully ecosocial story sustains a symphony of life systems *and* of diverse kinds of consciousness. This 'ecology of mind', rather than fixation on the single aim of ego-benefit, sounds the narrative calling of our time. We are invited by *guan* to outgrow the fragmentation of our interests and reinvent (eco)humanity as a mode of the ongoing transformation-wholing – not as a fragmented particle of a single-ordered whole, but as a participating member and a 'focusing' of an open 'fielding' of emerging Earth-human relations.

Ecohumane relationships for themselves and not as tools to externalized ends (wealth, status, domination) least impose on their environment. *Guan*ing as members of life systems, we are more inclined to respect and sustainingly care for those systems as well as for ourselves and the young in education, right livelihood and celebration. *Wuwei* (unforced, nonacquisitive) conduct moderating dysfunctional environmental abuse is simultaneously imparting and receiving the wholing-event (*taiji*) in resonant, mutually beneficial *guan* attunement. Contemplative *guan* restores in Earth-human relations the *re-ligio*, re-membrance, and reciprocity (*shu*) between ourselves and the natural cosmic order.

Guan allows us to experience all beings in *analogia entis*, i.e. as self-similar fractals of the field of Heaven, Earth and Humanity, or as embodiments of the potentials of the all-connecting quantum field. Developing his narrative of the cosmic "holomovement" wherein "everything is enfolded into everything", the physicist David Bohm analogously proposes that scientific research should be complemented by meditative practice relevant to the 'undivided wholeness' disclosed by contemporary as well as ancient research. This, others call a 'mature contemplative' orientation in the participation-observation of nature. Identifying *guan* as a meditative and contemplative method, Cheng echoes contemporary quantum physics in describing *guan*'s benefit in allowing us to maintain the link and identification with the ultimate source of being and becoming. Whether this is labeled a quantum vacuum field, Gaia, ever-present origin, or *taiji* is a matter of points-of-view which in *guan* become sustainably integrated, not simply left as fragments of human-cosmic self-narration. In the end, Cheng observes, "Scientific objectivity is dependent on nonscientific subjectivity and we need to transcend and integrate both".[9]

We are now, claims Berry, entering the Ecozoic Era whose 'awareness that the universe is more cosmogenesis than cosmos might be the greatest change in human consciousness that has taken place since the awakening of the human mind in the Paleolithic Period.' Analogously, we find the practical Confucian sensibilities that,

> ... although human nature in its original substance is completely identical with the ordering principles of the universe, the human mind has to be purified [cultivated] through learning before it can fully realize the principle inherent in human nature.[10]

In this story, uncultivated ego proves unsustainable, rendering us, says Berry, 'autistic' to the Earth and to the spontaneities of cosmos in ways that amplify our ecopolitical dysfunctionality. Hence, Berry speaks of the Great Work as "the most far reaching restructuring of being that we have yet experienced". Translating *guan* across time and civilization, Tucker agrees that "The art of Confucian spirituality might be described as discovering one's cosmological being amidst daily affairs".[11]

This is also the narrative of evolutionary systems theorist Kauffman's recent book, *Reinventing the Sacred*, and of what Berry emphasizes is the reinventing of the human in a living realization of ecohuman celebration. In this view, practical contemplative experience is sustainably functional conduct. The story goes on...

Hexagram for Observing (guan).

> We are not here to control. We are here to become integral with the larger Earth community.[12]

Notes

1   Thomas Berry, *The Dream of the Earth* (San Francisco: Sierra Club Books, 1988): 111-13; Chung-ying Cheng, "Philosophical Significances of *Guan* (Contemplative Observation): On *Guan* as Onto-Hermeneutical Unity of Methodology and Ontology", *International Studies of I Ching Theory* 1 (1995): 156-203; Guy Burneko, "Contemplative Ecology: *Guan* for a More-than-Sustainable Future", *Journal of Chinese Philosophy* 37.1 (March 2010): 116-130.
2   Cheng, 163, 167-8, 170-76; Menas Kafatos and Robert Nadeau, *The Conscious Universe: Part and Whole in Modern Physical Theory* (New York: Springer-Verlag, 1990).
3   Cheng, 170, 176-77, 187, 192.
4   Berry, *Dream*, 82, 87, 195.
5   Berry, *Dream*, 45.
6   Charles D. Laughlin, "Archetypes, Neurognosis and the Quantum Sea", *Journal of Scientific Exploration* 10.3 (1996): 375-400; Charles Laughlin and C. J. Throop, "Imagination and Reality: On the Relations between Myth, Consciousness, and the Quantum Sea", *Zygon* 36.4 (2001): 709-36; Bernard Haisch. *The God Theory: Universes, Zero-Point Fields and What's Behind It All* (San Francisco: Weiser, 2006): 17.

7   Cheng, 174, 184; Jones and Culliney, 647, 652; Robert G. Jahn, and Brenda J. Dunne, *Margins of Reality: The Role of Consciousness in the Physical World* (New York: Harcourt Brace, 1987): 324; Laughlin and Throop, 729.
8   Cheng, 162-63, 170; Berry, *Dream*, 195.
9   David Bohm, *Wholeness and the Implicate Order* (London: Routledge and Kegan Paul, 1980, repr. 1981): 143-44, 155, 177-78, 203; David Bohm, *Fragmentation and Wholeness* (Jerusalem: van Leer Jerusalem Foundation, 1976): 18, 23; Cheng, "*Guan*", 167, 175.
10 Berry, *Dream*, 82; Thomas Berry, *The Great Work: Our Way into the Future* (New York: Bell Tower, 1999): 190; Tu Weiming, "Ultimate Self-Transformation as a Communal Act: Comments on Modes of Self-Cultivation in Traditional China", *Journal of Chinese Philosophy* 6 (1979): 242.
11 Berry, Dream, 215; in Tu Weiming and Mary Evelyn Tucker, eds., *Confucian Spirituality*, vols. 1 & 2. (New York: Crossroad, 2004): 1.
12 Stuart Kauffman, *Reinventing the Sacred: A New View of Science, Reason, and Religion* (New York: Basic Books, 2008): 7-9; Berry, *Great Work*, 48, 161.

I've been called to cosmogenesis since gazing at the stars on boyhood nights in Rome, NY. The journey has taken me to intercultural and transdisciplinary work in Alaska and China, an interdisciplinary Ph.D. in the evolution of consciousness at Emory, and to university teaching, writing and research fellowships elsewhere in the US. Joined with love for my gifted partner Greta D'amico and my wonderful family, my enduring interest has been celebration of the nondualized life of things in ecohumane sustainability and its evocation in science, mythopoeia and spirituality – evolutionary systems cosmology, Chinese lore and contemplative experience. My home is The Institute for Contemporary Ancient Learning in Seattle. Publications include, *By the Torch of Chaos and Doubt* (2003), and a recent article "Contemplative Ecology" in *Journal of Chinese Philosophy* (March 2010).

MODULE 1
Green Building

Contents

*Dr. Matthew Hardy introduces Module 1 with his 12 Principles of Traditional Building. As Secretary of INTBAU (International Network of Traditional Building, Architecture and Urbanism) for eight years, Matthew was instrumental in raising global awareness to the need for reviving the wisdom embodied in traditional forms and practices. His 12 Principles read like a veritable testament, akin to Holmgren's 12 Principles of Permaculture, and we might expect they will become core subject matter in architecture programs across the globe. If you're not familiar already, please take a look at the influential work Matthew spawned at **www.intbau.org** and continues today with the sister organization, the Prince's Foundation for the Built Environment - **www.princes-foundation.org***

The 12 Principles of Traditional Building

Matthew Hardy, Ph.D. – Council for European Urbanism, London

Introduction

As we face a future more uncertain, more crowded and with both dwindling resources and reduced energy available in order to manipulate those resources, it may be sensible to assess what the traditional buildings of the past can teach us. The past may be a guide to our future in two of these key principles. Like the past, the future is likely to be a time of reducing resources, and it will almost certainly be a time in which energy is increasingly hard to find and correspondingly more expensive. We might also feel that one thing that the future will not have in common with the past is huge population growth, with its associated pressures on space, water, farm land and urban building plots.[1] I hope to show in the following article how all of these issues have been dealt with, with elegance and economy, in traditional building. I list these issues as 12 fundamental principles:

1) Closed Building Energy Cycle

Traditional building systems operate using a closed energy loop. For example, lime is created by burning limestone or clays using a renewable resource, wood, and the resulting hydrated lime is set using water. The set lime can be returned to hydrated lime by re-burning. Broken bricks can be ground up and added to the lime mortar mix as a pozzolanic agent to improve setting and durability,[2] as can the ashes used to burn the limestone in the first place. This is a completely closed energy circle, as the CO_2 produced by burning wood is reabsorbed by the trees in the next growth cycle. This system relies on sustainable management of woodlands.

2) Local Materials

A Scotsman observed to me that in his home village, every house was built of materials gathered within 400 yards (metres) of its site. This rule seems almost universal for simple buildings, due to the cost and difficulty of transporting building materials over long distances. As traditional societies broke down following industrialization, and more recently following engagement with the world financial system, the first visible changes to traditional dwellings are often imported or manufactured materials. High value buildings, however, such as churches and cathedrals, frequently used a range of materials imported from across a wide region. Thus we find churches across the UK using Caen stone, a limestone from Normandy, and Purbeck marble, a hard stone from the south coast of England. In each case, heavy materials were transported by water, a low-energy method of transporting heavy materials over long distances, but one which was nevertheless very expensive and limited in its use.

3) Build Up, Don't Dig Down

Nature has provided us with an abundance of natural sites and each one, with the exception of swamps within and near which we should not build, has its own degree of slope, from gentle to steep. Traditional building adapts to a variety of slopes without destroying natural contours. A good rule, explained to me by an elderly architect, is to place the main floor plane just above the highest point that it intersects on the site. This makes sure that water running down the slope cannot enter the main rooms. We should not level ground by cut and fill, a method only made available in recent years by oil-powered excavators, but sit our buildings as far as possible on the natural slope. Clearly we must excavate our footings down to solid material, but we need not move enormous quantities of earth so that our building sits on an artificial ground plane. Rather, we should enjoy the opportunity to elevate the main floor and the possibility of providing undercrofts and basements naturally accessible from the lower level. On steeper sites, we will find the happiest relationship to the ground if the long axis of the building is parallel to the contour. These simple rules explain the effortless grace with which traditional buildings sit on the ground.

4) Timber and Wood

In the traditional landscape, woodland comprises between a sixth and a third of the available area. Woods are not wild nature, but a resource carefully managed over the long time by each village, or more recently, by woodland management agencies of government. The key is to emphasise the difference between 'timber' and 'wood'. Timber is a large section of a tree that takes time to grow, and as a result is a very valuable resource, saved for very important constructions and for ships. Timber is grown on a 40-year or longer cycle and harvested as logs at the end of the period. By contrast, wood is a different resource, harvested traditionally every seven or so years. Wood consists of poles of small diameter, grown in coppices. Coppices are trees that are regularly cut to ground level and allowed to spring up again as a series of slender stems or poles. Poles are used to frame small buildings, including small houses, sheds, wagons and other important items like furniture, tool handles, and so on. Coppices are normally limited to species such as hazel, hornbeam, beech or ash.[3]

5) Maximum Volume, Minimum Surface Area

The first principle of traditional building is to enclose the maximum possible volume using the minimum of materials, thus minimizing surface area. This is limited by the available materials of course, but a characteristic of all traditional building is a very simple overall form with very limited projections. This principle produces large areas of flat wall pierced by openings for windows and doors only. Bay windows seem to have appeared only with the Industrial Revolution. An exception is the very elaborate forms of display on urban palace facades arriving with the wealth generated by the wool trade. Here, every rule of traditional building is exceeded with conspicuous display and ostentatious decoration. Returning to our hypothetical traditional dwelling, we are likely to see decoration limited to doors and windows alone, and limited in scope. We will also certainly see no more than one window per room, and only one above or adjoining the main door, given emphasis at all. In the colder regions, main rooms are baffled from draughts with smaller air locks and lobbies. In humid regions, care will be taken to align the openings so as to permit free passage of cooling breezes.

6) Build to Enclose Open Space

Traditional builders placed houses on urban sites on the front boundary. With private open space at a premium, and securing land and goods a priority, there was no question of setting back houses from the road. The front wall of a house was the outside wall of the public space. Privacy was ensured by raising the floor level so that window sills were above eye level outside. Over time, additional buildings would be erected on the side and rear boundaries to secure the plot from encroachment. Behind the dwelling, a courtyard or side yard gave access to smaller buildings for animals, storage, processing of food, workshops and other ancillary uses. The space was often used to collect water for the household, with sophisticated examples using a central well to collect water from the roof and paving, filtered through sand beds to remove impurities. With spaces around opening directly onto the courtyard, it was a lively and social place within the household, with more private spaces located further from the courtyard. It would most likely be paved, with perhaps a few small beds or pots for flowers near the dwelling.

7) Finishes Reflect the Use of the Rooms

Within the dwelling, if a richer household, one room would have better construction and finishing than all the others, and its use would be restricted to only special occasions. In simpler households, there would be only one room, or only one main room. These principles even applied to hall houses: the open frame would be constructed with the best face of each frame facing the owner's end of the hall, away from the entry door. The plan would be a simple rectangle, or series of rectangles, with the only irregularities coming from exigencies of the site or accidents of construction history. The most important room would be the largest. Decoration will be graded throughout the house, with the best mouldings and the finest finishes reserved for the best rooms, and the best windows and the best window trimmings reserved for the street front of the house.

8) Make 16-foot (5.5 metre) Rooms

By far, the majority of European traditional buildings are built to a system based on 16 foot (5.5 metre) spans. This relates comfortably to a maximum length of easily available timbers of around 20 feet (6 metres) – a standard

Barns in Bran, Transylvania, Romania.

Market roof in Villebois-Lavalette, Charente, France.

which seems to have applied throughout all time – and more importantly allows two rows of animals to be tethered within, facing the walls, while leaving a space to walk down the centre. The dimension allows for a comfortable space around a central table and can be divided into two smaller rooms with ease. In England, France and northern Italy, such rooms were floored over by a series of smaller wood beams running fore-and-aft, resting in turn on two major timber beams running parallel to the façade. The difficulty of obtaining these latter timbers can be seen in poorer houses, with timbers often crooked, bent, tapering or re-used from some earlier structure often seen. In richer houses, large straight timbers were ornamented with decorative chamfers and richly painted decoration. Flooring depends on the availability of boards. In England, upper floors are usually wide boards, parged underneath with lime plaster. In France and Italy it was common to bridge between the wood beams with terra cotta tiles, over which a lime screed supported tiles, making a very solid and soundproof floor.

9) Shed the Rain and Make a Useable Loft

The roof is a most important element in any traditional building. Keeping the rain off, and shedding it safely away from the walls, is essential. The governing principle seems to be to create useable roof spaces while minimizing both the eaves' height and the number of junctions in the roof plane itself. Roofs in most traditions are framed with timber or wood poles, with a tie beam carefully arranged to minimize the use of heavy timbers. Thus, simple vernacular buildings are pitched straight off a wall plate using widely spaced principal rafters and small common rafters supported at their mid span by underpurlins. In simple buildings, internal walls may well be called into service to prop sections of roof. Larger and more important structures are normally trussed across the full span, irrespective of whether support is available internally. Roof trusses tend not to be fully triangulated, so as to leave useable space for storage and attic rooms. The roof pitch is proportioned by simple numerical ratios, or angles constructed using compasses, never as an angle.[4] More importantly, the pitch in a particular tradition is derived from the water-tightness of the roofing material in windy conditions. This is why houses in the Alps, where there is regular snow, have a low-pitched roof of about 1:4 pitch, while houses in rainy London, where snow is uncommon, have much steeper pitch. The difference is that the stone slab roofs used in much of the Alps are relatively waterproof, as they are constructed with large irregular slabs with many air spaces, while traditional roofs in London were constructed with small fired clay tiles that needed to be overlapped three times at a pitch of about 3:4 in order to keep out rain. Later London roofs made of Welsh slate were reduced to around 1:2 pitch or less.

10) Animals Below, Hay Above – and other storage strategies

Traditional houses were home to more than the nuclear family of recent experience. Dwellings housing 'households', not families, were the centre of an agricultural production system that included animals, labourers, household help of various sorts and large volumes of stored food and provisions. In Europe, a house might include for example a huge loft in the roof space used for storage of dry provisions such as hay and grain crops, together with large basements and cellars for animals, oils, cheeses, fruit and other preserves. The household might only occupy one floor of the house, with the animals providing heat from below in the winter, and the hay above insulating the main rooms from the cold. The plan of a simple house might include housing for animals under the same roof, even in the same rooms in very simple houses. Together with horses, and working dogs and cats kept for pest control, the traditional house was home to more than humans. Larger house plans were composed of a number of 'apartments', consisting of three rooms ranging from small to large and opening into each other. Each apartment opened onto a central hall which served as a reception point for strangers. Only the most privileged personal friends would have been allowed into an apartment. Larger and richer houses still provided for animals, feed, food and wine housing and storage, but at some remove from the main rooms, and arranged into a larger and more conscious composition. The combination of storage and home allowed a farming household to plan for lean years and survive famines in a way that is completely unknown in the present day of 'just-in-time' deliveries and supermarkets with only two days of stock.

11) Build for Cyclical Maintenance and Repair

Traditional materials are not necessarily highly durable, but they are always highly repairable. As we have seen, the lime cycle is an infinite loop. Damaged or deteriorated bricks or stones can be removed from a wall and replaced by matching bricks or stones. Lime wash, a soft external finish made of lime, water and ochre, can be applied easily over an older coat without sanding, scraping or other preparation. Broken individual roof tiles or slates are easily removed and replaced as necessary. Timbers affected by rot or borers can be cut out and a new section spliced in to make a framework as good as new. Wooden windows can be repaired in similar fashion. And in every case, the materials are readily available from the same or other sources nearby. Lime, stone, brick, plaster, timber and other natural materials are never replaced by a newer model, superseded or retired from production. These cycles of repair and renewal echo the cycles of growth and decline in the natural world, and

*Re-roofing, building
museum, Sighetu
Marmatiei,
Maramures,
Romania.*

provide local jobs for the building trades, and for quarry workers, foresters, sawmills and lime kilns. The whole cycle supports and is supported by the local economy and money is kept in the local community. Repairs become a normal part of life, and can become rituals of renewal and new life.[5]

12) Only Heat the Key Spaces

Traditional buildings were economical with heat, as wood was a valuable resource that needed to be eked out over a winter. With a kitchen stove kept going most of the year, in simple houses the kitchen became a natural centre for the household to gather to socialize and share meals. In larger or richer households, a small room would be heated in the winter, with a larger hall open to the north serving for summer entertaining. External and/or internal shutters kept the heat out in the summer, and the cold at bay in the winter. Wall hangings and paneling helped to keep the radiant temperature up a little. The remainder of heating needs were supplied by warm clothing, and in very cold climates by the heat of animals living in the floor below. In large houses, particular rooms would be used at different times of the day and year. Great care would be taken with orientation of rooms, with small winter rooms facing sunward, bedrooms east, dining rooms west and summer living rooms north. Beds in cold countries were boxed in or draped around with curtains. Nobody expected to heat or cool a whole house to a constant temperature throughout the year.

Notes

1 We might imagine a 13th principle, Avoid Excess Population Growth, but there is not space for it here.
2 See Ian Brocklebank (2006): "The Lime Spectrum", Context 96, November 2006. London: IHBC for a good account of the range of lime strengths and traditional additives. Available at ihbc.org.uk/context_archive/97/brocklebank/lime.html
3 See Oliver Rackham (1986), *The History of the Countryside*. London: J. M. Dent for a full account of traditional management of woodlands in the UK.
4 See proportions.de for a comprehensive discussion of proportioning systems.
5 As in the well known examples of the Ise shrine in Japan, and the annual refacing of mosques in Mali.

Dr. Matthew Hardy, RAIA, FRSA, RIBA, is Senior Lecturer in Architecture and Urbanism at The Prince's Foundation for the Built Environment. After working at the Foundation to establish INTBAU (International Network for Traditional Building, Architecture & Urbanism) in 2001, he served as its Secretary until early 2009 when he moved back to look after the Foundation's academic education programmes. Matthew has lectured and published widely in support of INTBAU, editing the book *Tradition Today* for INTBAU in 2008 (with Robert Adam) and *The Venice Charter Revisited* in 2009. He has taught widely on both course-work and summer programmes, as an Honorary Visiting Research Fellow at Oxford University, Visiting Professor with the University of Notre Dame, and Lecturer with the University of South Australia. Dr. Hardy has also maintained a practice in architecture and urban design in Europe and Australia since registering as an architect in South Australia in 1983. He holds a Ph.D. in Architectural History from the University of Wales, a Bachelor of Architecture from the University of Adelaide and a Diploma from The Prince of Wales's Institute of Architecture. He is a Fellow of the Royal Society of Arts, an International Member of the Royal Institute of British Architects, a member of the Royal Australian Institute of Architects, and was recently elected Chair of the Council for European Urbanism.

Cordelia Osasona provides a captivating account of the traditional building techniques of a tribe of the Yoruba ethnic group, and how these techniques have evolved over the years. Cordelia continually weaves together details of construction, choice of materials and their processing, etc., with the larger social and cultural contexts within which these choices are made. Professor Osasona states in her conclusion, "The traditional builtform, in any culture, should be the starting point in the quest for a socio-culturally appropriate, popular building culture". In that sense, she has performed a valuable service for her region by documenting in detail its 'traditional builtform'. Should modernizing trends happen to reverse themselves, for whatever reason, this culture will have something to fall back on.

Traditional Building Form and Techniques in Africa

Cordelia Osasona – Obafemi Awolowo University, Nigeria

Introduction

The present research effort spotlights the Ijebu, a tribe of the Yoruba ethnic group in Nigeria, and examines the development of their indigenous domestic architecture. The village of Iwesi, on the outskirts of Ijebu-Ode, is used as the case-study for this research. Village elders, serving as key informants, supplied historical details of not only cultural origins, but also of construction techniques, local terminology for forms, materials and techniques, and other useful information. A critique of the local indigenous architecture (in terms of the forms, and the techniques and materials generating them) was the main thrust of the survey conducted.

It was discovered that the most popular building technique is cob construction, with floor-plans invariably rectilinear. A typical homestead is seen to either take the form of clustered living spaces centered on an impluvium, or be a loose aggregation of discrete units essentially unified by socio-cultural exchanges. The traditional kitchen, a major ancillary facility in a typical Yoruba home, is discovered to feature improvisations to increase its utilitarian value.

Description of the Settlement

Over 70% of the developed part of the present-day town of Ijebu-Ode is given over to residential buildings. Mud-walled traditional buildings bravely stand shoulder-to-shoulder with modern sandcrete-block, storeyed ones. The transition, for the most part, has been very gradual, and is commonly status-motivated: a petty-trader who starts off by living in a 4-room earth

house, feels he should move into a
6-room one made of laterite blocks
held together with cement, in
tune with a big boom in business,
and a 'promotion' to the status of
'businessman'.

For the most part, the pattern of
settlement is haphazard. A central
location of the *Awujale's* (the traditional ruler's or *oba's*) palace is,
however, apparent. This has not been
brought about by deliberate planning,
but rather, by the fact that in the
olden days, it was customary for the
oba's subjects to build their houses
roughly round his palace on all sides,
such that, with time, it became the

*The health facility in
the community.*

centre of the settlement. In the village of Iwesi, however, the house of the
village head *(baale)* is situated right on the outskirts of the settlement. Perhaps
this is not so surprising, when one considers that the settlement is very small,
and that the *baale* is more or less a figurehead, having no administrative
powers, whatsoever, vested in him. In fact, the village is directly under the
administration of the *Awujale*, and is noted solely for its seasoned drummers
whose duty it is to play at the *Awujale's* palace during festivals.

In the olden days, it was also customary for a market – the chief one – to
be situated in front of (or as near as possible to) the palace. The equivalent
of this central market in Ijebu-Ode is the Odo-Egbo Market which is near
the *Awujale's* palace. Other markets of note are Ita Osun and Ita Ale, a night
market. (The word *ita*, in the Ijebu dialect, means 'market'). Most markets
in the town are held on a 5-day rotational system.

Traditional Builtform

As far as building in Yorubaland is concerned, the word 'traditional' has
come to mean not only the indigenous, but also the prevalent type of
builtform using, to a greater or lesser extent, local materials and techniques.

Generally in Yorubaland, laterite is a great favourite for various forms
of construction (even up till today when it is difficult to refer to present
building styles as traditional). In the early days of the settlement, the laterite
was used in its 'raw', unmoulded form, as opposed to the present-day trend
of making it first into bricks. An area of land was set apart as a 'borrow-
pit', and the laterite was dug up by communal effort. This was normally
done during the rainy season, when there would be plenty of water available
for the treading (and general conditioning) process, which would follow the
digging. The laterite was then well-moistened with water and trodden under
dozens of unshod feet. This treatment was repeated about thrice (in the

course of about a fortnight), till the laterite was soft and fine in texture. It was then finally heaped up on the site (called *atebo)*, and covered with large plantain/banana leaves, to prevent it hardening quickly.

Another major accessory of the traditional builtform was the palm-tree. Palm fronds were used together with broad *gbodogi (sarcophrynium)* leaves, for cladding purposes, and the stem was cut up and used as trusses and purlins on the roof framework. Today, the fibre roof has been replaced by one of corrugated metal sheets – or even asbestos-cement. The joists were usually from the coconut palm (which had been fired for extra strength), or of the branches of other trees – chosen for their hardiness and termite-resistance. The oil-palm, coconut and other trees, were readily available in the forests.

Construction Techniques

Initially, there were no particular members of the society occupied in the building trade as a way to earn a living (as there are now); every man worth his mettle was supposed to build his own house (though, invariably, his neighbours rallied round and lent him a helping hand).

With the first settlers, the prevalent building form was the 'wattle-and-daub' type: palm stems were fixed in the ground (in a double row) at intervals of about 6-12 ins. (15-30 cm), and perpendicular ones were tied to each row with creepers, forming the outline of the building on the ground, and the space between the double rows (about 30 cm wide) was filled with ready-prepared laterite. The palm stems acted as reinforcement. The building was then roofed with palm fronds on a skeleton of trusses, joists, etc.

The next type of building form did away with the palm stem reinforcement, and using the laterite just like that, was popular till early in the 1970s, when a number of innovations were made. In this building system, a man decided to build a house of 4-6 rooms (each not usually bigger than 10ft or 3m square), and when he had set about it, some of his neighbours came round to help. He could either map out the four corners of his house by four wooden posts – which were later integrated into the building – or do without them. In either case, a shallow foundation (about 1ft or 30 cm) was then dug. The laterite was then brought from the *atebo* by the volunteer

More 'progressive' vernacular building – still predicated on the central corridor.

workers (a form of communal labour termed *ebese*) who would give it a 're-tread' on the building site. Several of the workers would then take up positions as 'bricklayers' *(onimonde)*, while the others formed a chain (or several chains) engaged in throwing the laterite from one to another, till it eventually reached the 'bricklayers' – a procedure called *ju si mi, ki nju si o* (which, literally, means 'throw it to me, and I'll throw it to you').

The foundation was laid, and left to dry for about 3-4 days, after which the walls of the house were built up gradually, stopping after every 1ft 6in-2ft (45-60 cm), to allow the laterite to dry for a few days. There were two texture alternatives to the finish of the wall. In the case of a fairly smooth finish, the *onimonde* (bricklayer), after each building session, attempted to smoothen the wall surface by scraping with a wooden 'knife'. The second alternative – the more popular one – was to leave the wall slightly pitted and rough as it was; this was particularly useful in the manufacture of *oguso* – fire kindling – since the wall surface was used as a kind of mould against which the pulp from the palm fruit was stuck, to allow it to dry. The walls were about 1ft (30 cm) thick, and in the course of building, roughly trapezoidal doorways and window-openings were left. In the days before the innovation of window shutters, these openings were made very small – 1ft-1ft 6in (30-45 cm) square – so as not to permit burglars, and high (about 5ft/1.5m from the ground) to discourage peeping, and so that they would be protected from rain by the overhanging eaves.

The roofing system was fairly complex, and there were quite a number of variations. The basic construction was a system of coconut tree (or other tree branch) joists with palm stem trusses and purlins (as has already been mentioned). One way of putting on the roof was to leave the sides open; this invariably generated a gable roof. The hipped roof was the other very popular roof-type. In either case (before the innovation of nails) the joists were passed through holes made for them at the top of the walls, and all the component parts were tied together with strong creepers. Mats of woven grass fibres were tied to the joists from the inside of the building, constituting the ceiling (in some houses, this was dispensed with), and the framework of the roof was covered with a very thick layer of palm fronds, over a fairly thick one of *gbodogi* leaves. The thickness of the leaves served to keep out rain. The top layer of fronds was firmly secured to the wooden framework beneath, by binding with creepers. The whole roofing process is termed *yele*.

The building thus provided served only as the actual living quarters (i.e. it was a collection of sleeping/living rooms, the latter popularly referred to as 'parlour'), with perhaps a workroom for the man of the house, if his occupation was such as could be safely carried on in the house (e.g. as in the case of a *baba l'awo,* a traditional medicine-man, or diviner). The kitchen *(akata)* was quite detached from the house, being a separate building entirely.

This kitchen too, was built of laterite, but was on a much smaller scale than the main house. It had large, low windows – to let out smoke and let in plenty of air. It was roofed in the same way as the house, but without the mat ceiling, so that the rafters were visible and readily accessible for hiding away odds and ends. The kitchen also served as the granary, there being no need for large, separate storage structures, since farm produce was strictly for domestic consumption, rather than for trade. A shelf of tree branches fitted to the mud wall was festooned with corn-cobs which had been left in their shucks to dry first, the outer coat being used to string them up. The corn was fired from time to time to preserve it from insect pests. Conveniences such

Close-up of sequence above. (As repairs became necessary, the latest materials and techniques were used).

as a pit latrine and a bathroom were also separate from the house, and were nothing more than a palm stem or bamboo screen with, occasionally, one or two fronds thrown across the top.

The walls of the house were coated with a concoction called *eboto* – cow dung mixed with charcoal and special dark-green leaves *(ejinrin)* to form a fairly thick paste, which gave the walls a dark, glossy finish; it was also waterproof. Doorways were covered with mats or fitted with heavy doors of hewn logs which were carried bodily, and put in place at night-time, or whenever it was necessary.

Compound walls, though a common feature in the past, have completely (or nearly completely) disappeared. They were either of laterite (in which case they were a continuation of the actual walls of the buildings within the compound) or of bamboo poles/palm stems interwoven with creepers and vines. The walls enclosed the main house, the kitchen, toilet, bathroom and perhaps a shack for livestock. Today, where there is any fencing, it invariably delineates the domestic property of an individual – not necessarily a lineage grouping.

As remarked earlier, building techniques have undergone several changes, one such being a change from the use of palm fronds to corrugated (metal or asbestos) sheets for roofing. This has been accompanied by a lowering of the window level, and the introduction of shutters for the now wider windows. Proper doors are also now in use. Perhaps the most significant thing about the 'modern' traditional builtform, is the fact that the laterite is now made into bricks before use. These bricks are of two main sizes (approximately 30 x 23 x 13 cm, and 30 x 12 x 13 cm), and are not of a high standard of workmanship. In the building process, the bricks are held together with sand-cement mortar, and plastered over with the same mixture. There has also been the introduction of fascia boards in the roof structure. Even today, paint render is still optional – more a reflection of economic realities than aesthetic indifference. Generally, the outhouses have steadily maintained their positions outside the main house (though, here too, there has been a touch of modernity as, by and large, palm fronds have been replaced by corrugated metal sheets). A few buildings however, with their owners bent on making a statement of being socially 'savvy' (based on the main town having progressively encroached on Iwesi with the attendant concessions to progress that must be made), feature conveniences as tenuously-attached appendages of the back regions. Also, increasingly, the kitchen, as a separate building, has been replaced in its cooking function by borrowing space within the exaggerated central corridor of most homes, for the activity. A main doorway, in which a gate of flat lengths of wood is used in conjunction with a proper door, is fairly common. The pieces of wood forming this gate could be beautifully carved, and are nailed down, side by side, on two perpendicular pieces running top and bottom.

The rooms were usually bedroom-and-parlour combinations, and could also serve as a store for food items such as yam and cassava, or as a workshop. In the case where the bedroom was also the workshop, it was larger than normal, and could be partitioned into two – either with cloth or mats. Where a courtyard was not fully developed, the un-built part served as a playground for children, and housed livestock which were left to roam about during the day. The courtyards were also used for entertaining during festivities. (In the village of Iwesi, in the early days, this was the only available festival ground, since the status of the village was such that it did not require a large arena for elaborate festivities).

Functional Adequacy

In many ways, the materials employed in the traditional builtform, were very adequate for the purposes to which they were put. The use of laterite in building was a good economic measure, since it was readily available and cost nothing. When dry (after having been thoroughly prepared), it presents a very hard surface to the atmosphere, which is able to stand the test of intense insolation and heavy downpour (provided it is aided by a generous roof overhang). The thatch for the roof was also readily available, and is very good as a thermal interceptor (i.e. it prevents the full impact of the sun's radiation from being transmitted to the interior of the building). When laid very thick and on an incline, it also prevents rain-water from getting into the house. Using such materials as laterite and thatch, a building can be easily and cheaply maintained to give the shelter and comfort it has been designed to give.

A sheet-pan roof, for as long as it remains new and shiny, performs the same functions as a thatch one, though at a much higher cost. (The shiny surface reflects most of the heat incident on it – as compared with the storing and filtering technique of thatch.) When rusty, however, it tends to transmit most of this heat to the interior of the building, thus building up an oven-like atmosphere, which is doubtless very uncomfortable. As far as durability is concerned, the corrugated metal sheet has an edge over the thatch roof which has to be changed relatively frequently (usually, not longer than about five years).

Conclusion

Taking the whole traditional structure into account, one sees that the traditional builtform was a direct response to the traditional way of life of the Ijebu. Their simple, unsophisticated ways were reflected in their simple uncomplicated buildings; their spontaneous reliance on nature for survival could also be seen in their turning to her for the materials to build their dwelling. The earth houses with their palm frond roofs blended perfectly into the landscape of the original virgin land. The organic nature of the configuration of the traditional houseform lent itself readily to their social structure; in the event of a significant increase in family size, additional sleeping accommodation could be contrived without too great an upheaval to the building. (The expedient for occasional increases was the provision of sleeping-mats, which could be spread almost anywhere).

The traditional builtform, in any culture, should be the starting point in the quest for a socio-culturally appropriate, popular building culture. This is particularly true of developing economies. Modern architects in such regions of the world would do well to study and improve upon it, bearing in mind the fact that it has stood the test of several hundreds of years of innovations and has, to a large extent, persisted – in spite of them.

References

Information Division, Ministry of Local Government and Information, Ijebu-Ode Government Printer; Abeokuta.
Denyer, S. (1978), *African Traditional Architecture*, Heinemann; London.
Dmochowski, Z. R. (1990), *An Introduction to Nigerian Traditional Architecture*, Vols. 1-3, Ethnographica; London.
Gardi, R. (1973), *Indigenous African Architecture*, Van Nostrand Reinhold Co.; New York.
Osasona, C. O. (2005), *Ornamentation in Yoruba Folk Architecture*, Bookbuilders Editions Africa; Ibadan.
Rudofsky, B. (1964), *Architecture Without Architects: A Short Introduction to Non-Pedigreed Architecture*, Academy Editions; London.

This article first appeared in INTBAU Essays, Volume 1, Number 18, available at:
http://www.intbau.org/archive/essay18.htm
Used with permission.

Cordelia Olatokunbo Osasona is a registered Nigerian architect, and a Fellow of the Nigerian Institute of Architects (NIA). She obtained B.Sc. and M.Sc. degrees in Architecture from the University of Ife (now Obafemi Awolowo University), Ile-Ife, and is the first female architect to be trained by the University; she also obtained a Master of Art (Art History) degree, from the same institution. She is an Associate Professor, and was recently head of Architecture at OAU (2006-2009). Since her appointment in 1985, she has been teaching various courses including Freehand Drawing, Architectural Graphics and History of Architecture; in addition, over the years, she has coordinated Design Studio activities for various classes. She also teaches architectural conservation and restoration, which she has used to spearhead students' involvement in heritage property-upgrading in Ile-Ife. In 1992, she was briefly at the Centre for Architectural Research and Development Overseas (CARDO), University of Newcastle, courtesy of a British Council (Higher Education Grant) fellowship.

In the second of a series of articles in this Module describing vernacular approaches to Green Building, Thana Uthaipattrakoon provides an historical account of traditional building techniques in Thailand. As with everywhere else, the choice of materials was decided by what was available from the local ecology – in this case bamboo. Over the years, however, traditional materials have become associated with 'poverty', and now everyone wants a concrete house to show how wealthy they are! The article does a good job dispelling the tendency to romanticize the 'traditional village'. Thana, a professionally trained architect from one of the most innovative schools in Asia, also describes his experiences introducing the 'mud house' as an alternative to concrete.

Natural Building in Thailand

Thana Uthaipattrakoon –
Arsom Silp Institute of the Arts, Thailand

From the caveman era to a time when human beings first began developing actual house-building techniques, 'Natural Building' has revealed itself to be a basic human skill requiring nothing but simple materials. Throughout this long period of gestation, human beings were learning about the basic relationships between local society and geography, climate, flora and fauna, and so on. From this, Natural Building has developed into a more sophisticated vernacular architecture which is unique from place to place, depending on the differences of local context.

Southeast Asia is very humid with plentiful resources of forest, biomass, and biodiversity. In olden days, even though there were thousands of tree varieties and a lot of wood for construction, the lumber-harvesting and milling machinery was not yet developed. Most of the housing was made from bamboo and covered with leaved roofs. Only houses of the richest people with servants, royal family buildings, and religious buildings, were built from timbers and burned brick.

Teak wood is one of the most important economic products of Thailand. The exports to Europe began in 1777 – when British merchants made a deal with the governors in the Northern provinces – and lasted until 1896. During the King Rama V epoch (1910-1935), the government established its first Forestry Department. The Department developed a forest concession and invited a British man, Mr. H. Slade, to be the first Director General in charge of monitoring this concession.

However, as if hiring a fox to overlook the chicken house, the concession led to widespread deforestation all over the country. Tree cover was reduced to 53% by 1961 and by 1978 only 34% remained. This rapid deforestation resulted in emerging environmental problems throughout Thailand – for example, drought and flooding in many places. Because of these unprecedented ecological disasters, in 1989 the government decided to close the concession permanently. By that time Thailand had only 28% of her original forest cover remaining.

Apart from the concession, Thailand also witnessed a new phenomenon: Western influence on local agricultural practices to promote the cultivation of mono-crops for export. This was a result of the first National Economic and Social Development Plan that was introduced by the World Bank after the Second World War. The adoption of the western-style development model brought Thailand firmly into the global economy, with the rapid development of infrastructure and utilities, such as the construction of roads, railways, and reservoirs for power generation. All this new building caused further decline in the forest cover. As a solid symbol of entering the modern western development model, these constructions were mostly done with inflexible, relatively expensive, non-recyclable concrete.

The most significant changes occurred within the cities, whereas the rural people were still, of necessity, living harmoniously with Nature, cherishing a more simple life. They continued using natural local materials for local construction. Eventually 'the tide of development' invaded the rural areas as well. For monetary reasons, some of the villagers were encouraged to damage the forest in order to grow mono-crops. Some of the villagers were even deported according to the Forestry Department's selectively enforced attitude, believing that the villagers were destroying the forest when in fact it is black-market smugglers who are behind any unnecessary pillage. The Forestry Department is able to deport people by using the Forest Reserve Act, whereby government can announce that the community and the community forest is suddenly 'reserve' area, a distinction prohibiting people from residing there.

Workshop in Nakornratchasrima Thailand. (Mud is chemical free... safe to everyone).

With the fast pace of deforestation, Thailand had to import wood – an important building material in vernacular architecture – from neighboring countries for the very first time. As the prices rose to the point where people could no longer afford these imported woods, they replaced wood materials with concrete and cinder block. These materials became the standard for construction in Thailand, and have remained so until the present day.

Traditionally, bamboo was the most prevalent material for construction in remote areas, the chosen vernacular for village culture. The advantage of bamboo is that it is quite abundant, light-weight, easy to work with, and grows exceedingly fast. Yet bamboo was relegated to controversy when Thai law began identifying bamboo as a *temporary* building material; therefore, the owner of a bamboo house is unable to get citizenship because in a census record those people are officially considered to be *transitory*. For these reasons, hill tribe people, who have a strong traditional bond toward bamboo houses, were forced to change. If they are not recorded in the census record, they are unable to procure an ID card. This means they are technically not 'Thai', and therefore unable to qualify for social welfare or benefits from the government.

When bamboo can no longer be used, and concrete and wood become increasingly expensive, it seems that owning a strong, secure house built by one's own hands becomes ever more out of reach.

In 2002, the origination of the Mud House Project opened a new vision and new solution to Thai society. The Project began to publicize and support the notion of building one's own home using simple local materials with community participation. The Project's main strategy was to conduct workshops at locations throughout Thailand using participatory learning processes. Although the 'mud house' might not be the right solution for all, it surely can be a viable alternative for certain groups in certain contexts. From the very beginning, the Mud House Project focused on grassroots community development. It soon became very interesting, however, to discover that most of the people who are interested in the mud house come from the city. Perhaps this is because people who live in the city feel distant from Nature and long for its soothing touch. Unfortunately, the mud house is not a very viable solution for urban areas. The combination of a fast-paced lifestyle, no available local materials, and no supporting legal structure, make building mud houses in the city not only against the law, but also very expensive, since all material needs to be purchased and imported, and outside laborers and craftsmen need to be hired.

Mud house workshop with monk in Laos.

In rural areas, the majority of people have grown less appreciative of the graceful simplicity of the mud house. Many villagers have been changing their life-style from the old sustainable ways, and now strive for what money can buy; and in the construction market, that usually means a concrete house.

When I first started working with the Mud House Project, I had an opportunity to travel around the country. Things were so very different from what I had learned in school. One of the villagers shared with me that, nowadays, the corporate chain vendors have infiltrated everywhere, even into the most remote of areas. They have everything you could want up for sale, such as vegetables and fruits – and even western-style instant food and factory-produced snacks such as candy and sodas. The villagers prefer to buy these consumer goods even though they can grow some of them in their own back yard.

"Why don't they just pick stuff from their own garden so they don't have to pay for everything," I asked wonderingly.

"Because they want to show their neighbors how wealthy they are. Whoever gathers stuff from their backyard will be considered as poor," answered my guide.

From this perspective, and with this (one might say, 'globalizing') attitude, building houses at a reasonable price has become a symbol of poverty. On the other hand, owning a concrete house with its associated debt has given people the reputation of being rich, and has brought them respect and admiration from the community.

As a natural builder, there are times people have come to me because they have no option to buy and own a house. In many cases, they become sad after our conversation when they find out that the mud house is not a good choice for them either – maybe because they have no money or time, or live in a low-lying, flood-prone area, or perhaps have no access to materials. So, despite its elegant simplicity and affordability, the mud house still does not fit every circumstance or need.

In my opinion, the appearance of the mud house as an alternative spurs people to start asking questions about our society and larger context, serious questions like: "Is there any possibility for us to own an environmentally-friendly house without placing ourselves in debt for the rest of our lives?" I think of the ecovillagers as a group of people who consider themselves to be innovators ready to seek answers and try new methods in order to open the way for friendly relations with our world.

Thana Uthaipattrakoon was born on 13 Dec 1978 in Bangkok, Thailand. Thana graduated from Faculty of Architecture from Silpakorn University in 2000 and worked as a junior architect for one and a half years. Thana lived, studied and worked in Bangkok before he joined the natural building workshop which changed him forever. He decided to quit his job and became a mud building facilitator. At that time villagers were threatened by a government dam building project. Thana held a month long event to help villagers build their own houses and community buildings; a whole mud community. He then became a natural building manager in 2005. There are now six mud house learning centers that work closely with the workshop group and many more all over Thailand. Thana is currently working on a Masters in Community and Environmental Architecture, Arsom Silp Institute of Arts, Bangkok, Thailand.

Martin Stengel is an enthusiastic Green Builder! In this primer to natural building in temperate climates, the author moves deftly between providing useful information based on experience to sharing what at other times is more of a whimsical tale. Martin demonstrates how Green Building appropriately responds to issues in each of the Four Dimensions of the EDE curriculum; yet he even goes beyond that by justifying how the widespread acceptance of natural building will be an enlightened act of planetary evolution. The health and beauty which Martin sees as intrinsic to building with natural materials becomes no less than inspiration for the soul.

Green Building in Temperate Climates

Martin Stengel – Sieben Linden, Germany

Introduction

Having a warm and safe home is one of our basic needs as human beings. Having this need met is essential to our wellbeing, our capacity to face the day with energy and joy, and to offer our hospitality. The concentration of economic power in big cities lures people away from their homes in rural areas in both industrialized as well as in developing countries – therefore new housing is urgently needed around the world's growing cities. At the same time, the ecological standard of people's basic housing needs, especially since the Second World War, does not foster human health nor meet the people's need for beauty to grow and regenerate. What's more, this housing consumes enormous amounts of heating energy because of the low standard of insulation, which just isn't coherent with what's needed in the planet's current ecological situation. It seems quite clear: We urgently need to modernize, rebuild and retrofit our living structures! And there's no need to wait for miraculous solutions – everything we need is readily available!

Considerations in Temperate Climates

Housing in temperate climates calls for certain characteristics that a "good house" should meet:

- High insulation values in all parts, reducing the amount of energy needed to maintain a comfortable climate within the house, keeping energy costs to a minimum
- Enough space to live and work inside as winter can be cold and long

- good humidity resistance since wet periods also can be quite long
- a durable life-cycle, as constructing in moderate and cold climates is on average much more expensive than constructing in warm and hot climates
- a non-toxic and even health-supporting quality, as people pass many hours a day within their four walls
- last but not least: *beauty* – to stimulate our creativity and love for ourselves, each other and the planet

An increasingly important consideration for the design of new houses is the expected end of cheap and abundant fossil-fuel energy. This will affect the use of many of our conventional building materials, which require high energetic inputs for their production and distribution. 'Peak Oil' will inevitably drive up energy prices, so the need for increased energy efficiency is now becoming obvious to everybody. The need to reduce carbon emissions to mitigate climate change is emphasizing the same kinds of questions. The consequences are that we now have to consider not only how we will heat and cool our living spaces and in what quantities but also how we will provide the materials needed to construct them. Heating energy can be supplied on a renewable basis only if the average energy demand of each house is significantly reduced. There just isn't enough biologically productive area on this planet to grow enough biomass to meet the energetic demands of our existing highly inefficient buildings.

During the EDE held in the ecovillage of Sieben Linden in Summer 2009, the group of participants created a list of all qualities expected by a 'Green Building' that would connect with the four dimensions of Ecology, Economy, Social and Worldview. After studying the list we realized that all these qualities would be met by a holistically designed and constructed house built mainly out of timber, strawbales and earthen plasters. Sieben Linden is a place where all the dwellings have been built out of these ingredients for the past ten years: "Gosh, we *can* do it!"

A Smart Solution: Building with Strawbales

Building with strawbales is both a quite old and at the same time very new technology. Very soon after the first horsepower-driven balers started to change the face of traditional agriculture, the first simple strawbale homes were erected by poor workers on farms in Nebraska, USA, a region lacking wood as a building material. The oldest still-existing houses are now one-hundred years old, still being used and in good condition. Modern lifestyles and methods forced this building material to disappear – until in the late 70s alternative thinking pioneers in the US again started to rediscover this useful material, compatible for an energy conscious future. The last two decades can be seen as the real beginning of strawbale construction as a viable future tradition, with now thousands of more or less owner-built houses in the US,

Canada, Australia, China, Mongolia and most European countries. It's a fast growing, very creative, and at the same time constantly professionalizing movement.

In the following, I try to sort the characteristics of strawbale building under the Four Dimensions of the EDE curriculum, knowing that conscious readers are aware of the fact that many of the topics mentioned also relate to other Dimensions than the one in which they are listed.

Ecological Aspects

Renewable materials like strawbales and wood bind carbon dioxide during their lifetime as growing crops and trees. Choosing these materials for the construction of an environmentally-sound house means sequestering carbon from the atmosphere into the fabric of the building for up to one-hundred or even two-hundred years. If the plants are grown according to organic farming principles, as in combination with other crops, the emission of other greenhouse gases like nitrous oxides can be avoided, and even more carbon can be sequestered by building up new soil (keyword: 'carbon farming'). Making up the balance of CO_2 emissions during production of the insulating material including carbon incorporated in the material, the use of strawbales instead of conventional mineral wool saves about 25 tons of CO_2 – which means that energy put into the manufacturing of the mineral wool can be more sensibly applied to building a strawbale house and then heating it for about ten to fifteen years.

A strawbale house at Sieben Linden built entirely by hand.

Following the principles of passive solar design, and installing a controlled ventilation system with heat recovery, it is possible to achieve heating energy consumption of only 15 kWh/sq.m. This is more than ten times lower than that of the average building in Northern and Central Europe! The remaining amount of heat energy needed can be provided by very modest systems using wood, biogas and/or solar power. If a higher technical investment is possible, solar systems with seasonal solar storage tanks, best in combination with a local heating grid, can be appropriate. When plastered with clay or lime, strawbale walls can additionally reduce the need for heating and cooling by moderating indoor temperatures during changing weather conditions throughout the day and year.

In 2002 and in 2006, parts of Sieben Linden underwent carbon footprint studies, carried out by the universities of Kassel and Berlin.[1] The studies found that the emissions for housing were 90% lower than the German average, including construction and heating. In the case of one strawbale building built only by hand with natural and reused materials, the overall

result was *below zero*, meaning that more CO_2 is now sequestered in the built-in materials than had been emitted during the construction process.

Strawbales and wood can be produced without any additional chemicals. They are the cheapest available insulation material that can be delivered in perfect organic quality. At the end of the building life-cycle, the three main elements straw, wood and clay (or maybe lime) can be easily disposed of and restored to the Earth. They simply go back into the natural cycle fertilizing new organic growth without leaving troublesome residues.

Fostering Regional Resilient Economies

The Woodland Classroom at The Sustainability Centre, UK, built from local softwoods 'in the round' that are usually converted into paper or woodchip.

Strawbales, wood, and clay as the main resources for a natural strawbale house don't need intensive investment or concentrated production facilities which then require long distances of transportation to the consumer. Strawbales are the only building material provided directly from the producing farms themselves, with no need for further industrial processing. Farmers are given access to a new regional market, providing a product of high value based on the biological productivity of their region.

These are the reasons why large-scale business and industry so far have not been interested in developing, testing, standardizing and patenting methods of strawbale construction. The international community of engaged strawbale builders is doing a lot of the labour of developing and testing themselves, on a voluntary basis, driven by their fascination with the advantages for society as a whole. They are publishing most of the results as 'open source' through books, films, magazines, and a flood of internet resources. Through the publication of tests under many different conditions, and with the hands-on skills learned in workshops, the growing knowledge is made available to anyone who is interested. By acquiring these skills, these pioneers are preparing for the creation of resilient communities, ready to face shortages in energy and other resource supplies.

Availability of Straw

Twenty-percent of the annual total strawbale mass produced in Germany, for example, is available for non-agricultural purposes (data 2003). This is more than enough for constructing the approximately 190,000 one- and two-family houses that are built in Germany every year. Still, it is important to mention that straw is not at all a waste product, as some people like to call it. Nature works in cycles and everything that is taken away from fields needs to be replaced in order not to deplete the fertility of the soil. Our strawbale houses will feed forests and fields after the end of their lifetime.

Labour versus Money

As the state of our global economy seems to be moving further away from 'reliable', and as people all over the world have varying access to financial capital, it is a profound statement of security and resilience if the need for financial income can be reduced by economic self-sufficiency. Not only can people grow food in their own or the community's gardens, but building a house can be done with your own head and hands and those of some friends or economic partners. Working directly on the construction of one's own house reduces the need to earn money by selling one's labour on the market in order to pay back debts and interest through credit buying. The more uncertain employment possibilities become in industrialized countries, the starker will be the difference between conditions of families who have built rather than bought their new home.

The cost of the construction materials for a high standard strawbale house is about 50% of the total cost of building it. By using simple construction techniques, reused material and aiming at a lower standard even less investment is possible. The cost of erecting the building out of these materials is dependent upon the builder's knowledge, practical skills, organizational talents and time. Therefore, natural building with strawbales can provide affordable housing for low-income social groups in many parts of the world, especially in rural areas.

Creating Social Community

A socially healthy community is profoundly based on its economic conditions. The possibilities of meeting the needs of people by following the principles of a regionally resilient economy have been shown above. Mutually helping each other within neighbourhoods will create bonds that work as a basis for creating even more together. Along with this, building with strawbales has shown an incredible interest amongst people wanting to immerse themselves more fully into world changing activities. Working on a strawbale construction site means acquiring new skills and gaining experiences of personal empowerment. Many enthusiasts have joined networks of like-minded people in different countries, inviting interested people to assist in strawbale workshops or 'public wall-raisings' (this is a ritual in some places where locals are invited for a day of raising together the strawbale walls of a new building). The annually organized European Strawbale Gatherings (ESBG) demonstrate both a growing and professionalizing move-

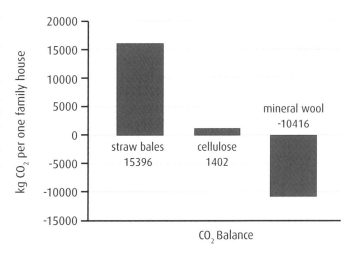

ment of alternative builders and a cross-fertilizing environment of culturally creative people.[2] While this movement typically seems to attract ecologically-conscious people that are searching for alternatives to our destructive modern practices, building with strawbales is also attracting the attention of people with no 'green' background at all, simply because of its surprising advantages: "Hey, is this what's possible with ecological standards?" they might be thinking. "Let me have a home like that, too!"

Last but not least, natural materials are an invitation to creativity and playful work. With a firm basis in professional design and sound construction techniques, there remains a lot of space for open-ended artistic expression: from playing with the motion of rounded corners or other shapes to moulding beautiful pieces of art spontaneously at the time of applying the earthen plasters on strawbale walls. Herein lies a strong healing aspect for any human being – and whoever has had the opportunity to live in a beautiful self-built house knows how deeply satisfying it can be.

Reconnecting with NATURE

Choosing to build with strawbales and clay becomes a personal process of looking at the world more holistically, with a consciousness that allows one to step out of familiar mainstream paths with their associated separation from Nature. It is often a rational *and* emotional choice to live surrounded and protected by natural materials as a sensitive human being, a being with a physical and emotional body that says 'yes' to a shell that lives and breathes too. Healing our relation with the earth-dust (a shaman friend of mine would even say 'stardust') from which we are made will synergetically contribute to the healing of the planet as well as ourselves.

Living in rooms made out of natural materials provides a major condition for becoming and staying healthier. Strawbale walls are never cold or hot. Earthen plasters are famous for absorbing odour and regulating humidity; they even have shown a high capacity to protect from electro-magnetic radiation. And touching the smooth surface of finished clay plaster can become quite an intimate sensory experience with Mother Earth...

Conclusion

Constructing with strawbales is a future-building, individually and collectively mind-shifting, and culturally creative practice. It contributes to protecting our natural habitats, fostering regionally resilient economies, and providing healthy and beautiful environments for human beings to live in. Compared to actual mainstream building methods, this is still a relatively unknown art form. But if we look at all the characteristics of this 'ancient-modern' technology and its flexibility to be combined with many other sustainable technologies – social, physical, *as well as* spiritual – I can see its promising potential as being one of the widespread construction standards of our near future, especially for human beings that are changing the world.

Notes

1 University of Kassel (2002): 'CO$_2$-Äquivalente verschiedener Lebens-und Wirtschaftsweisen'
  and
  Technical University of Berlin (2006): 'Stroh im Kopf statt Stroh im Haus'
2 For Europe see: www.strawbale-net.eu/; more internationally see: www.thelaststraw.org/

Martin Stengel is a graduate engineer with emphasis on alternative energies and sustainable housing. He has been living in community for 17 years and is one of the founders and planners of the ecovillage of Sieben Linden. He is skilled at group facilitation and community building; he leads singing in choirs; he is coordinating editor of the Eurotopia directory; and, he has been co-teaching and facilitating the Ecovillage Design Educations in Sieben Linden since 2007.

*Roshni Udyavar takes us to India with this account of passive design considerations, opening our eyes to the fact that intelligent design produces energy efficiency **and** comfort for the inhabitants. What's more, vernacular knowledge everywhere was sensitive to micro-climatic conditions; therefore, there is much to learn from the store of traditional building. While grounded in the past, Roshni points knowingly to the future: "Design of buildings with respect to climate, thermal comfort and energy efficiency is the most definitive future trend in architecture." Indeed, this is the synthesis of ecology and architecture.*

Designing Buildings for Thermal Comfort & Low Energy Footprint

Roshni Udyavar Yehuda – Rachana Sansad's Institute of Environmental Architecture, Mumbai

Introduction

It is logical that a building's design will influence its energy consumption and the thermal comfort of its inhabitants. Building design here refers to form, orientation, design of architectural elements such as openings, shades, roof, etc., use of materials and massing – all of these 'passive' features of a structure. These passive features influence a building's energy consumption for heating or cooling, ventilation and day-lighting. Unlike active elements such as fan, air conditioning or artificial lighting, they are an integral part of the structure. They are passive features which use solar energy to provide thermal comfort to inhabitants by using principles of heat and energy flow in the immediate environment.

Passive solar architecture is a holistic approach to design, which relies on knowledge of basic building physics to evolve technology which can be applied to architectural elements. It produces a design which is responsive to local climate, and therefore has social and environmental relevance as well as global appeal for its energy and resource conservation principles.

Energy Efficiency in Buildings

Energy efficiency in buildings can be achieved by:

i.   Passive solar design of buildings
ii. Use of renewable sources of energy
iii. User-end measures in energy conservation

Use of renewable energy requires higher capital investments while the user-end measures cannot be regulated except with the use of energy conserving devices and equipments. Passive solar design of buildings achieves energy efficiency without any substantial increase in capital investment. At the same time, it can make the building thermally comfortable. By some conservative estimates, the building sector world-wide could deliver emission reductions of 1.8 billion tonnes of CO_2. A more aggressive energy efficiency policy might deliver over two billion tonnes or close to three times the amount scheduled to be reduced under the Kyoto Protocol (Achim Steiner, UN Under-Secretary General and UNEP Executive Director, Oslo, March 2007/ SBCI report).

Passive design principles such as optimum orientation of buildings, it is estimated, can reduce the cooling load by 30 - 40% (Y. P. Singh, Anoj Kr. Singh, 2004). Day-lighting is another major source of energy consumption in commercial buildings. Most offices in India, for example, use artificial light during the day, consuming up to 60% of total energy consumption. This amounts to immense wastage since working light level requirements in most offices varies from 200 - 300 Lux, which is only 2-3% of the design sky condition[1] in India, which averages at 10,000 Lux (Arvind Krishan, 2007).

Thermal Comfort of Occupants

Thermal comfort can be defined as a mental state induced by physiological conditions in which a human being feels comfortable. For a long time, scientists around the world searched for a definition of thermal comfort and its variables. It was agreed that humans feel comfortable during particular seasons of the year and times of the day as compared to the rest and are, therefore, more productive at these times. This came to be called 'the comfort zone'. The British department of Scientific and Industrial Research, headed by Drs. H.M. Vernon and T. Bedford arrived at certain conclusions in their experiments and investigations. Further, C.E.P. Brooks showed that the British comfort zone lies between 58 to 70°F; the comfort zone in the United States lies between 69 and 80°F; and in the tropics it is between 74 and 85°F; with relative humidity between 30% - 70% (Brooks, Charles, Ernst, 1950).

The thermal comfort can vary with individuals, type of clothing, the nature of activity being carried on and the sex, as women and persons over 40 years are found to have a thermal comfort temperature one degree higher than others.

The Olgyay brothers were the first to propose a bioclimatic chart. This chart was built up with two elements – the dry bulb temperature as ordinate and the relative humidity as abscissa. In the center of the chart is the comfort zone. On the whole, Olgyay's bioclimatic chart effectively demonstrates that climatic parameters are not independent. American scientists have tried to establish a physiological measurement, combining the effects of temperature, humidity and air movement. This resulted in the effective temperature scale (ET) (Houghton F.C and Yaglou C.P., 1924).

The consideration of microclimatic conditions to a building's design is even more relevant than the macro-climatic analysis. For example, the presence of tall structures may shade buildings and hinder the movement of wind, while the presence of paved surfaces may reflect and re-radiate heat. The presence of sea or water body creates microclimatic conditions experienced as land and sea breezes which cannot be ignored. Plant and grassy covers reduce temperatures by absorption of insolation and cooling by evaporation.

Passive Solar Design or Bioclimatic Architecture

This has been an important field of study since Victor Olgyay's 1960s research on finding a measure for human thermal comfort with the invention of the (temperature and relative humidity) bioclimatic chart. In fact, the practice of bioclimatic architecture dates back to the beginning of agriculture and society almost 10,000 years ago and is visible in vernacular architecture around the world which was dependent on passive design in the absence of active measures such as lights, fans and air conditioners.

Several passive design strategies such as the solar chimney, the Trombe wall, the wind scoop, the malkaf, the courtyard, the wind tower, the earth air tunnel, etc. have been observed in vernacular architecture around the world designed in response to the particular climate of the place. These principles can be incorporated into modern buildings as well.

Vernacular buildings were designed to achieve thermal comfort with minimum energy inputs. Traditional examples include Buddhist caves, Taj Mahal, Agra, the Gol Gumbaz, Bijapur, and traditional temple architecture throughout India, while modern examples include the NMB Bank headquarters in Netherlands, the CII Green Building Center (a LEEDS Platinum rated building) and the IGP Complex, Gulbarga, Hyderabad among many others.

Building Physics

Architects seem to have a fear or lack of interest for all that is mathematical and lack an understanding of the basic laws of physics. The fact that this knowledge is presented in the way it is, makes it even more difficult to understand and even more improbable to influence his basic thinking.

TOMBAZIS

Right: sketch of an earth-air tunnel; Far Right: principle of a Trombe wall.

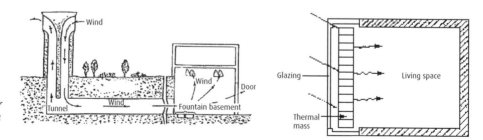

Knowledge of building physics can not only be a vital tool and skill for an architect but also can enhance design and form. It includes the principles of heat and mass transfer in buildings, which is studied with respect to orientation, materials, massing, finishing, and so on. The first step in this subject is analysis of the climate under consideration.

Rudimentary climate analysis tools which are still in use include the sun dial, the solar path diagram, the wind rose and wind square diagram, Psychometric chart, and Radiation square. Mahoney tables and bioclimatic charts are used to analyze data obtained from a meteorological department. Computer analysis tools include Autodesk software, Ecotect as well as Energy Plus and Design Builder software.

Orientation

Orientation – one of the key aspects of passive design – affects the potential capture of prevailing wind and solar radiation for a building, which are usually transmitted inside through openings or fenestration on the building envelope.

The latitude of a place and the orientation of building determine the geometric relationship between a building and its environment. In the northern hemisphere, north-south orientations are considered best while south-east north-west is considered desirable. It is difficult to provide shading on east and west facades through shading devices alone because of the horizontal angles parallel to the horizon as the sun rises and sets. The Balcony is an effective element that has evolved to deal with shading on east–west facades in India. However, the scarcity of space today often leads people to dismiss this feature thus leading to increased energy consumption in the bargain to increase internal space.

According to simulations conducted by Prof. Y. P. Singh (Dept. of Arch., MITS, Gwalior) and Anoj Kr. Singh (Research Associate, Dept. of Arch., MITS, Gwalior) in Jaipur, the amount of solar radiation per unit area on north and south facing walls is much less compared to that on the walls facing east and west. Hence, for minimum solar heat gain by the building envelope, it is desirable that the longer axis of building should lie along east and west directions. When solar angles (contributing to heat gain) and wind direction (required to orient buildings for natural ventilation) are contradictory on a site, the building can be oriented within a range of 0 to 30° of prevailing wind direction to suit the solar angles without losing any beneficial aspect of breeze; buildings can be oriented at 45° to the incident wind for diminishing the solar heat gain without significantly affecting the air motion indoors.

Opening and Fenestration

An opening represents a thermal break in the building's envelope. Fenestration is the entire assembly of the openings including the glazing,

Earth-air cooling at BCIL Collective Bangalore.

shutter, frame, vertical and/ or horizontal shading devices, louvers, light shelves, curtains and blinds. The design of fenestrations and its integration with the building form poses a huge challenge to the designer. If optimally designed, they can provide glare-free daylighting, natural ventilation and a vital link to the external environment. If poorly designed, they can cause visual and thermal discomfort through glare and heat gain.

In their research paper on analyzing the effects of design parameters on thermal performance of buildings (in the context of composite climate), Ar. Rajeev Garg and Ar. Rajesh Jain of the Department of Architecture & Planning, Indian Institute of Technology, Rourkee (JIIA, December 2007), have simulated the model of a single room building. The base case is a building with four walls, no fenestrations and sunshades. The solar heat gain in this model has been compared with other models with similar dimensions but with additions of windows, sunshades, doors, etc.

Thermal simulations were carried out for composite climate on May 30 for all the models oriented North. As the indoor temperatures were compared, it was found that the model with no fenestrations had the minimum heat gain as compared to the other three models. Shading the walls in addition to shading the openings considerably reduced heat gain, which is directly proportional to the number of fenestrations. Thus, fenestrations significantly contribute to solar heat gain and hence should be designed with utmost discretion. Large openings on north and south facades are useful as they can be shaded with horizontal devices, while smaller opening are preferred on the east and west phases, since they require vertical shading.

Vernacular Architecture

Vernacular architecture provides the best examples of architectural elements employed for thermal comfort. The use of thick walls in the Bungas of Rajasthan provides a time-lag for heat transfer, their round form minimizing heat gain per square meter of surface area. The different sizes and types of courtyards throughout India – from Rajasthan, Gujarat and Maharashtra to the Konkan belt up to Kerala – present a wide variation in courtyard design; in addition to providing privacy and an open-to-sky space, they also let in ample daylight and air circulation throughout the house. Hot and humid zones from Kerala, Maharashtra and Sri Lanka witness the absence of walls and the predominance of the roof as a design element. Different designs of the belvedere can be witnessed as it makes use of the prevailing breeze and the stack effect in coastal areas. In the hot arid regions, thick walls, compact, usually round forms, and courtyards use principles of thermal storage, ideal surface-to-volume ratio and radiative night cooling respectively.

Scope & Future

Design of buildings with respect to climate, thermal comfort and energy efficiency is the most definitive future trend in architecture. Architects will need to understand the organic processes which sustain biological life and use these principles to design sustainable buildings which will not only reduce their energy footprint but also make buildings in a real sense the 'third skin'.

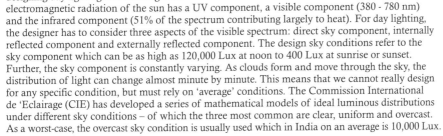

Traditional jharokha in Rajasthan.

Notes

1 Design sky conditions refer to the assumption of average sky condition that is used while designing day lighting in a building. The electromagnetic radiation of the sun has a UV component, a visible component (380 - 780 nm) and the infrared component (51% of the spectrum contributing largely to heat). For day lighting, the designer has to consider three aspects of the visible spectrum: direct sky component, internally reflected component and externally reflected component. The design sky conditions refer to the sky component which can be as high as 120,000 Lux at noon to 400 Lux at sunrise or sunset. Further, the sky component is constantly varying. As clouds form and move through the sky, the distribution of light can change almost minute by minute. This means that we cannot really design for any specific condition, but must rely on 'average' conditions. The Commission International de 'Eclairage (CIE) has developed a series of mathematical models of ideal luminous distributions under different sky conditions – of which the three most common are clear, uniform and overcast. As a worst-case, the overcast sky condition is usually used which in India on an average is 10,000 Lux.

Roshni Udyavar Yehuda is an architect and environmentalist. She heads the postgraduate department of environmental architecture at the Academy of Architecture, Rachana Sansad, Mumbai since 2003. From 1997 to 2002, she was closely associated with internationally acclaimed environmentalist, Dr. Rashmi Mayur, while working in his organization, International Institute for Sustainable Future.

Elke Cole knows what it takes to build a good house. Her approach is intimate and homey, like a warm conversation with a good friend. Her design criteria are profoundly personable and people-centered: she is building the house for real people, specific people – the people who will be living there. Reading Elke's homily may cause a little bit of sadness, for you will come to realize that the vast majority of us are living in comparatively cold, sterile, industrial-like dwellings – and what does this say for the state of the world? Elke's houses are real 'homes', overflowing with the one essential quality that can animate and bring life to its inhabitants: 'soul'.

Building as if People Mattered: A Good House

Elke Cole – OUR Ecovillage, Vancouver Island, Canada

Introduction

A good house is like a good pair of shoes – it fits comfortably, with room to wiggle but not too loose to collect debris. It is made of good materials and put together with skill, like smooth leather becomes a beautiful shoe by the hands of a shoemaker. Like a good pair of shoes it ages gracefully, doesn't need constant polishing to look good, and having a few wrinkles just shows how much you love being there. Good shoes support your feet, which in turn support your posture and whole body. A good house supports not only your body but also your soul, giving you refuge and rest. And a good house is timeless as is a good pair of shoes – not giving in to fashion's whim.

The Fit and the Support

Perhaps we all agree that a comfortable shoe is hard to find. What's comfortable for me won't be for you: we want to find the right fit for each of us. With a shoe that's a little easier to accomplish than with a house design: the house has to fit more than one person most of the time. It is a process of inquiry that, with help of inspiration and creativity, leads to a custom layout. Questions to ask are addressing what happens in the space: what do you do in any of the rooms you wish to create. Drop the labels for a while – let's not assume too much. What do you ask of a space to be able to do what you want to do: does it need to be bright? Warm? What does it feel like to be there? How does one space relate to others? What else might happen in the same space?

Now the typical trap is to make too much space for everything – just in case. A little discomfort here and there is a small price to pay for a cozy place.

If your living room feels like a hotel hall it is probably too big. If we can't see into each other's eyes or hear a quiet word when we sit together, we're too far apart. Intimacy and relationship come from bumping into each other. We learn respect by finding boundaries, not by avoiding them.

One of Elke's soft and cozy creations, with ornamentation built right into the wall.

Think about all the people in the world who live in small one-room houses. They have few belongings, and their house is their shelter and safety. In societies like that people know how to be together – they feel unsafe when no-one else is there to sleep beside them. And they share what there is: I have been humbled a few times by the incredible sense of generosity and hospitality.

So what does it take? How simple can we make it and still have our needs met? A place to sleep: just wide enough and long enough – perhaps not very tall. Make it cozy, with curved edges, let the morning light wake you. Keep out the toxic vibrations of the world: no phone, no electronics. Switch off the electricity so you may rest. Keep your clothes someplace else – perhaps close to the bathing area.

A place to wash or bathe: soothing water runs over your body, the air is warm and there's space for elbows and knees.

What about the toilet you say? Well perhaps it has its own little place: with a little window for a view and some fresh air or some poetry to read.

A place to cook and prepare food: where things are at hand and within easy reach, surfaces open and easy to clean. Here food is at the center: bins and containers to store, dry places and cool ones, stimulating the senses. Food and hospitality go hand in hand – allow for someone to be on the edge of the kitchen to talk or snack, and have the dinner table right close as well.

A place to eat: a table surrounded by seats good for an intimate dinner for two or a party of a few. Inviting conversation, within reach of the stove where the food is prepared. Comfortable enough to linger after the meal is finished.

Finally: a place to hang out – alone or with friends, with a book or a movie. Warm and cozy in winter, bright for doing things, allowing for stuff to tuck away, like favorite books, some candles, pieces of Art. The play place that connects to outside – opens up on warm days, lets the sun in.

You may have a few others, more specific places that you need for work or recreation, or for keeping stuff. I believe the basic needs are very similar for all of us, and if we can come back to a level of simplicity we will be rewarded.

What is the effect on dreamlife for a person sleeping in undulating curving space as compared to a person sleeping within four rigid square walls?

The Materials

Good materials like good food are materials that haven't been highly processed or chemically created – things like Wood, Earth, Stone and Wool. In other parts of the world it looks like Bamboo, Palm-thatch and Clay.

Point #1: Work with what's local, perhaps even on the site. Claysoil is found in abundance in many places and can be used for cob, light clay, earth plaster and floors without needing to be fired or chemically treated. Combined with straw and sand, natural pigment and some horse manure it is probably the most versatile material from structure to finish. Earthen homes have a special quality that no one can resist: thick walls, soft edges, often curved shapes with built in seats stir our soul. We want to stop there and stay for a while, let our eyes wander and feel the grounding energy. Earthen walls have the capacity to uptake humidity from the indoor air when there's excess, and release some back when there's not enough, balancing the relative humidity around 50%. This wonderful attribute means that we don't require mechanical systems that deal with excess moisture.

Let's also note here that earth building is fairly easy to learn: people of all ages can participate in workshops and enjoy working together to acquire the skills while making new friends. To understand that you could build your own home is very empowering.

A house is of course more than its walls: it needs a good foundation and a good roof, some insulation, heat, windows and more. For a low ecological footprint foundation we can consider options that combine a concrete footing with a stemwall of stone or earthbag.

There's nothing wrong with using wood if we pay attention to the methods of harvest. Ideally you'd cut down a couple of trees to allow solar access and mill them up to have rafters or floor boards. It's not always that simple though; and you may go to a local mill to source your lumber. Wherever possible it's best to leave the wood round: it's strongest that way.

One of the hardest things to choose is the roofing. Natural choices would be slate, wood shingles or thatch. Back to the question here: what's local? 'Living roofs' or 'green roofs' are becoming more and more common but still require a waterproof membrane. They improve insulation value, filter rainwater and can grow a crop if built for that.

In a colder climate we want to insulate. Nature offers some choices here too: sheep's wool, dried sea grass, straw, and hemp can be used to fill cavities.

Good materials are all around us if we pay attention and learn to use them.

Timelessness and Aging

Have you ever seen a piece of wood that has been touched thousands of times in passing? The hands slowly polish it resulting in a beautiful patina. When a building is designed carefully with attention to such details, and with the use of good materials, we experience a 'timeless' quality'. The designer's reference for this has been *A Pattern Language* in which Christopher Alexander and his team lay out the pieces that in combination make a whole that is both functional and beautiful. The patterns at work in good buildings are independent from technology and new developed things – they address our soul.

Natural Houses have a powerful impact on visitors. There's an impulse to sit down and stay a while. Exhale. People go and touch the walls that are finished with clay plaster, showing bits of straw. Eyes light up when they meet sculpted elements. And the realization that you can do it yourself is the most liberating discovery: Now the good house is within reach.

Placement and relationship to the natural surroundings are at the beginning and the end of the life of a house. When holistic design is applied, the house will be connected to place: garden, access, sun, and trees. When built from local materials we see harmony in color and surface. And if further we can stay close to the original state of a material, it will have the possibility of a graceful ending: compost or back to the earth.

Hopefully this will happen many generations later.

Elke Cole is a Natural House Designer, builder and educator. She lives at O.U.R. Ecovillage on Vancouver Island, Canada, where she coordinates the 'Natural Building Skillbuilder' programs and has her consultation and design business Houses That Love You Back. Elke's work takes her around the globe with projects in Africa, India, and Costa Rica. Her designs are based in Permaculture and value relationships between owners, builders and the natural environment presented at the site.

Elke is one of Cobworks founders. Working with groups on design and leading workshops on building projects has earned Elke a solid reputation in the Natural Building field. Elke is available for consultation, architectural design and to facilitate natural building and design workshops. Please visit **www.elkecole.com** , read her blog: **On building and being** or email **elke@cobworks.com**

Accomplished author, seasoned builder and experienced kibbutzer Jan Martin Bang provides here a comprehensive checklist for the would-be eco-builder – from the choice of materials to site-specific ecological considerations. What may be especially helpful, however, is Jan's attitude. The developed world could be viewed as a vast dumping ground of high quality, high embodied-energy materials. To the keen eye, these disposables are valuable building components. When this attitude is put into practice, we don't design our buildings first and then go out and purchase the materials; instead, we gather the materials first and then design the building around what we've got. The French call this 'bricolage'.

Building With What You Have

Jan Martin Bang – Camphill Communities, Norway

Context Considerations

Before building we need to know our context:

- The general climatic and environmental context, which will determine whether we have to concentrate on heating or cooling, bringing water in or getting rid of it
- The availability of materials, whether they be mud, wood, stone or recycled
- The social and financial context

Design

Design should reflect spiritual, social, economic and ecological values. A house designed for a dozen residents does not have to be much larger than many large family houses in the affluent West today.

- Spiritually we need space for meditation, contemplation and sacred ritual. Is this a private thing, a group activity or a combination of both?
- Socially it is important for us to decide if we all want to live together in one big room, or whether each individual or family needs to have their own house and garden.
- Our ecological aims are also quite specific in their determination of our design. What kind of heating? What kinds of materials? How do we deal with toilets and waste water?

Designers should ask site specific questions. Where are the sun and the wind? Do we want sun in the dining room and kitchen for the morning time?

Perhaps we orient the living room toward the west, so we can gather in the evenings and watch the sunset. Storage of food and fuel can be along the wall opposite the sun. Food stays cool, and the woodpile will protect from cold polar winds. Large solar facing windows let in the winter sun. An overhang gives us a place to sit and shade from the hot summer sun. This is design in action, working with the realities of the environment and the needs of the human being.

Site Planning

- Renovate if possible
- Evaluate site materials
- Locate building to minimize ecological damage
- Consider solar energy in siting and landscape
- Consider existing landscaping
- Consider transportation

Design

- Smaller is better
- Energy efficiency is top priority
- Optimise material use
- Landscape holistically considering energy and food
- Design for recycling
- Consider grey-water recycling and use
- Design for future reuse of materials
- Avoid health hazards such as radon

Site Work

- Protect top soil
- Isolate chemicals from ground water
- Minimize job-site waste creation
- Manage operations using ecologically responsible contacts and partners

Equipment

- Efficient heating and natural cooling
- Efficient lighting, window placement
- Efficient water heating; consider solar
- Consider ventilation efficiency

The Earth Sanctuary at Findhorn – a famous example of building with what you have.

Social Aspects

We are what we live in. When we plan our buildings, we are also planning what kind of society we want to create. We make the buildings, and then the buildings make us!

Which Materials?

Many modern building techniques are infatuated by the global dimension. What is suitable for Rangoon is also thought to be good in Reykjavik. The way to overcome this is to look at local indigenous traditional techniques:

- What materials did they use and how?
- Are these materials still available?
- Has the environment changed, the forests cut down, the quarries built over or used for landfills?
- Are the traditional materials privatised and therefore not available?

Countries in Europe or North America have large amounts of high-grade waste which could be used for building. For example, at Earthaven Ecovillage in North Carolina, one building was based on using crates thrown out by a local business, the free materials determining the shape and construction of the building. Hurdal ecovillage in Norway made a deal with a local manufacturer of doors and windows to buy discontinued models and designed many of their initial buildings around the sizes and shapes of these windows and doors.

Our design would be based upon balancing available materials and ambient conditions.

Materials

Most houses built in the western world today rely on industrial materials, steels, alloys, plastics, wood that has been shaped and impregnated, often chopped up and put together again, and various forms of artificial stone. These modern materials represent an enormous energy cost in terms of production and transport.

If we take as our starting point the cost of felling, sawing and transporting timber, estimated at 580 kWh/tonne, we can compare other materials:

- Timber   580
- Bricks   2,320
- Cement   2,900
- Plastic   3,480
- Glass   8,120
- Steel   13,920
- Aluminium   73,080

Stone

Because of its weight, transport over long distances is expensive but if you have stones lying around on your site, you can save lots of money. Stone requires skill to work with. Unless you are an experienced dry-stone wall builder you need to use a cement matrix to hold the stuff in place. You need to be aware of the geology; some stone weathers badly.

The easiest and most effective way of using rough stone is to build a box of wood and fill this with stones, cement and reinforcing. These wooden boxes can be built in sections which are dismantled as the cement sets, and which can then be moved along to make the next section.

Earth

You can make a test of your particular earth by taking a sample, shaking it in a jar of water, and letting it settle for a few hours. The courser material will settle at the bottom, the finer in the middle, and the organic matter on the top. Ideally a mixture of between 50-70% sand, 10-20% clay, and a good addition of chopped straw is the best for an all round plaster. The simplest plaster I've used was just a mixture of earth, sand and a little cow dung to make it hard.

Adobe are earth bricks, dried in the sun, and cemented together using the same earth mixture as a bond. Pisé involves building a framed box, ramming damp earth in hard, letting this dry and then moving the box upwards to then ram in the next layer. In both cases with an earth plaster finish on the inside and outside, you have a heat retaining wall, thermal mass, breathing qualities to give good air and a healthy inner climate.

Each building becomes a unique creation, an unreproducible work of art appearing at an unrepeatable juncture of time and space.

Bricks and Blocks

A step up from the adobe earth brick is to include a greater percentage of clay, and fire the bricks, turning the material into a kind of stone. By adding cement and other materials, you can skip the firing and use the chemical hardening process instead. Ordinary bricks are standard sized, but you still need skill and experience to lay good walls.

Building blocks are typically much larger, and shaped for things like corners, strengthening courses and door or window surrounds. Making your own cement blocks is pretty easy. In the 1960s the Appropriate Technology folks developed a lever operated press to make bricks from earth with a small percentage of cement added. The Cinva Ram, as it is called, has decades of experience behind it and tens of thousands of homes have been built with it.

Tiles and Pottery

Tiles for roofing can be made in the same way. Fired tiles are waterproof, and will last for hundreds of years.

Glass

Some modern windows are very high tech, very expensive, and efficiently minimise heat loss. At that end of the range, with aluminium alloy frames, triple plated, vacuum spaced, possibly photo sensitive glass, you need to consider the embodied energy and the processes that go into the components. At the other end of the range, scavenging windows and frames from houses about to be demolished, you can find the cheapest and most environmentally friendly solution. Get hold of the windows before building the house, so that you can plan the window sizes right from the start.

Metals

Today we use a wide range of metals in our houses, both for structural purposes, and fittings and connections. They are precious resources, mined, heavily processed and often transported far, with all the embodied energy problems that this entails. On the other hand, with careful forethought they can often be recycled quite effectively, and that has an enormous bearing upon the energy use.

It is worth bearing in mind that certain metals have health hazards. Lead in pipes and in paint is perhaps most well known, but there are many others: mercury, nickel, zinc, silver, arsenic, etc.

Timber

Untreated timber is clean, can be shaped with fairly simple hand or power tools, can be fitted together with joints or pegs, usually ages well, and can be recycled in many ways when we have finished with the building.

Various kinds of timber behave differently, some withstand water by their very nature, some split easily giving us shingles for the roof. Others again are soft and easily worked into decorative elements. They come in many colours and often with delightful graining. Combinations of different timbers can be a real joy to live amongst.

Timber treated with arsenic to avoid fungus rot is highly toxic.

Our buildings can once again become the reserve of fine craftsman, as in this impeccably notched cabin in Norway. This kind of skill cannot be mass produced.

Grass and Stuff

Canes, reeds, bamboo, grasses and straw all belong together. Straw houses are as old as the earliest shelter building. Examples of vernacular architecture from other parts of the world include mudhifs of Iraq made of reeds, Balinese bamboo houses and the reed shelters used around Lake Titicaca in Bolivia.

Straw Bales (SB)

Modern strawbale houses have been standing for nearly a century already. The original load bearing construction of the Nebraska SB

house is being increasingly replaced by a post and beam structure where the bales are used as infill.

SB houses have the advantage of being built from an organic, renewable material. SBs breathe, depending upon the plaster you apply, and have an insulation far higher than that which is generally demanded by building codes. The actual wall construction, both bales and plaster, requires a group effort by people who need no special skills, though they do need an experienced guide.

Natural Fibres

Today the tipi and the yurt have made a comeback in alternative circles, and are viable forms of quick and relatively cheap housing. Wool, cotton, linen, silk, sisal, jute, rayon, kapok and coir are all worth considering.

Hemp used to be produced in vast quantities in many parts of the world and was the basis for rope and coarse material for literally millennia. As a crop, it requires very little protection against pests and diseases, and as a product, it would fit perfectly into a system which wants to grow and use organic, natural fibres.

Generally, fibres would form components of your indoor fittings rather than the materials from which you build, for example: curtains, carpets, wall hangings and lots more, not to mention clothes, bedclothes, towels, etc.

Paints

Paints consist of a pigment floating in a liquid, either water or oil, and today can contain many compounds which are a hazard to our health.

If you can, find suppliers of natural paints and varnishes. These suppliers exist in small numbers and are following a pattern not so different from the organic food market of a couple of decades ago.

Junk and Recycling

All over the world we are knocking down old buildings as fast as possible, and often many usable components are shoveled into landfills. Planking, beams, windows, doors, plumbing fixtures and furniture can all be salvaged and reused. This is not appropriate for the mass- produced modern industrial house, but rather to the individual, tailor-made, hand-built house. This is ideal for an Ecovillage, where we can create our own cottage industry, collecting materials, storing them and using them. The ecological saving is significant and reduces the embodied energy costs of a building.

'Earthships' is a concept developed by Mike Reynolds in New Mexico during the 60s and 70s. Old car tyres are stacked up and filled with earth, creating massive thermal walls. Tin cans are cemented together with mud to make insulated interior walls. The idea of using junk not only makes our building cheaper, it also fills a need in getting rid of and making use of an energy-embodied resource.

Plastics

Most plastics are made from oil, and once made can be recycled almost indefinitely. This makes it a useful and flexible material. The biggest drawback is that many plastics contain gases that leak out slowly. Another drawback is that plastics give off poisonous gases when burnt, and are heavy industrial products. Given that we can minimise these two problems, plastics have a place in our list of building materials.

When building with what you have, a structure is never entirely complete. As new materials are gathered, new opportunities arise for extension or embellishment.

A Check List for Materials

- Avoid ozone depleting materials
- Avoid materials with high energy costs
- Utilize local material
- Look for locally recycled material
- Minimize use of old growth lumber
- Minimize materials that off-gas
- Minimize use of pressure treated wood
- Minimize packaging and resulting waste

Jan Martin Bang is an ecovillage activist with 16 years experience as a kibbutz member in Israel and seven years as a Camphill co-worker in Norway. He writes for *Landsbyliv* (Village Life), the Norwegian Camphill magazine, and is an active member of the Norwegian Ecovillage Trust.

He has written a book on Permaculture Ecovillage Design published by Floris Books in 2005, called *Ecovillages: A Practical Guide to Sustainable Communities*. A second book, *Growing Eco-Communities: Practical Ways to Create Sustainability* was published by Floris Books in 2007. *Sakhnin: A Portrait of an Environmental Peace Project in Israel* was published in 2009, and he is currently working on two books about the Camphill movement.

He can be contacted at: **jmbang@start.no**

MODULE 2
Local Food

Contents

This article on soil restoration begins Module 2, since healthy soil is the foundation of all local food practices. With the rigor of a soil scientist and the observant tenacity of a permaculturist, Achim Ecker introduces us to the fundamentals of this essential activity. Visitors to Achim's native ecovillage in Germany, ZEGG, instantly notice the increase in wildlife and lushness of vegetation as compared to the surrounding terrain. Achim refers to this as 'Paradise'; and after reading his article, it will become obvious that any chance of regaining Paradise on Earth must begin with healthy soil restoration.

Healthy Soil Restoration: The Key to Sustainability

Achim Ecker – ZEGG, Germany

"The best thing that humans can do is build topsoil."

Healthy Soil = Healthy Plants = Healthy Food = Healthy People

The first 30cm of soil are vitally important for the development and sustainment of Life on Earth. This level, the humus top-layer, feeds plants, animals and humans with all the necessary nutrients. This is how it has always been. Since the beginning of industrial agriculture, however, we witness an alarming loss of this vital topsoil. Worldwide, 24 billion tons of fertile soil annually are washed or blown away, or are simply destroyed. This huge mass of material would suffice to cover the entire agricultural surface of the United States.

The Role of Healthy Soils

The key to sustainability is to begin with soil restoration. It sounds so simple yet can be quite profound: Ultimately, soil is our only source for healthy food/nutrition. In addition to air and water, it is one of the essential environmental systems, which together make up the basis of life for us humans, for the flora and the fauna. Only healthy soils are capable of sustaining biodiversity, genetic and natural resources. Healthy soils are indispensable for the production of food and for the storage of water and energy. Healthy soils also have active microbial life that are capable of breaking down and utilizing many pollutants.

Soil life – micro-, meso- and macro-fauna – is a key indicator. These soil biota are the managers, or underground stewards of the Earth. Worms, in particular, break down organic material into smaller forms that can be digested by microbial beings such as bacteria and fungi. These in turn further digest the organic matter in order that minerals can be more easily assimilated by plants. Worm castings (worm poop) are Nature's best fertilizer, and worms can create 60 tons of worm cast per acre per year.

The amount of soil organisms is unimaginably large. Just one gram of healthy soil contains approximately 600 million bacteria, 400,000 fungi and 100,000 algae. On one hectare of soil this amounts to more than 20,000 kg of microorganisms within the upper 15 cm. In addition there are 4500 kg of higher organisms at work in and on the soil.

Soil testing.

Decaying organic matter may well be considered as fuel for bacterial activities in the soil, which operates as a factory producing plant nutrients. Soil bacteria, the agents of decomposition, use carbon mainly as fuel, and nitrogen as building material for their bodies. Bacterial activity will not occur in the absence of water or mineral elements such as calcium, magnesium, potassium, phosphorus, and others. These, as well as nitrogen, are essential. Soil organic matter is the source of nitrogen, the basic component for all proteins and amino acids.

Natural Recycling

Decomposition by micro-organisms within the soil is the reverse of the process represented by plant growth above the soil. Growing plants, using the energy of the sun, synthesize carbon, nitrogen, and all other elements into complex compounds. The energy stored up in these compounds is then used more or less completely by the microorganisms whose activity within the soil makes nutrients available for a new generation of plants. Organic matter thus supplies the 'Life of the Soil' in the strictest sense.

Soil History

Soil, that incredible medium in which our food is grown, is made up of three basic elements – water 25%, air 25% and solids 50%. The solids are made up of organic (humus - living and/or once living, now decaying) and inorganic (non-living such as rock and mineral) matter. It is the amount and variety of organic matter in the soil that determines how potent and fertile it is. The exact composition of humus is still a mystery to chemical science today.

Once upon a time, most parts of Europe (and the whole world!) were densely forested. A thick deciduous forest layer kept moisture in the ground, prevented erosion, and was a continuous source of organic matter. The high productivity of most virgin soils has always been associated with their high content of organic matter, and the decrease in the supply of these soils with cultivation has generally been paralleled by a corresponding decrease in productivity.

The glacial residue of pulverized rock offered minerals in solution for plant growth. As the plants found nitrogen to combine with these minerals, they grew, expired, and began to accumulate in the soil. Finally, when the rocks were more completely weathered so that they provided less minerals, an equilibrium point was reached at which the accumulated organic matter held in combination most of the minerals that could be turned into soluble forms.

To re-establish this equilibrium is the main goal of all soil restoration.

Soil Restoration

Coming from these considerations, the protection and improvement of the soil layer are key concerns of the ecological work done at the ZEGG. In the state of Brandenburg, with deep post-glacial sands, the soil is well aerated but water drains right through taking precious nutrients with it. In the forests, average humus layer is no more than 2 cm deep. In open terrain, a thin grassy sod covers pure sand. Originally the soil was very poor in organisms and vitality. One problem is the low amount of rainfall, amounting to only 500 mm per year, together with the sandy soils and their poor capacity to store water.

A soil rich in diverse forms of organic matter is a healthy soil. Such soil will contain life forms such as bacteria, fungi, molds, worms, insects, plants and more. This rich variety, or biodiversity, is what will ensure the plants receive an abundance of nutrients in the correct balance. Crops will thrive! Healthy soil is the foundation for a prospering organic vegetable garden and fruit orchard. Our two main strategies of soil quality restoration at ZEGG are: improving organic matter content and re-establishment of soil dwelling populations (microbes, fungi, worms, insects, etc.) by creating good life conditions for them. We have steadily increased the humus layer by mulching with old straw, leaves and hay from the parks and public gardens of the Belzig municipality, and with cardboard. Mulching creates a habitat for a multitude of organisms and fungi, which make nutrients available to other plants.

Leaf compost.

Fresh organic matter is characterized as a rule by a large amount of carbon in relation to nitrogen. So, initially, the decomposition will draw nitrogen from the soil: the mulch layer needs nitrogen for its decomposition. After the breaking down of the mulch, thanks to the soil life activity, there will be more nitrogen available. Each time the process will be faster. The restoration of soil organic matter, thus, is often a problem of increasing the nitrogen level. This is the basic principle behind the use of legumes as green manures. In building up the organic content of the soil itself, it will often be desirable to use legumes and grasses rather than simply to add organic matter, such as straw and compost, directly. Legumes draw nitrogen from the air and deposit it in the soil; the amount in the soil is further increased when their own remains are added to it.

"Shit makes flowers grow!" Together with urine it contains high amounts of nitrogen and minerals. We eat the plants (or animals that ate the plants). Plants contain nitrogen that we pass on in concentrated forms. On some of the mulched areas at the ZEGG, we also spread the compost from our dry toilets, as the nitrogen, phosphorus, the innumerable microorganisms, fungi and worms promote decomposition of the organic material into rich, usable humus. Initially we scattered clay dust, which forms a mineral compound with humus, thereby improving its ability to retain nutrients and water, preventing their loss by leaching into the groundwater in our sandy soils.

ZEGG harvest.

Another valuable method of soil restoration is the use of green manures. These include peas, beans, lentils, clover, alfalfa (*Medicago sativa*), lupines (*Lupinus polyphyllos*), broom and black locust (*Robinia pseudo-acacia*) – all members of the pea family (*fabaceae*). Over a period of several years, we have sown a large variety of green manure plants, which now freely propagate themselves. Alfalfa (*Medicago sativa*) was especially important to us in re-cultivating the land. It is able to extend its root system down to an astounding depth of more than 10 meters, enabling it to remain lush and green even during the driest of summers. In this way, it makes water and minerals from deep levels of the ground available to many other plants, and permeates the soil with veins of humus.

We use a mulch mower and subsequently leave the plant material lying on the ground, in order to recreate a natural layer of humus.

Using Local Resources

For about 12 years now, our local town of Belzig has been supplying us with profuse amounts of autumn leaves. Before this, they would drive them to the garbage dump about 10 km away. They actually had to pay to deposit this 'waste'. Ever since they have been bringing it to us, they have been paying less, driving less, and wasting less energy. We let these leaves sit for awhile, and then spread them under trees and bushes, or cover and consequently feed entire grasslands with the intention of cultivating them with vegetables afterwards.

The leaf mulch has proven to be particularly beneficial in the forest, as in addition to improving the soil it suppresses the dreaded grasses. Leaf mulch contains seeds from a host of other trees and shrubs which all contribute to transforming a typical, post-modern pine monoculture into a full mixed-use forest, combining a variety of fructiferous trees with the usual understory plants. Leaf mulch provides these seeds with the perfect conditions for germination and early growth (cool/damp stratification).

Additionally, in the forests on the grounds of the ZEGG, we created so-called Benjes – hedges from brush-wood – providing habitat for hedgehogs, snakes, toads, amphibians and birds. The slow decomposition of organic material over time steadily improves the soil. These hedges retain water and slow down winds. Birds settle on them and drop seeds, which can then sprout and grow protected from game. Since we began our soil restoration work, vitality has already been considerably improved and a large variety of micro-organisms, insects and fungi, but also birds and many other animals, may be observed. A very particular healing dynamic has been initiated, which is especially obvious during dry spells. We have been able to reduce watering to an absolute minimum, while the vegetation remains vibrantly green for much longer periods. While we strive to improve the soil in large parts of our land, other areas are left untouched as rough pasture, forest biotope, etc. We very rarely enter these enclaves, leaving them to themselves as much as possible, so that they remain sanctuaries for the animals and nature spirits on our terrain.

When neighbors and guests enter ZEGG, they instantly notice many more birds and much more lush vegetation than just a hundred meters away. Birds thrive on this richly set table of a healthier food chain. Every year a greater variety of birds come to enjoy this and help us with our gardening. An herbalist discovered more than 80 healing herbs growing wild here. The enriched soil life has given us 'Paradise' and has provided natural ground to support a higher diversity of plants, insects, birds and animals – and higher diversity means higher resilience in extreme times. Just remember: the basis of all this is a healthy soil: it is the Mother of health for all that live upon it.

References

http://www.zegg.de/zegg-community/ecology.html
Sustainability and Ecology at the ZEGG Community by Achim Ecker.

Achim Ecker, born in 1959, has lived at ZEGG for more than 25 years. He has been deeply involved in the development of the ZEGG-Forum and has trained and supervised groups at ZEGG and in Europe, South America and the USA. He has a deep care for people and for our planet. At ZEGG he is the chief landscape designer creating fertile soil and an edible landscape on glacial sand using intuition and permaculture knowledge. He studied permaculture with Fukuoka in Greece and with many others in Germany. He also works as an eco builder on the multi-facetted challenges of retrofitting and insulating existing houses with renewable materials. He is motivated by a deep caring, compassion and love for people and life. Achim always seeks new edges to learn and teach. For the last 15 years he has been teaching integral Forum and awareness training in German, English and Spanish. His homepage is: **www.zegg-forum.org**

This essay about the local agricultural techniques practiced at Konohana Family has truly global implications. Michiyo Furuhashi writes with genuine heartfelt belief in the importance of her work. Key to the vitality of all the interweaving systems at Konohana Family – ecosystem, soil system, and the bio-systems of plants and animals, including human – is the production of 'Konohana-kin', a microbial-based solution. Konohana-kin, teeming with beneficial micro-organisms, is freely applied as the foundational nutrient layer; thus, all living systems at Konohana Family share this microbial source. After reading this essay, you will want to begin feeding Konohana-kin to all your kin also!

Organic Growing for Community Self-Sufficiency

Michiyo Furuhashi – Konohana Family, Japan

Agriculture of Konohana Family

Konohana Family, established in 1994, is an agricultural community of 71 people living together, crossing the boundaries of blood relationships. The basis of the Family's life is organic agriculture, growing various kind of produce such as rice, cereals, vegetables, poultry for eggs, bees for honey, goats for milk, and tea and fruits. We also produce miso and soy sauce with the traditional method, and a variety of processed products, living a self-sufficient lifestyle rich in variety. We produce almost everything by our own hands except salt, sugar, some spices, vinegar, and oil.

We develop and engage in various businesses and activities such as delivering our rice and vegetables using the brown-box scheme, offering educational programs to local people and visitors regarding ecovillage development and organic agriculture, accepting guests requiring mental care, and cooperating with the Ecovillage Design Education (EDE) program.

We produce food in small quantities but with great variety, including 10 varieties of rice, 217 varieties (88 items) of vegetables, nine varieties (five items) of cereal, and 36 varieties (25 items) of tea and fruit.

Our production area is eight hectares of rice fields and eight hectares of vegetable fields. This land is scattered around our neighborhood and 90% of it was fallow land which we have been allowed to use free of charge. In order to achieve the greatest degree of self-sufficiency possible, we sow and cultivate the same land several times consecutively, adjusting timing for continual harvesting of vegetables in season.

We follow Nature's way as our model. Nature does not have an ego, maintains harmony, and ensures that its members rely on each other. In order to live in harmony with others naturally as compassionate individuals, we hold meetings every night to reflect back on and openly discuss any issues or thoughts which may be causing any one of us concern. We have never skipped a single meeting even once over the last sixteen years.

The agriculture of Konohana Family, similar to our way of life, uses Nature as a model. Soil that can grow healthy crops is a rich ecosystem with rich biodiversity.

Generally, when we say 'soil' we mean the collection of microorganisms, small insects, their droppings, dead insects, dried leaves and other organic matter. A good example is a healthy natural forest where the forest bed is squishy-squashy when you walk on it. Crops are grown using this refuse generated from the infinite activity of life and other broken down organic matter as nutrition.

Trees in the forest look as though they are growing without doing anything; however, they actually live through connection with other life forms. Many life forms such as microorganisms and small insects are contained in the soil of healthy forests. Fallen leaves on the ground are broken down and turned into nourishment by the microorganisms and the insects. Konohana Family tries to duplicate the same conditions in our fields. In addition, what makes the crops grow is not only soil: adding the light of the sun, water, wind, air and human love makes it possible to produce healthy food full of life's vital energy.

Types of Organic Fertilizers

In the last 15 years, Konohana Family has been practicing a type of organic agriculture which fully utilizes organic fertilizer obtained from local sources. Table 1 shows the locally obtained types of organic fertilizer categorized by C/N ratio.[1] High C/N ratio materials are used for compost, to cover the surface of cultivated soil as organic mulch[2] and/or for plowing back with the residue of crops to make new soil after a crop has been harvested. Low C/N ratio materials are used as sub-materials for compost, as an enhancer to break down crop residue, and for anaerobic fermented bokashi[3] or soil bokashi. Since the low C/N ratio organic materials are easily effective, we generally let them go through a fermentation process with microorganisms.

Table 1: Locally Obtained Organic Materials.

High C/N	chaff, grazing, fallen leaf, reed, turf grass, paper sludge, charcoal, smoked charcoal, green leaf, rice straw, straw, buckwheat straw.
Low C/N	poultry manure, cow manure, goat manure, rice bran, tofu refuse, wheat refuse, soybean refuse, cooked water of soybean, water of washed white rice, cooked water of buckwheat noodles, kitchen waste, fresh leaf.

Until recently we primarily used this kind of fertilizer. However, from July 2009 we have been experimenting with the 'The Carbon Circulation Method' (CCM). In the CCM, we do not add any manure, but rather keep adding high C/N materials such as used mushroom beds, wooden chips, and half-raw grasses. As a result, we can get twice more harvest than the conventional method. We have observed good results in our experimental fields, and we intend to steadily shift to this method.

Konohana-kin (microorganisms)

We develop microorganism-based materials using these raw organic fertilizer sources to utilize in our fields. Among those, I would particularly like to introduce Konohana-kin (kin means 'microorganisms' in Japanese). Konohana-kin is a fermented microorganism solution where effective locally adapted microorganisms are selected from natural ingredients and then compound cultured. We consider it to be a basic necessary material for use in any organic product. Ingredients used are tofu refuse, brown rice amino acid, pine needles, loquat leaves, bamboo leaves, herb, citrus peels, stevia (produced by ourselves), molasses, and finally microorganism materials (EM2, EM3, EM4) which we purchase.

We believe that the primary source of fermentation is the microbial communities already existing in the other natural ingredients since the additive proportion of EM materials is only 1/100 each. The process promotes accelerated lactic fermentation in the existing microbial communities such as natural lactic acids and yeasts with the fermentation being induced by EM. We arrived at the present production method of Konohana-kin after a long time of trial and error, which also took hints from sake brewing technology. It is not merely a cultured solution of microorganisms but rather can be brewed at a consistent level of quality as in sake and soy sauce production. The production method is explained on our website (in Japanese) and we welcome observation and provide training.

Konohana-kin is an indispensable material for production of composts and bokashi, and we feed fermented foliage mixed with Konohana-kin to our chicken and goats, and also add it to the food for our bees. Organic matter resulting from daily living such as leftover water from cooked soybeans and water of washed white rice are subjected to lactic acid fermentation using Konohana-kin and used to make an activate solution of microorganisms which we sprinkle on soil, and/or mix for making compost. With these effective microorganisms in the intestines of our animals and in the organic matter applied to our fields at work, we expect the development of a compatible relationship in the ecosystem between the crops and animals. As for livestock, we are able to raise them without using any antibiotics or chemicals, and realize a significant improvement in fodder and in their breeding environment by using the microorganisms.

Our Basic Attitude about the Use of Organic Matter

We believe that the organic matter acts as a lever to activate the natural ecosystem in the soil. Looking at the bigger picture, having organic farmland

*The Konohana-kin
of the Konohana
Family live out their
lives at the foot of
Mt. Fuji, and are
no doubt nourished
by the subterranean
geothermal activity.*

means circulating the local organic matter and converting organic waste into a useful resource.

It is said that the soil is not simply a container for fertilizer but that it is actually a living society and a soil-ecosystem, and the microorganisms living there gain more than 95% of their energy and nutrients from organic matter in the soil. Plants also naturally have a system to absorb the necessary nutrients for growth from the substances circulating in the soil which are generated by soil-microorganisms. The natural ecosystem has a mechanism for plants to spontaneously generate the necessary nutrients, and many creatures' lives are supported by the plants to balance out the system.

Applying this principle to the field, it is possible to promote the action of soil-microorganisms and activate the soil-ecosystem by collecting and processing various local organic matter and turning it into organic fertilizer in the field. As a result, it becomes possible to produce stable and high quality food products. The organic matter is not simply a replacement for chemical fertilizer; it is utilized to adjust the soil-ecosystem which is the basis of crop production by combining various ecological technologies and putting them into practice.

The Utilization of Konohana-kin for Bee Keeping

Currently, it is difficult to obtain safe food throughout the world. We use Konohana-kin not only in basic farming but for raising livestock and beekeeping as well. Recently, a phenomenon in which bees are disappearing is occurring worldwide, including in Japan. This is called Colony Collapse Disorder (CCD), and this is a phenomenon in which a large numbers of bees disappear overnight with no discernible cause.

One of the possible reasons is a virus. It has been observed that the immune system of bees is weakened by investigating the bees which are left in the hives. Resistance to the virus can be improved by enhancing their immunity. We expect to enhance the immune systems of animals and plants when we use Konohana-kin, and clear results have been obtained. We consider that the more we use Konohana-kin, more resistance is developed to various diseases. The breeding environment of bees has worsened in Japan as well, and by applying chemicals to the disease bacterium and parasites as in normal bee keeping, those organisms grow stronger. Thus, it goes into a vicious circle, which means more chemicals need to be applied. Konohana Family does not use antibiotics, so parasitic infestation is very low. Therefore, the use of chemicals against general parasites is purposely de-emphasized. An environment is created that excludes bacterium harmful toward life by putting priority on good bacterium through the spraying of Konohana-kin in the beehives and mixing it in their food and water. The enzymes refined from Konohana-kin have the ability to circulate life, so naturally it works for the health of the bees effectively. It is also thought that the surviving good bacterium enhances the immune system of bees, and that creates a condition of disease resistance.

History of Konohana's Agricultural Practice

Konohana Family gradually began converting its production method to the 'Carbon Circulation Method' (CCM) starting in July 2009. Until then, we had utilized the organic fertilizer that can be obtained locally as mentioned above.

     The quality of the local land was poor, particularly in the beginning, so we applied local organic material such as fallen leaves, reeds and poultry manure to the soil. Later, the area of land that we cultivated increased so we could not get enough fallen leaves and reeds for all fields; therefore, we applied 1.5 tons of poultry manure per 10 acres of land. This method gave good results at the beginning. However, insect damage and plant disease grew worse. Those phenomena made us realize that we put too much fertilizer, so we reduced the amount to between 400 and 800 kg per 10 acres. As a result, we had no problem with komatuna,[4] carrots, and daikon, but in spite of the reduction of fertilizer, we still had pest problems with cabbage and broccoli. We discovered CCM later as we sought a new solution.

The Carbon Circulation Method (CCM)

We began to grow leafy vegetables such as komatsuna, rocket salad, and cabbage with this method in July. Currently (October 2010) we are harvesting them and we have observed significant improvement over the previous crops. All crops are shiny, the leaves are thick and rich in color (which differs from the results gained by applying excessive fertilizer), and the taste is consistent.

     Here is the procedure: Shred green manure and mix with soil, then add the activated Konohana-kin solution[5] and a small amount of raw rice bran. Till the soil surface to a shallow depth of 5 centimeters. Wait for one week as the activated micro-organisms break down the green manure and increase in numbers. Then, one week later, till the soil deeper to 15 centimeters. Two weeks after mixing the green manure in the soil, the soil is set to plant seedlings and sprinkle seeds. Here, Konohana-kin provides an opportunity for good bacterium and indigenous bacterium to increase their numbers, and plays a role in encouraging fermentation rather than decay. Until now it was thought that immature green manure prevents growth; thus we had always waited for three months after tilling with the green manure.

     Life and death always follow each other in the natural world. With CCM, life energy is passed on from one generation to the next. For example,

*A particularly
delectable palette
of fine alimentary
creations – the
ingredients produced
entirely within the
ecovillage.*

let us say that there were not enough minerals in the soil. If Sorghum is grown in the field accumulating minerals and used as mentioned above as green manure, the life of the tilled Sorghum is not lost, rather it is broken down by micro-organisms. At the same time, it supplies minerals and acts as a source to nurture new lives.

The agriculture of Konohana Family is called 'Natural Farming'. This does not mean 'not doing anything' and totally depending on Nature, but rather engaging the human element *as part of* Nature. That is the way of our agriculture. We think that we can make sustainable food production possible by putting thought into the process: increasing the circulation, concentration, and availability of materials in Nature, and by introducing organic matter at appropriate times for the local climate and land.

Conclusion

The food self-sufficiency ratio of Japan is 41% by calories; which means that, indeed, 59% depends on imports from foreign countries. The self-sufficiency of food in an ecovillage is not just an ecovillage issue. If the ecovillage can be self-sufficient, and reuse kitchen waste as a composting resource, that can be a model for the local society, and also encouraging for the local residents. As food self-sufficiency becomes possible throughout the region, it will contribute to improving national food self sufficiency, and as a result, we will not need to import crops from overseas anymore. Further, through the reduction of waste, we can contribute to the reduction of global warming. Currently, only 22% of the world population lives in developed countries like Japan. Hidden behind the achievement of a rich dietary life for ourselves, dependent as it is on food imported from overseas, there is the exploitation of food-producers from poorer countries. We believe that demonstrating food self-sufficiency in an ecovillage will have great influence as a socio-economic model for society as a whole.

Notes

1 C/N ratio: The carbon/nitrogen ratio can, amongst other things, be used in analyzing sediments and compost. Carbon to nitrogen ratios are an indicator for nitrogen limitation of plants and other organisms. (from Wikipedia).
2 Cultivated soil: The cultivated part of soil in rice-paddies and fields. Most crop roots are within cultivated soil, this becoming a very important source of nutrient and water.
3 Bokashi: Bokashi is the softening effect of fermented organic fertilizer. Sources of organic fertilizers are diverse: oil-seed cake and meal, rice bran, poultry manure, fish meal and born.
4 Komatsuna: Dark leafy green Japanese vegetable of Brassica family, looks similar to spinach.
5 Activated Konohana-kin solution: Add molasses to Konohana-kin as feed, and heat up to 30 degree Celsius to maximize its activity.

Michiyo Furuhashi is a Japanese environmental educator and founder of the Japan Ecovillage Promotion Project (JEPP). Since 2007, she has lived in the Konohana Family (**www.konohana-family.org/files/welcome3rd_e.pdf**), a leading ecovillage in Japan. She is in charge of ecovillage education and international communications. She also sings in the Konohana Band. Michiyo is a board member of Gaia Education and the Global Ecovillage Network (GEN), is vice president of the GEN Oceania and Asia region and is GEN's amabassador in Japan. She organized the first Ecovillage Design Education (EDE) in Japan from 2008-9 and is organizing another EDE in 2012 for the general public and especially the people affected by the 2011 mega earthquakes and tsunami.

This article traces the history of the Federation of Damanhur – undoubtedly one of the most magical places on Earth – in relation to its agricultural production. Author Capra Carruba, with the help of friends, weaves an enchanting tale that highlights the priority of food in a growing community. From a few visionary city folk scratching out some terraces on a muddy hillside to now value-added production distributed within a regional market, the story is one of determination, confidence and trust. Capra only hints at the underlying spiritual values that keep the community together – yet if you look a little closer, you will find that it is these spiritual values that sustain Damanhur.

Rebuilding Cornucopia: How to Create a Community Garden

Capra Carruba and Friends – Damanhur, Italy

Cornucopia – a symbol of food and abundance; also referred to as the food of worship and holiness

Introduction to Damanhur

The Federation of Damanhur is a thriving eco-society in the foothills of the Alps of Northern Italy. Damanhur, one of the oldest non-monastic intentional communities in the world, is a society based upon ethical and spiritual values. Its growing population of nearly 1,000 citizens has united to create a consortium of more than 80 businesses – including art studios, various services, green building companies, agricultural cooperatives, as well as a variety of other innovative business models. The territory of Damanhur extends across the Valchiusella and Canavese region of Piedmonte and includes nearly 600 hectares (1,483 acres). The heart of Damanhur is 'The Temples of Humankind', an extraordinary underground complex, often described as the Eighth Wonder of the World. This artistic masterpiece is dedicated to universal spirituality and to the re-awakening of the divine in every human being. Damanhur is a model community, based on action, optimism and the idea that every human being lives to leave something of him or herself to others and to contribute to the evolution of humanity as a whole.

Damanhur was not born as an agricultural project; yet self-sufficiency emerged as a strong objective for us from the very beginning. This led to

An enterprise originally begun on crude terraces has grown into a sophisticated regional exemplar.

the development of an elaborate structure for food production and distribution. In this article, we intend to share the most important lessons we have learned over these past 35 years, including the difficulties we have encountered and the solutions we have pioneered as a result. While much of our situation is unique, many of the solutions are concrete examples with broader application.

So now, the story of a community that began with just a few people, mostly young city folk, inspired by the spiritual dream of a new civilization. These were visionaries who developed our own model of society, which included sustainable agriculture as a focus. Thirty-five years later, we produce not only enough for our own community needs but also surplus for the surrounding local community: vegetables, wine, bread, olive oil, cheese, and meat.

From Family Garden to Self-sufficiency

In the late 1970s, the first citizens of Damanhur purchased a muddy, hilly piece of land and christened it their capitol: Damjl. With no previous experience in agriculture, the founders did their best to create and cultivate terraces into a family-style garden. The group's main focus at the time was the construction of the underground Temples of Humankind, which was built entirely by hand, in secret. The physical demands of construction heavily influenced their diet and nutritional needs.

Soon, out of necessity, certain community members began to specialize in farming. Food production began to become more efficient. Just like our artists and builders, who were learning their crafts from the ground up, our farmers too were starting from scratch.

Damanhurians were pioneering a new civilization and were doing so with an increasing sense of urgency. Their goal to create a new paradigm for human existence led to radical choices. Perhaps the most important of these was a year-long experiment in complete self-sufficiency, which took place in 1985. The project, known as 'Olio Caldo', which means 'Hot Oil', a term taken from an ancient myth, included not only food but also clothing, shoes, tools, bags, furniture, and transportation. Any and everything used by the group participating in this project was produced by the group.

This year-long experiment later extended to the entire community. The teachings from this experience profoundly impacted the values of the growing society. The possibility of freedom from dependence on an outside distribution system of anonymous people and goods gave our community the confidence that we could feed ourselves and produce what we need. Yet we also learned practical lessons, including the realization that even the most motivated individuals cannot sustain a lack of nutritional variety for months or years. Perhaps this is possible in smaller groups but not on a large community scale.

Even today, the 'Olio Caldo' experiment continues to have resonance in Damanhur. We give immense value to what we produce ourselves, which has both important economic as well as social ramifications. In that period, the community had about 100 members. Decisions were centralized and the economic strategy prioritized the purchase of larger houses as well as additional land and equipment for farming. As with all agricultural concerns, the challenges were and are immense. Our relatively small companies grow organic in a mountainous region with a short growing season, which is itself economically challenging. Climate conditions further impact this equation. It has been a priority to educate our community to eat seasonal local fruits and vegetables.

As sustainable agriculture evolved and the community grew, we transitioned from family-scale to professional-level production. In the days of our small-scale gardens, it was fairly easy to adapt tastes to the products available in the greenhouse or in the fields. If tomatoes were abundant, we found new tomato recipes and ways to preserve them in sauces. If salad was scarce, we simply ate more of the other vegetables. What we didn't produce, we could buy at the market – or better yet, we could barter our products for those of our neighbors.

As Damanhur continued to grow, our agricultural needs became more complicated. Citizens arrived from other parts of the world, bringing with them diverse tastes and food expectations. Entering a model for sustainability required new citizens to adjust their expectations and come to terms with basing their diets on local organic produce and seasonal foods native to an elevation of 480 metres.

Food can be a touchstone for many aspects of our lives and suddenly dinner was psychologically charged with needs that went way beyond what was on the menu that eve! In Italy, the country that invented 'Slow Food', expectations for exquisite cuisine run especially high. Coming to terms with agricultural planning and limited resources, satisfying our diverse tastes – while at the same time guaranteeing a sufficient economic outcome for the

At Damanhur, all lifeforms are treated with respect, for all are understood to be components of an interdependent web.

farmers – have been difficult challenges. All of these substantial questions led us to invest significant resources in our agricultural chain.

In the 1990s, agricultural companies took responsibility for food production, while the community still offered significant support. Producing for the community meant creating several cooperatives with qualified workers, introducing appropriate mechanization, having structures to store, conserve and create food products, as well as adequate vehicles to transport fresh fruits and vegetables. Creating food products to sell commercially meant we needed authorization from the national health administration and food labels that complied with Italian law.

There were many complex considerations to take into account – from acquiring the needed investment capital to developing adequate distribution channels. When we were making marmalade at home for the family, we could do as we liked. When we decided to put our products on the shelves of the local markets, profits needed to cover costs, and questions arose about quantity and variety, punctual delivery and use of excess food. In the first few years, while these questions were still being answered, the formation of cooperative consumer groups was critical. These developed later into the first and largest organic food store in the area, 'Tentaty', located in Damanhur Crea, which serves as an important distribution point for locally-produced foods and products.

Current Production and Agriculture in Damanhur

Today, the basis of our self-sufficiency is two-fold. Some crops and meat production are centralized, serving the community as a whole. In parallel, each nucleo-community cultivates a family garden, with greenhouse, to satisfy their individual needs for 'home grown' fruits and vegetables. In a community-wide initiative, bee keeping has been embarked upon by each

*Buono amicos
– consapevole e
dignitoso.*

Damanhurian family, in response to the global crisis of declining honeybee
populations.

Self-sufficiency is an ongoing learning strategy and a project with many
implications, and we are gradually moving towards our goals. As of today,
we have 60 hectares for growing crops and hay. By 2011 we will be 100%
self-sufficient in meat production; for dairy products 80%; grain production
70%; vegetables between 70 and 100%, depending on the season; wine and
olive oil 40%. Damanhur also has ample chestnut forests in an area we call
the Sacred Woods.

Damanhur's several agricultural companies include farming, wine
production, fruit trees, wild plants and herbs, cheese making, a bakery, and a
seed bank for preserving the diversity of local plant life. A molecular biology
laboratory for testing to insure that our food products are absolutely GMO-
free completes the picture.

The Spirit of Damanhurian Agriculture

Farming in community, for those who take on the task, is a mission of passion.
What feeds this passion is the direct connection to energies beyond this
human realm, and the collaboration with those energies to not only sustain
our community, but to allow it to thrive, and contribute to the evolution of
humanity on this planet. The constant research to maintain a harmonious
ecosystem puts our farmers into contact with the essential aspects of life,
mediating between nature and our physical survival, in collaboration with
plants and animals, on both material and subtle planes.

Nourishing ourselves with other beings, both plants and animals, implies
a great responsibility. It is not enough for our meat to be organic. The animals
who make this sacrifice for our table must be provided both a high quality
of life, and a dignified death. The tomato and greens in our salad must be

recognized and respected as intelligent life-forces.

Respect towards all living beings translates into diverse and conscious farming methods. With the common denominator of 'organic agriculture', a variety of methods for growing have been explored within the community. This research includes permaculture, biodynamic agriculture, radionics, and hydroponic cultures. Beyond our collaboration with nature to sustain ourselves physically we have also engaged in fascinating and completely experiential contacts with nature, like playing music to plants and then creating the means for the plants to express themselves musically. There also exists, within Damanhur, a unique field of research involving metal devices which direct vital, intelligent energy, called Selfica.

An ideal of self-sufficiency is to create an unbroken chain, where there is not only vital production but also little waste: In addition to meat and milk, cows produce manure, which is in turn used to fertilize the fields of hay and grain, which then is used to feed the cows, who again provide our meat and milk.

In the history of humankind, many rituals have been practiced around the time of planting and harvest. As a community, we echo and reinforce those ancient and universal rituals of gratitude and harmonious collaboration with the energies and intelligences of the plant and animal kingdoms. In addition to our rituals for planting and harvest, each day, when Damanhurians sit down to eat, we offer a very old and beautiful prayer, thanking the fruits of the earth, of the air, water, and beneath the earth, the animals and all of the elements — alchemical nourishment for our bodies and our essence. And we ask that our behavior be conscious and worthy.

> Noi ringraziamo i frutti di terra, di aria di acqua e di sottoterra, gli animali e tutte gli elementi nutrimento alchemico al nostro corpo e alla nostra essenza. Sia il nostro comportamento consapevole e dignitoso.

This article is the result of a joint effort of many people. I wish to thank Fauno, Gracchio, Sciacallo, Quaglia and Betsy for their precious contributions.

Christine Schneider was born in 1968 in Northern Germany and has lived since 2001 in Damanhur, where she chose the name Capra Carruba. She has studied political science and has worked as a consultant in Organization Development and training, presently in her own company SOLIOS. Capra teaches metaphysics and community building in the University of Damanhur. Her great research interest is what makes communities work and how transformation can be realized. Capra is Secretary of GEN in the twin office of Damanhur.

EcoVillage at Ithaca (EVI) has become a shining example of sustainable community development, and is probably the most replicable model in North America. In this article, Executive Director Liz Walker writes about their agriculture programs. At the height of the growing season, EVI's West Haven Farm feeds 1,000 people per day off of 10 acres, mostly through its CSA and outlet to a farmer's market. There is also a tradition of outreach to Cornell University and Ithaca College. Yet perhaps what is most impressive is the regional network of local food production and education that has developed with EVI at its center ... Liz Walker and her ecovillage are setting precedents.

Bringing the Harvest Home: CSA Farming and Farmer Education at EcoVillage at Ithaca

Liz Walker – EcoVillage at Ithaca, New York, USA

It is a clear summer day in mid-August. Jen and John, our resident farming couple, work with a dozen helpers to bring in the day's harvest. They pick bright red and sun-gold tomatoes and three kinds of beans. Huge heads of romaine, green leaf, and butter lettuce overflow their containers. Zucchini, patty pan, and yellow summer squashes abound, along with purple shiny-skinned eggplants. The air in the barn is redolent with the aroma of herbs – dill, basil, and cilantro.

Everyone works quickly. Soon the Farm's 200 shareholders will come to pick up their weekly allotment of organically grown produce. People will stop and chat with friends, as children play in the sandbox. And they will pick bright bouquets from the flower garden to add color and scent to their homes. The bounty of this place will find its way to kitchens and tables throughout the ecovillage community and beyond to the greater Ithaca area.

West Haven Farm was the first part of the EcoVillage at Ithaca (EVI) vision to manifest. Established by Jen and John Bokaer-Smith in 1993, the 10 acre (4 hectare) farm is certified organic by the Northeast Organic Farming Association (NOFA). Unlike other farms, it will never feel the pressure of developers eager to create another subdivision, since it is protected by EVI's permanent conservation easement on 55 acres of land (about a third of our total acreage), held by the local Finger Lakes Land Trust. The Farm is also a Community Supported Agriculture (CSA) farm.

CSA: we're all in this together

A CSA farm creates a wonderful web of connection between people and the land. By joining a CSA, people can enjoy organic seasonal food produced close to home at the same time as they help sustainable agriculture to flourish. Shareholders pay a portion of the farm's expenses and in return receive a weekly bounty of freshly picked vegetables, herbs, and flowers all through the growing season (from late May to early November in upstate New York). Farmers benefit by having a guaranteed market for their produce,

Planting at West Haven Farm.

and consumers have the satisfaction of eating well – a dynamic that is both reciprocal and personal. As Jen told me, "The relationships we develop with our members nourish us, just as the food we produce nourishes our members."

West Haven Farm is not only supported by its CSA members, however. Although 60 percent of the farm's crops do go to members, another 40 percent go to the Ithaca Farmer's Market, and 1 percent goes wholesale to EVI (for our community meals several times a week) and Greenstar (a local natural foods cooperative). That adds up to 101 percent, which accurately represents what the couple puts into the farm. All in all, West Haven Farm feeds about 1,000 people a week during the growing season. As a casual gardener, I find it astonishing that 10 acres can be so intensely productive.

Part of the secret of the farm's success has to do with the way that our farmers nurture the soil. John and his right-hand helper, farm manager Todd McLane, literally feed the soil by applying green and composted manure, planting nitrogen-fixing cover crops, and practicing crop rotation. Their efforts are restoring land previously depleted by years of poor farming practices. And healthy land produces healthy crops.

The land now produces veggies with exceptionally high nutrient values. In fact, at EVI a popular folk remedy for colds calls for soup made from Jen and John's fresh produce. Eat the soup for dinner, the saying goes, and you'll feel better by morning. I've tried it and it's true.

Today the farm is a very successful operation. The couple farms 8½ acres (3.4 hectares) of veggies, 1½ acres (0.6 hectares) of fruit, and a 1 acre (0.4 hectare) apple orchard in a nearby town (which they work cooperatively with another farmer). They grow 250 varieties of seed, including about 50 types of flowers and just about every type of vegetable you can grow in the Northeast, except asparagus. They planted lots of fruit trees in 2001 – apple, peach, apricot, pear and plums – which are now beginning to bear fruit.

Knowing how delicious their strawberries are, I was not surprised to find how succulent their other fruit is, too. It gives me great pleasure to bite into a crisp apple or juicy peach grown on our own land!

New Ownership Model:

Despite its success, West Haven Farm has required tremendous dedication and sacrifice from Jen and John and also created a financial stretch for its owners. While the non-profit EVI, Inc. owns the land they farm (which the farm leases for a very low rate), they have had to invest about $200,000 of their own money to build a small barn and a permanent greenhouse, install a pump and expand the existing farm pond, acquire hoop houses to protect early seedlings from frost, install a ten foot deer fence, and much more. They had to take out a second mortgage on their home, and after 12 years of farming, started to feel burned-out. They tried to sell the farm, but few people met all the criteria. They were looking for experienced farmers who had enough money to buy the business, and preferably wanted to live in community. Many candidates visited and some even seemed to fit the bill, but nobody actually made an offer. Just when it looked as if we might be losing a very important on-site farming enterprise, Jen and John decided to try a new model, and bring in investors. They found a handful of families (mostly residents at EVI) who wanted to invest in long-term food security. These investors were able to help pay off the couple's debt, in return for a share of the modest profits.

A Groundswell of Local Food and Farming

In the meantime, the potential crisis spurred the hatching of another vision. For years, West Haven Farm had offered a modest level of educational

Who has not experienced the smell of a production greenhouse in full bloom? This is where hobby turns into science.

programming for occasional interns, or tours for Cornell University students. What would happen, we pondered, if our non-profit educational organization, the EVI-Center for Sustainability Education, worked jointly with West Haven Farm to provide hands-on educational opportunities for budding farmers?

The idea got traction at a special fundraising dinner, held in the fall of 2008, which featured Cornell University President David Skorton and his wife, Dr. Robin Davisson, as keynote speakers. Skorton and Davisson each spoke passionately about local food, and recounted how Cornell was beginning to change its buying habits to source 25% of its produce from within 100 miles. Clearly the university, which feeds 24,000 people daily, and has a $9 million annual grocery budget has a lot of economic clout. (In 2009 the policy grew to include 33% of the produce purchased by the University.) One of the issues brought up by the speakers was the need for more local farms as the demand for locally-sourced products multiplies.

After the dinner was over, my friend and former EcoVillage neighbor Joanna Green came up to me. "Liz, I know what I want to do with my life now," she told me, her face glowing with conviction. "I want to be the person who makes this idea happen." Under Joanna's guidance, 'this idea' became a fast-growing program, Groundswell Center for Local Food and Farming. Joanna took early retirement from Cornell, where she had worked for over two decades in sustainable agriculture education and research. Drawing on her extensive network of contacts in local food and farming, she put together a terrific advisory board, including representatives from Cornell Co-operative Extension, Ithaca College, graduate students, farmers and more.

> The Groundswell mission "is all about helping youth and adult learners develop the skills and knowledge they need to build sustainable local food systems. Our focus is providing hands-on, experiential learning opportunities with real working farms and food businesses in the Ithaca, NY area. Through collaboration with area schools, colleges and universities Groundswell offers programs of study for beginning farmers, students, community members, and professionals." (www.groundswellcenter.org)

After over a year of careful organizing, Groundswell Center taught its first 'Summer Practicum in Sustainable Farming' in the summer of 2010. Fourteen young adults spent eight weeks learning through hands-on training at three local farms – West Haven (a vegetable farm), Kingbird Farm (a horse-powered farm that specializes in grass-fed beef, pork, poultry and eggs), and Northland Sheep Dairy (featuring production and marketing of gourmet sheep's milk cheeses.) The Practicum included in-depth field-trips to visit other local producers and retailers, some academic study, and students enjoyed preparing their own local foods lunch each day of the program with the help of a nutritionist from Ithaca College. They ate delicious, seasonal food which they had often harvested themselves, and in a closing dinner for supporters of the program, several students noted that

the lunches were a huge hit. "It was the first time I really learned how to cook with vegetables," one young man in his mid-twenties said. "I found out they were really good." Students earned six credits through the local community college, but even more important than the credits was the life-long knowledge and appreciation they learned for local food and farming. A number of the students felt the program had changed their lives.

Groundswell also initiated an innovative program that was first developed by farmers in the Hudson Valley. The new Finger Lakes CRAFT (Collaborative Regional Alliance for Farmer Training) offers advanced training to aspiring farmers in the Ithaca area. The CRAFT approach builds on the training provided by individual farmers to their interns and employees during the course of the growing season and includes nine day-long training sessions at one of the three farms mentioned above. The CRAFT approach has been highly successful in increasing the quality, depth and breadth of new farmer training in several other regions in the US and Canada. And communities with a CRAFT program tend to attract the most serious and committed trainees, which is a great benefit to participating farms. We're excited to be developing this program right here in the Ithaca area.

I asked Joanna how she felt about Groundswell's progress. "In a way, Groundswell is a culmination of decades of work – a weaving together of many of the existing strands in the local food system with some new ones, notably: EcoVillage at Ithaca, Cornell Cooperative Extension, the farms, the community college, Cornell, Ithaca College, and local public schools," she told me. "It's also a very replicable model I think."

In October of 2010, the Groundswell Center won a major grant from the United States Department of Agriculture (USDA) to support the training of new farmers and urban market gardeners.

Groundswell's New Farmer Training Project aims to increase the number, diversity, profitability, and environmental sustainability of area farmers by providing training, mentoring, business planning support, and affordable access to land at EcoVillage at Ithaca.

"We are making a three-year investment to develop a strong, multicultural, social and economic support network for beginning farmers," said Joanna. "We'll be bringing together young and old, white, black, immigrant, affluent and limited resource, beginning and experienced farmers to learn from one another and to strengthen our local food system."

Recognizing the diversity of potential farmers in our community, the project will address the needs of three target groups:

- Start-Ups – those recently started in farming on their own, yet needing further training, mentoring, and business planning support in order to succeed;
- Farming Interns – those able and willing to spend two years working and learning on established farms;
- Market Gardeners – urban gardeners interested in developing small-scale commercial enterprises to serve local community markets.

In addition to supporting beginning farmers in our own community, Green believes the project will make the Ithaca area a magnet for serious aspiring farmers nationwide, who are looking to gain hands-on experience and training before starting their own farms in other regions.

Thanks to Joanna, Jen and John, Todd, and other farmers, the Finger Lakes is a good place to learn how to grow delicious food, and a great place to eat. I'm glad that our abundant land at this ecovillage can be put to such good use.

Liz Walker is co-founder of EcoVillage at Ithaca and Executive Director of the non-profit EcoVillage at Ithaca – Center for Sustainability Education (**www.ecovillage.ithaca.ny.us**), in Ithaca, NY. This is excerpted in part from her popular book, *EcoVillage at Ithaca: Pioneering a Sustainable Culture* (New Society Publishers, 2005) as well as her new book, *Choosing a Sustainable Future: Ideas and Inspiration from Ithaca, NY* (New Society Publishers, October, 2010).

For permaculture connoisseur Maddy Harland, the idea of an impending food shortage would be unthinkable. Within a network of forest gardeners and plant propagators in Britain, enthusiasts like Maddy trade and share root stock, seeds and cuttings to disseminate a cornucopia of food plants that you'll never find on the supermarket shelves. Indeed, Maddy calls the current availability of variety and nutrition in consumer societies 'pathetic', and entreats us to explore and experiment with the bounty that Nature has to offer. The ensuing vision is called "The Age of the Edible" – a sustainable future where families and communities cultivate and establish local varieties from Nature's store in a primordial human practice that contributes to not only food security but spiritual nourishment.

The Age of the Edible

Maddy Harland – The Sustainability Centre, England

One common concern that people share with me is how we are to feed ourselves once the cheap and ubiquitous supply of supermarket food has dried up along the agricultural and transport system that both rely so heavily upon oil. My response is that we have only touched the tip of the proverbial iceberg when it comes to food. What we eat, particularly in industrialised cultures, is incredibly limited: on average, a few kinds of meat, fish, common vegetables and fruits and one or two grains. Yes, we eat exotic vegetables and fruit out of season, flown in from the far corners of the world, but mainly the conventional western diet is pathetically limited as well as unhealthy.

In 1996/7 I worked closely with Ken Fern on his seminal book, *Plants For A Future – Edible and Useful Plants for a Healthier World*. Ken is an extraordinary pioneer who has researched, grown, experimented and eaten plants that inhabit all ecological niches, from the woodland and forest to the field and aquatic edge. He has created a database of 7,000 edibles, medicinal and other useful plants (www.pfaf.org). Ken opened my eyes to the potential little known plants and made me think about our cultural predisposition towards eating supermarket food, preselected for cosmetic appearance plus their ability to travel and store well so that they have a longer shelf life. The industry may be in part promoting organic, seasonal and sometimes local varieties but it is still selecting mainly monoculturally grown crops and F1 hybrid seed. The results are bland, limited and erode our understanding of the potential repertoire that is available.

Imagine then the invigoration of local 'heritage' seedsaving and seed swapping, plus a voyage of edible discovery by intrepid growers and the trans-national exchange of information, plants and seed by permaculturists and other experimenters. A global, grassroots movement is quickly growing that will usher in the age of the edible. What stories will emerge as we open our minds to the delights of new perennial and annual foods?

A caveat: ecologists and earth restoration specialists have a legitimate concern that exotics i.e. non-native plants outcompete natives. One salutary example is Japanese Knotweed. This plant, introduced as a garden ornamental exotic (though it an edible) but has escaped the garden and now colonises in the wild. It is almost impossible to eradicate and grows through tarmac and concrete. Another example is European blackberry released into the fragile ecologies of Australia where it grows in large impenetrable thickets, outcompeting the native species. When experimenting, we need to be sensitive to where we release untested plants and encourage a resurgence in growing ancient native edibles. Because "In nature there is no containment", we must experiment with caution, especially in fragile ecologies.

It is in my garden I experiment with informed caution. I do not plant species that are invasive yet I grow numerous unusual edibles and I encourage others to expand their repertoires. My favourite story is of

Wineberry making the most of the vertical wall space and underplanted with Chinese greens.

a rare variety of apple, a 'Bardsey Island', planted in the forest garden. How I got hold of this unusual tree indicates the hidden potential of undiscovered plants that are waiting to be found… For centuries pilgrims (Celts and later Christians), followed the setting sun to visit and often die on the remote island of Bardsey at the end of the Lleyn Peninsula, Wales. Indeed three trips to Bardsey were considered the equivalent of a pilgrimage to Rome.

"These days most pilgrims to Bardsey are tourists; popping over for a quick picnic and to take photos of the ruined medieval abbey, the seals and mainly, of course, themselves," wrote Ian Sturrock, a nurseryman who was to rejuvenate this rare variety. "Our feathered friends also visit the island and with the birds come the 'twitchers' and Bardsey has the oldest bird observatory in the UK."

Ian tells of how his friend Andy Clarke, a birdwatcher, found an old, old tree growing up the side of one of the island's houses. Both the fruit and the tree were free from disease. A nibble revealed a delicious crisp apple with a lemony flavour. To cut a long story short, Andy brought back two apples for Ian, a nurseryman based in Bangor, who couldn't identify the tree from his extensive reference library but knew immediately that it was a potentially delicious variety. The National Fruit Collection people also failed to identify it. The lone tree was unique. Ian was given permission to propagate the tree and thereby preserve it for posterity. He grafted several hundred trees to several different rootstocks and set about making them available to fruit growers all over Britain who would be willing to give him feedback.

On the island, the tree is lashed by gales most of the year, and often loses most of its leaves to salt and wind-burn. Consequently it only produces fruit occasionally. The tree is completely free of the diseases that flourish in the damper conditions of the mainland, particularly scab on the fruit, and canker in the wood. In 2005, nobody knew when the tree flowered and whether or not the blossoms were frost tolerant. (The island is frost free.) Did the tree produce a regular crop? The mother tree crops irregularly because spring's salt laden gales often kill the blossom. When was the best time to harvest the fruit or how long it can be kept? These and many other questions remained a mystery.

Tim Harland and I were very keen to trial the tree as we grow apples on chalk in the middle of the Hampshire Downs about 12 miles away from the English coast. We have 23 varieties of earlies, mids and lates. The chalky soil isn't great for a number of our varieties and we have had canker and scab. Ian sent me a tree and we planted it in the winter of 2005. It is a vigorous and healthy tree. Even in its first season in 2006 it blossomed, but to establish our precious charge we removed all of the flowers for three years and let the tree put its energy into its roots. In 2009 we let it be. The tree blossomed in May and set its fruit successfully. It showed no signs of frailty in wind and heavy rain and began cropping in mid to late August. The next year it cropped again.

I can confirm that tree and fruit are scab resistant, and yes, the apples are really good: crisp, sweet, reasonably large and with beautiful hues of reds and yellows. The skin goes a little waxy after a week or so in normal temperatures but the apple remains crisp. I don't know how long they store for and I doubt I will find out until the tree is larger. They are simply too good to save. I must be more scientific next cropping season! My gratitude goes to Andy for realising he had found a jewel and to Ian for his skill with grafting and generously letting us plant one of the trees. It's top of my list of apples and I want to go to Bardsey Island itself and meet its Mother.

Besides the Bardsey Apple, I have been experimenting with other less usual edibles like the South American tuber, Oca (*Oxalis tuberosa*), honeyberries (from the Lonicera family), and summer truffles inoculated on hazel. Another edible that crops year after year in our forest garden with little husbandry is the Asian or Nashi pear. This is sold in supermarkets as a premium priced exotic pear in Britain but it is so easy to cultivate at home. It has a beautiful low growing, spreading habit, resonant of its Eastern origins, pretty white flowers in Springtime and hardly needs pruning. The pears are the shape of apples, are crisp and juicy. They are pleasant to eat and make excellent wine.

Less aesthetic but equally useful is a perennial kale given to me by permaculture friends in Wales. Whilst admiring their forest garden I came upon a healthy kale bush and Andy simply pulled off a few lower storks and advised me to put them in a pot with compost, no complicated propagation techniques required. They rooted enthusiastically and I planted them out in early spring. In their first season they were munched by slugs and plagued by hungry pigeons. I covered them with cloches made from large water bottles with the bottoms cut off and by autumn they had recovered. In late October and November, the plants provide the family with healthy greens on a weekly basis, a time when most of our annual vegetables are finished and the greenhouse is growing plants for the 'hungry gap' in the Spring. Since establishing this perennial kale, I have cut storks and passed them on to other friends in the colder region of England. They too have been pleased with the plant's productivity and good taste. This is a plant every cool temperate vegetable gardener should have a place for.

Fruit of the deliciously fragrant Asian pear.

Another favourite is a more modest plant, pink purslane (*Claytonia alsinoides. C. sibirica*), given to me by Ken Fern. This is an attractive little edible that likes shady damp places in my garden where little else that I can eat will grow. It tastes like pea shoots, self-seeds and has lovely little pink flowers. It is a useful addition to salads and is effortless to grow. My kind of edible!

This year, we have also planted a new batch of trees from the Agroforestry Research Trust such as Nepalese Pepper (*Zanthoxylum alatum*), Chinese Dogwood (*Cornus kousa chinensis*), Yellowhorn (*Xanthoceras sorbifolium*) and ground cover plants like Rubus nepalensis. Chinese Dogwood particularly interests me as an edible because it is such a beautiful tree. I see no reason why kitchen gardens and forest gardens shouldn't be places of beauty as well as being functional. We need to feed the spirit as well as the body.

A visit to Martin Crawford's forest garden at the Agroforestry Research Trust in Devon, England and a thorough read of his wonderful catalogue reveals that there are many more plants that we can grow and experiment with even in cool temperate climates. I do not have room for a nuttery or more standard trees in my forest garden – it is full! – so I am gradually adding smaller perennials that I can slot into the shrub and ground cover layers. Each year I also try out new vegetable varieties, usually given to me by a friend who has saved the seed. My experiments with edibles are just a fraction of what is possible and I know that my eclectic garden is a drop in a vast ocean of marvellous possibility.

The moral of these stories is that we are only just touching on the potential of vegetables, fruits and nuts that can be cultivated on our planet. Think how many more undiscovered edibles there are waiting to be found, propagated and shared. I imagine the growing global network of plant enthusiasts sharing information and plants, experimenting with organic, low maintenance polycultures and opening the minds of others to an exciting world of culinary possibilities. Let's herald in the Age of the Edible and celebrate the potential for more new discoveries.

References

Ian Sturrock's nursery: http://www.bardseyapple.co.uk
Plants For A Future: Edible & Useful Plants For A Healthier World by Ken Fern, Permanent Publications, 1997.
Agroforestry Research Trust http://www.agroforestry.co.uk

Maddy Harland is the co-founder and editor of Permaculture Magazine **www.permaculture.co.uk** and Permanent Publications **www.permanent-publications.co.uk** She co-founded The Sustainability Centre in Hampshire in 1995, a recycled naval base on 55 acres of the South Downs, now a thriving education centre and community. Maddy is also a founder of Gaia Education. In 2008, Tim and Maddy's company won The Queen's Award for Enterprise for their 'unfettered dedication to promoting sustainability internationally'.

Seasoned permaculture veteran Chris Evans provides a comprehensive report of his extensive experience designing and implementing village-scale water catchment systems in Nepal. The connections between catching, storing, and efficiently using the precious resource of water in the production of local self-reliant food systems is made vivid. Also vivid is the whole systems permaculture thinking that went into the designs. Chris' report provides optimistic testimony that villagers the world over have the techniques to restore and revitalize their degraded landscapes; what is required is more widespread application of educational programs like the EDE to bring this knowledge to where it is needed.

Village-Scale Water Catchments in Nepal

Chris Evans – Designed Visions, Wales

Background

The hills and mountains of Nepal contain thousands of very distinct watershed areas that are characterized by steep slopes between both smooth and rugged high ridges, and valley bottoms with alluvial plains of varying width depending on their height in the watershed. Soil on the relatively young Himalayan slopes is extremely susceptible to erosion, especially during the monsoon, and nutrients are typically easily leached. The valley bottoms act as a natural conduit for this leached fertility leading to productive flat land where crop productivity is generally high. Meanwhile, on the slopes there is a constant struggle for farmers to hold on to valuable fertility, and labor inputs are high in attempts to replace lost nutrients. This is mainly done through animal manure produced after trees have been cut for fodder which is carried often long distances from ever denuding forests and fed to livestock such as cows and buffalo, together with leaf litter used as bedding. The resultant compost is then carried to the fields.

The problems of erosion of young soil on steep slopes are exacerbated by the monsoon, when 80% to 90% of the country's rainfall (annual average 1,600mm) falls in just four months between June and September. There is usually a small amount of rain in winter that falls as

Run off from a well-forested watershed on the left entering a river from an eroded watershed on the right.

snow in high elevations (above 2,000m), followed by a long dry season from February until the monsoon breaks again in June.

In the monsoon the soil becomes quickly saturated with water. In farmed or grazed areas with less permanent vegetation there is less storage capacity in soil and biomass, and this is where soils are more quickly eroded and leached. Run off from these slopes is soil-laden, turning rivers turbid and causing siltation of riverbeds and plains lower down in the watershed. Well-forested watersheds have a much greater capacity to catch and store water, and run off from these areas is much clearer.

Villages in the hills and mountains are often situated in **keyline** areas, where the slope changes from roughly concave to convex, and permanent springs are the clean water sources. Higher up slopes less permanent springs are found that

Elevation planning around keypoint (key area).

	Ridge or Plateau	Upper Slope	Middle Slope (Keypoint)	Lower Slope	River Plain
Site characteristics	• thin soils • flat/gently undulating • windy, frost • moist • low temps • less surface water	• very steep • good light • cold but no frost • cold air drainage • thin soil • springs	• good light • no frost • cold air drainage • thicker soil • springs • well drained	• frost settling • sheltered/ less wind • temperature extremes (hot/cold) • well drained • deep soil	• flat • deep soil • flooding • temperature extremes (hot/cold) • water run-off collects
Limiting factors	• soil erosion • fire danger • wind & frost damage • difficult access	• fire hazard • soil erosion • difficult access • cold air drainage	• soil erosion • water pollution	• frost • soil erosion • water pollution	• wind damage • flooding • river bank erosion • water run-off may contain contaminants
Opportunities	• plantations, fruit • pasture • deep water storage for drinking water, power (HEP) • access • wind power	• afforestation, orchards • water storage • wind power • >18% slope under trees	• settlement area • min. tillage • small dams for water collection/ distribution • agroforestry/ orchards • H.E.P.	• terracing • agroforestry • irrigation easy • cultivation • H.E.P.	• cultivation • irrigation easy • shallow water storage • aquaculture

issue during the monsoon but that dry up when the rains stop. The figure above describes limiting factors and opportunities offered by such landscapes.

Storage of Water

In more arid or evenly rainfall-distributed regions of the world, water storage in dams and ponds is a key productive feature of water-related design. The conditions in steep sloped monsoon/dry season regions are peculiar, however, because of the huge volume of water in relatively short periods. Here, a need is actually to divert water run-off from potentially erodable or leachable soils into water courses as the soil becomes saturated. Water storage structures such as dams, ponds or tanks become filled within days of the monsoon starting, and have little further use until the monsoon ends when they will quickly become exhausted and are not able to be recharged during the dry season. While there are benefits of this it is less likely that they offset the capital and labour costs involved in construction. There is the additional risk of water bodies created on sloping land actually causing erosion due to their weight and over-saturation of soil. Sites would need to be carefully selected where this risk is minimal, and small-scale systems prioritized.

Therefore the key strategy for collection and storage of water is in the biomass and soil: maintaining a permanent canopy and/or cover to the soil, with plenty of biomass to soak up precipitation – three inches of mulch can absorb an inch of water. Methods to do this, such as agro-forestry, mulching and green manures are described below. Thus the soil is covered, overland run off down the slope is slowed down, and an added benefit is that there is lots of organic matter to feed the soil life, made up of macro- and micro-organisms such as earthworms, bacteria and fungi.

Conservation and Use of Water

In the hills and mountains of western Nepal the Himalayan Permaculture Centre (HPC) has developed some innovative and integrated ways of working with water conservation and use in its work. Some of these are described below.

Non-cement Drinking Water

HPC uses a way of constructing drinking water systems without the need for cement, developed by their own technicians over the last 20 years. Instead of using cement for tanks, local resources of stone and wood are used, along with a certain type of moss that is planted into the mud mortar of tank walls, rendering them leak proof. Typically, a small, local spring is identified and is directed into a tank sunk into the ground and lined with stone using clay mortar, into which is planted the moss. The tank is covered and the area around protected from livestock and usually planted with trees. HDP (polythene) pipe takes the spring water to the user village – there may be break tanks on the way if the slope is steep and/or long – where typically 1 to 3 tap

Non-cement water tank filled with water, which will now be covered with a wooden trap door.

stands (depending on the size of the spring) are built, also from stone and wood rather than the conventional cement. One village may use more than one spring to supply its drinking water, and springs can be used even if they are seasonal. This has meant that systems can be constructed at 10% of the cost of conventional cement-built systems, due to not needing cement, sand nor skilled technicians to construct it with (all of which are needed again if the scheme breaks down). Non-cement systems, however, are cheap to build and maintain and both can be done by the villagers themselves, as they use the same local tools and the same resources used to construct the systems in the first place (i.e. mud, rock and wood).

Waste-water from tap stands is directed towards areas needing irrigation such as kitchen gardens and tree nurseries. These factors combine to make the technology more participatory, productive, cost-effective and sustainable. After construction, village stakeholder beneficiary groups are encouraged to set up micro-finance schemes where each household puts in a small amount each month (typically 5 to 10 Nepalese rupees, or about U.S.12 cents) that they use if new pipe or tap fittings are needed, that is that they can't make from local resources. Since 1990 over 40 small and medium scale systems for around 2,000 households (around 12,000 beneficiaries) have been established in various hill villages of Surkhet, Jajarkot and Humla districts, and most are still in good working order. This innovative system was nominated for the Water Globe Award 2003 in Austria.

Micro-irrigation for Kitchen Gardens, Nurseries, Fruit Orchards and Agro-forestry

The systems used combine drinking water with micro-irrigation in order to increase and diversify outputs from each activity. In this way, drinking water is piped to taps arranged around the periphery of each village. From here, shorter pipes attachable to the taps provide water for drip and sprinkler irrigation to areas of kitchen garden and nurseries for fruit and multi-purpose agro-forestry seedling production. Meanwhile, grey-water from washing activities at the taps is also used for irrigation purposes. This work involves both retrofit and repair of existing drinking water systems that have fallen into disrepair as well as construction of new systems.

Water Conserving Activities: Mulching

Mulching is a well known method of water conservation, where biomass cut from adjoining areas is layered as a covering on bare soil. This protects it from the drying influences of sun and wind and the impact of raindrops.

In addition, extra nutrients for soil macro- and micro-organisms are provided, and weeds are controlled. It is less known perhaps that rocks make excellent mulch – like a biomass mulch they cover and protect the soil, conserve water and keep weeds down. There is the added benefit of heat absorption creating a warm microclimate around and below the rock that is beneficial to soil life. They are especially useful for mulching around individual valuable trees such as fruit seedlings.

Green Manures/Cover Crops

These are crops grown specifically to benefit the soil, and are water conserving in the same way as mulching (in fact they can also be called a "living mulch"). An example is mustard, which can be sown during a fallow period between two other crops, and dug in (or cut and mulched) to the soil. The nutrients accumulated and locked up in the plant during its growth are then returned to the soil with interest, as well as covering the soil to provide benefits as described above in mulching.

Swales

It was described above why it is not always the best strategy to hold water in the landscape, where saturation of soil can lead to land slippage. However, on slopes that are not too steep nor too long, and in small scale systems, there can be advantages of swaling the land. Swales are a ditch dug on the contour that has the result of slowing overland and sub-soil flow of water, allowing it to percolate into the soil. They are especially good when above and below the swale is planted with grass, shrubs and trees as part of orchards and agro-forestry systems that soak up the extra water and accumulate it in biomass. This can then be recycled back onto the land as mulch, or fed to livestock and returned as compost. Other crops such as firewood, timber, bee forage, etc. can also be gained. Swale planting can also be integrated with windbreaks (see below).

Windbreaks

Shelter belts of trees and shrubs of varying heights act to protect fields from the drying effect of wind. This is especially so when fields have been freshly ploughed and are bare of biomass on the soil. These lines of plants, often on terrace edges and farm boundaries, have a multitude of other useful functions such as providing fodder, fuelwood, timber and poles, mulch material, nectar for bees, etc. close to the farms, thus reducing reliance on often depleted forest resources.

Grey-water Use

As well as the recycling of grey water from tap stands for nurseries, kitchen gardens etc. as outlined above, HPC has developed ways of using domestic waste-water from household use, which it demonstrates and trains to local villagers. Normally, water is carried from taps or springs in containers and used for cooking, dish washing and general household duties. Grey-water from these uses is normally thrown away with little or no further use. By strategically locating the hand and dish washing area close to a kitchen garden, or laying a pipe that carries it there, this water also can be recycled for productive means. Some washing is also done over compost heaps to provide moisture for faster breakdown of biomass during the dry season. In this way, what was a limiting factor of water has been linked to a waste product that had not been used.

Low-water Use Rice Cultivation

There are many types of cultivation that can be used as part of water conservation strategies. One of them, the **System of Rice Intensification (SRI)** is a relatively new technique for rice cultivation. It involves four major changes from conventional rice production:

1. The seedlings grown in the nursery beds are transplanted after just 8-12 days, or at the 2-leaf stage.
2. Seedlings are transplanted singly, not in a bunch.
3. Seedlings are transplanted at a wide spacing, from 25 to 50cm apart.
4. Much less water is kept on the paddies, and the soil is allowed to dry out ('crack') from time to time.

Paddy managed under SRI has shown good increases in yield. Double yields are not difficult to achieve, and some farmers have achieved up to 4 times their normal yield. The benefits are:

- rice production increased (up to 16T/Ha has been documented)
- less water needed (minimum around 15-25% of normal practice)
- less seed needed (about 12% of normal practice)
- no extra external inputs needed
- can use local/traditional seed
- more straw
- due to better soil and water management there is:
  - less pests and disease
  - better quality grain
  - more fertile soil

SRI also has great potential to combine with other methods such as no-till (see Fukuoka), mulching and green manures within the rice crop, as well as intercropping with other crops.

The Himalayan foothill states of Himachal Pradesh and Uttarakhand have achieved one of the most rapid extensions of SRI to date. Starting with just 40 farmers in 2006, there were 597 farmers using the new methods in 2007 while this year, there are about 13,000 farmers using SRI. See http://ciifad.cornell.edu/sri/ for more details of SRI.

Conclusions

The settled hills and mountains of Nepal offer tremendous potential for diverse annual and perennial cropping systems. This potential can be reached through sustainable management of water resources in the catchments of the plethora of rivers that run through the country. Starting with conservation and regeneration of existing resources of forest, soil, water and biodiversity, many techniques exist that can help to increase soil moisture to the benefit of crop diversification and ultimate improvement in productivity. Permaculture design can help to integrate these methods within traditional cultural and social systems to create a flourishing economy as well as domestic self reliance.

A stand of SRI rice nearing maturity. Each clump, with up to 80 tillers, comes from one seedling, planted here at 40cm spacing.

Chris Evans has lived and worked in Nepal since 1985, co-founding the Jajarkot Permaculture Programme (JPP), a diverse array of projects spanning 65 villages, and a membership of 12,000 farmers.

In 2001 he published the Farmers Handbook of over 40 farmer-friendly appropriate technologies (see http://www.green-shopping.co.uk/books/ebooks/free-ebooks.html). He currently works as advisor to the Himalayan Permaculture Centre (**www.himalayanpermaculture.com**).

Beside his grass-roots experience in Nepal, Chris has taught permaculture in UK, India, U.S.A. and Mexico. He currently lives in South Wales, where he teaches local permaculture courses and is involved in the transition initiative in his local town. He is also a partner in Designed Visions (**www.designedvisions.com**), a permaculture education and design consultancy.

Suzanne Foote describes in moving eloquence how locally adapted food systems are vital to the maintenance of indigenous cultural traditions – you could say that local food systems are the basis of local cultural traditions. Through her work with the Sioux Nation, Suzanne developed multiple programs to restore place-based agricultural practices. These programs have resulted in increased health, community pride, and a sense of self-determination. Suzanne relates the Sioux creed that food is sacred, and so its production and delivery cannot be entrusted to elements outside the community. There are profound lessons here for all of us who have adopted the practice of growing our own food.

Reviving the Past to Sustain the Future: Native Sioux Agricultural Systems

Suzanne Foote – Manitou Institute, Colorado, USA

Every year, native plant species and traditional farming practices are increasingly vanishing globally. Since the early 1500s, well over half of all native crop species have been lost as well as the knowledge of traditional native agricultural practices. A collective effort must take place now to save remaining seed species and revive traditional agricultural practices to ensure future food security and cultural integrity.

Years ago, Sam Moves Camp, a Sioux Medicine Man, told the Lakota Nation that they must return to their traditional core diet of native corn, beans, and squash as well as wild-crafted foods indigenous to the Lakota people. Sam gave very specific directions and delivered a compelling message to his people, stating

> we must get back to the land – this is a priority. We must acknowledge the spiritually-based, ecologically sound relationships and traditions of the Lakota and the plant species that we have evolved with and depended on. Together we must preserve our ancient food crops for our future survival as a people.

He also declared that, "If these traditional food crops become extinct, our culture and our spirit also will become extinct."

Sam's message correlates with several prophecies, such as those of Padmasambhava, or Guru Rinpoche as he is also known. In eighth century Tibet, he warned that certain conditions will come to pass in our time because of humanity's behavioral patterns. People will die of starvation even as there is food to eat because the food itself will become lifeless.

In direct response to these kinds of messages, a Native American non-profit organization – Ta S'ina Tokaheya Foundation – was established in 1989 on the Pine Ridge Indian Reservation. Ta S'ina Tokaheya, meaning 'First Robe', is the Lakota name of the founder: Michael Burns Prairie Sierra, a member of the Oglala Sioux Tribe. Michael had been searching for many years to find a way to address the Third World living conditions present on the Pine Ridge Reservation.

Ta S'ina Tokaheya Foundation promotes economic self-sufficiency through sustainable/organic farming, seed-banking based on traditional farming practices, and Ti O'sapaye development (sustainable community development based on traditional Lakota models). Green building and wind energy enterprises also were incorporated. By utilizing affordable and sustainable lifestyle alternatives and reviving and incorporating traditional Lakota principles, this model has served as an example and opportunity to improve quality of life for other reservations and non-reservation communities.

A key component of Ta S'ina's work was the creation of a Native American seed bank to preserve ancient seed species. These seeds are vital to providing a consistent, reliable, and healthy food source. Traditionally, the Lakota were nomads who obtained their food primarily by hunting buffalo and harvesting wild-crafted foods. Eventually they adopted native farming practices from surrounding plains tribes. On reservations today, however, the Sioux diet, like that of most tribes throughout North America, is heavily reliant on federal food commodities. Every registered member of the Sioux Tribe receives white sugar, white flour, powdered milk, eggs, lard, coffee, and canned meat.

As cultural traditions eroded on reservations and government food subsidies replaced the incentive for practicing sustainable food production, traditional diets based on hunting/gathering and agriculture vanished. As a direct result, death rates from diabetes, obesity, heart disease, and cancer have soared among Native Americans. However, preliminary studies have indicated that this trend can be reversed by a return to the ancestral Native American, Paleolithic diet of protein and fiber found in corn, beans, squash, grains, greens, deer, bison, and other wild-crafted foods. The traditional diet, high in fiber and protein, normalizes blood sugar levels, suppresses cravings for processed foods, and significantly reduces the occurrence of diet related diseases.

Over the past two decades, Ta S'ina Tokaheya Foundation has focused its activities on the collection and cultivation of endangered seed species to preserve crops that have evolved in Native American cultures. The ultimate value of seed-banking native seeds is to preserve the inherent genetic memory they possess. This genetic memory contains a natural resistance to harsh climate conditions and an inherent resistance to pests and disease. These seeds are extremely hardy and reliable and are naturally acclimatized to particular bioregions; they are also high in nutritional value. Since these seeds were the source of survival foods for the plains tribes,

Seed project plots and Medicine Wheel garden of the Ta S'ina Tokaheya Foundation.

their cultivation and perpetuation is essential not only for their nutritional value but for future food security. These efforts have provided ways to simultaneously reclaim Native heritage and improve health conditions. In addition, the sale of surplus crops and related value-added products has contributed to a growing local economy by creating sources of income for participating members of the Lakota community.

The endangered Native American Seed Preservation Project, a program under Ta S'ina Tokaheya Foundation, researched traditional scientific planting methods used by the plains tribes hundreds of years ago. These methods included techniques to prevent cross-pollination, such as utilizing various plant barriers to separate agricultural plots. Companion planting also was used. As an example, pole beans would be planted with corn for fixing nitrogen levels in the soil. Floodplains and bottomlands were typically selected for garden plots.

The seed project primarily implemented Hidatsa farming techniques as the Hidatsa women were among the most advanced farmers and ecologists of the plains tribes. The Hidatsa and Mandan knew the importance of keeping strains of corn and squash pure, because each variety had a special use. There are nine principal varieties of corn that were cultivated by the plains tribes: Ata'ki tso'ki – hard white corn; At'ki – soft white corn; Tsi'di tso'ki – hard yellow corn; Tsi'di tapa – soft yellow corn; Ma'ikadicake – gummy corn; Do'ohi – blue corn; Hi'ci ce'pi – dark red corn; Hi'tsiica – light red corn; and At'ki aku' hi'tsiica – pink top corn. The Hidatsa would refer to the cross pollination of corn as the 'traveling corn'. To maintain the integrity of the various strains, they configured their fields to prevent cross-pollination by creating barriers of sunflowers and separating the cornfields by variety.

The Ta S'ina Tokaheya Foundation began the seed project by selecting a 5 acre bottomland parcel outside of Oglala, a site which had the richest soil on the Reservation. The parcel was hand dug by members of the Lakota tribe, ranging from children to elders from the community. The gardens have brought community members together and have fostered a sense of pride. A half-acre mandala garden was designed in the shape of the Morning Star and a medicine wheel garden was designed and planted with medicinal herbs. The mandala garden represents the Lakota belief that all Lakota life originates from the Morning Star.

We, the co-founders of the foundation, [the author, her husband at the time Michael Sierra, and sister Kristina Mayo] engaged in a vigorous seed collection and location campaign in 1992 and began with a letter to SeedSaversExchange requesting heirloom Native American seed species. The request for heirloom seeds was later published in the SeedSaversExchange

1993 *Harvest Edition.* The response was overwhelming. Rare seeds were donated from individuals, seed banks, and universities throughout the US, Canada, South America, and Africa. We received many native varieties of corn, beans, and squash that date back as early as the 16th century from Fort Berthoud. These particular seeds originated from peoples of the Hidatsa, Mandan, Arikara, and Sioux Nations. Other seeds were located and collected from USDA seed storage facilities.

We were able to acquire and grow out all nine corn varieties mentioned previously, and this practice continues through 2010. Gummy corn seed was the most difficult to obtain, perhaps because it was one of the least favorite varieties used by the plains tribes. Throughout the Ti O'spaye cornfields,[1] companion planting was used by growing multiple varieties of dry climbing beans. One of the most prolific and flavorsome varieties is the 'shield figure bean,' which was grown by the Hidatsa 150 years ago. Dry pole beans climb the corn stalks while fixing nitrogen levels in the soil.

Pests such as grasshoppers have been a big problem in the plains and have wiped out entire crops throughout Nebraska and South Dakota. To remedy this, turkeys, guinea hens, and chickens roam free throughout the gardens eliminating grasshoppers and depositing manures. They also provide eggs and meat for consumption within the Ti O'spaye while excess is sold to the local community.

The Lakota view food as very sacred. The 'three sister' groups – corn, beans, and squash – are used for ceremonial purposes. During harvest season, a 'giving thanks' ceremony is performed. Women prepare a large feast using all the crops from the garden while ceremonial foods are placed in Nature to show gratitude for the abundance of food and seed. Everyone from the Ti O'spaye (community) gathers together for this celebration. The children and elders are inevitably the most enthusiastic participants. Both men and women go to the sweat lodge to pray and give thanks. For several weeks after the last harvest, seeds are collected, dried, and stored. Pumpkins and squash are sliced and dried to prepare soups during winter months.

Ta S'ina's garden is augmented by a 30'x36' greenhouse to propagate seedlings and to extend the growing season. Crop pollination is enhanced by two adjacent bee colonies which produce several pounds of honey annually in addition to by-products such as propolis, the glue which holds bee hives together, and beeswax. Many more saleable and value-added products are produced from the garden and a proposed line of cosmetics is in the making.

Ta S'ina also initiated an alternative housing project. Within close proximity to the garden, two model homes – one adobe and one straw-bale – were constructed from local materials, both utilizing solar energy. These models are very important because, shockingly, over 80% of the existing homes on the Reservation are without a heating supply, lack sufficient insulation, and were built with toxic materials.

Ta S'ina Tokaheya's programs have established a working sustainable community model, an 'ecovillage' if you will, through integrating traditional values and knowledge and by renewing a sense of cultural identity.

Currently, the primary focus is on sustainable energy systems and production. The Foundation is working very closely with the tribe in these areas, with the result being the creation of a whole new economy on the Reservation.

As a closing, I would like to share Michael Sierra's message to Ta S'ina's Tokaheya's Ti O'spaye:

> When we first began to come together as young men and women, we started a process of restoring our customs and traditions. As a result we became healthier and also restored our own pride and dignity because of the completeness and beauty intrinsic in our way of life.
>
> Because of our culture we learned to work towards building a better future for the next seven generations. However, we could see the reality of the conditions our people have been subjected to in America. We realized it would require our full commitment and begin with accepting the responsibility ourselves to change our environment.
>
> Ta S'ina Tokaheya culminated to become the focus of our efforts for modeling a way of life that incorporates a foundation based upon continuing the restorative efforts and practices of our Spirituality, that encompasses our role as 'Caretakers of Mother Earth', that utilizes sustainable and renewable concepts and technologies, and permits us to endeavor to achieve economic self-sufficiency.

Notes

1 Ti O'spaye is the Sioux word for community. Ta S'ina Tokaheya Ti O'spaye is one of many Ti O'spayes throughout the Reservation.

In the early 90s, Suzanne Foote helped found and establish Ta S'ina Tokaheya Foundation, later serving as one of the directors. In 1995 she formed Earth Origin Seeds, a program under the Manitou Institute, which focuses on sustainable agriculture and seed preservation. Currently she is serving as the Executive Director of both the Manitou Foundation and the Manitou Institute. Since 1988, the Manitou Foundation has provided land grants and financial support to various wisdom traditions for contemplative retreat centers, educational groups, and environmentally sustainable projects. Through Hanne Strong's vision, the Manitou Foundation established the world's largest intentional interfaith community. The Manitou Institute was later formed in 1994 to support local spiritual and environmental projects and programs, and to administer the Manitou Habitat Conservation Program, a local land conservation program.

MODULE 3

Appropriate Technology – Energy & Infrastructure

Contents

*This lead article for Module 3 was written by Gunnar Olesen, the European Coordinator of the International Network for Sustainable Energy (INFORSE). Gunnar relays his experience designing, installing and managing an effective community-scale energy system. The centerpiece of the system is the 'Stirling engine', which, when linked with a wood chip boiler, provides a combination of heat **and** energy. The important concept of 'pulsating district heating' is introduced. Detailed specifications also are provided, making this article an interactive read for anyone wishing to compare notes with their own systems.*

Stirling Engine: Efficient Heating for the Ecovillage

Gunnar Olesen – Hjortshøj Ecovillage, Denmark

Overview

The heating system in the ecovillage 'Andelssamfundet i Hjortshøj' near Århus, Denmark, is an outstanding example of a local heating system. It is designed to supply 105 energy efficient households plus community buildings and an institution. The system supplies heat from a wood-chip and a wood pellet boiler, and from a small (35 kW electric) combined heat and power plant utilizing a 'Stirling' engine. The scheme also includes decentralised passive solar heating, allowing the network to be disengaged during summer. Twenty-three houses use pulsating district heating to reduce heat loss throughout the network.

Organisational Structure

Andelssamfundet i Hjortshøj is an intentional community started in 1991 on the edge of the village Hjortshøj, located near the small Danish city of Århus. The aims of the community include enabling interested people from the Århus area to live a more environmentally-friendly lifestyle, including use of local renewable energy supplies, and to create a living space with more community activities than normally found in existing suburbs. The ecovillage is organised around 'house groups'. Each house group organiser is someone or some collective who has bought land in the community from the municipality that owned it previously, for the purpose of building houses. There are four kinds of house groups: 1) where community members bought the land together, 2) two groups of socially constructed housing (rented), 3) one group organized around a co-housing plan, and 4) a group consisting of individual houses developed by a local development company. The heat supply for this complex social mix is managed by a heating association with status as a 'cooperative with limited responsibility', and recognised according to Danish regulatory law as a heat-supplying entity. For the first groups to be developed, the heating cooperative operated on the basis of an exemption from the obligation to have heat supplied from the municipal district, while in the newer developments, the heating cooperative has the sole right to supply heat according to Danish regulation of energy supply.

Comfortable solar-enhanced life at Hortshoj ecovillage, Denmark.

The heating cooperative is managed by a board consisting of one representative from each house group. The Board is responsible for the financial affairs of the cooperative, and for extension projects, etc. Work on the Board is voluntary; the cooperative as a whole employs a paid accountant. Sometimes, however, board members are paid for work related to new developments. This has been the case for the preparation and installation of the Stirling engine and for the new development utilising pulsating heat supply. A consulting engineer has been advising the Board on new developments using the Stirling engine and pulsating heat supply.

The heating station operates automatically, while adjustments, general maintenance, and the solving of smaller problems is done by a group of volunteers, one or two from each of the house groups. While the work is voluntary, in some house groups the chores are divided, so that the person(s) involved with the heating station are not having other obligations in the group during that period. A 'chimney sweeper' has the overall responsibility for the operation of the heating station. When the station is in operation, he cleans the boilers and performs safety checks every week or every second week, depending on the season.

Development and Current Status

Until 2002, the heating was provided solely by a wood pellet boiler; however, in 2002 it was decided to upgrade the heating station with a wood chip boiler and a Stirling engine for combined heat and power production. The Stirling engine was installed in 2007-2008, but due to technical problems was not fully operational until later. By the end of September 2009, total power production was just above 1000 kWh. After a number of improvements, including measures to reduce vibrations and noise, the testing is now ongoing. We expect automatic operation soon, including automatic exchange between operation and stand-by modes.

In 2008, it was decided to supply 23 new houses in an extension of the ecovillage with an innovative heat supply – called pulsating district heating – where heat is provided for only part of the day. During that period, a heat tank in each of the houses is charged up to store heat for the rest of the day. This saves up to 50% of the heat loss in the network. All the new houses are individual-detached, so the network losses were potentially large using the existing technology as compared with the heat savings delivered with the pulsating method. The first one of the 23 houses was connected to pulsating heating in December 2008. By 1 October 2009, 8 houses were connected to the new heating technology – and the rest should be on-line through 2010. These new houses are also being connected to the control system of the pulsating heat and to remote heat metering. The automatic control of pulses and remote metering was installed during October 2009. For the 2009-10 heating season, various modes of pulsating heating will be tested, and the results will be gathered with detailed remote metering.

Future plans include:

- Buying an electric car for the community car-sharing club. The car will then be placed at the community parking lot beside the heating station and will be charged from the Stirling engine, when it is running. The car club is starting to analyse costs, availability, etc. A decision can be expected late in 2010.

- Buying solar PVs that can produce electricity in the Summer, when the Stirling engine is turned off. This will be done at the scale of individual houses, not by the heating association as a whole. Currently one house has installed a small PV system, with only a few others expected soon.

Economy

To join the heating cooperative, each member pays 135 Danish Kroners (DKK), including 25% VAT per square meter of heated area, plus the cost of a meter. The heat price is set to cover costs including depreciation of investments. There are separate tariffs for winter and summer months, giving those with good passive solar heating a benefit, as prices are highest in the summer. The current prices are 0.85 DKK/kWh (0.1139 €/kWh) during winter and 1.00 DKK/kWh (0.1340 €/kWh) during summer. All payments are determined according to consumption; no fixed charges are applied. The main investments have been the original heating station (548,000 DKK, 57,000 Euro in 1995), the new heating station with Stirling engine, including installation (4,662,000 DKK, 622,000 Euro in 2002-04), network components, including new development with pulsating heating (500,000 DKK, 66,000 Euro) – totaling 5,710,000 DKK, 761,000 Euro. The investments have been covered by a loan for the original heating station of 548,000 DKK (57,000 Euro), a loan for the upgraded heating station with Stirling engine, with a municipal guarantee, of 1,850,000 DKK (247,000

Euro), subsidies/support for the heating station of 2,570,000 DKK (343,000 Euro), subsidies for the pulsating heating of 97,000 DKK (13,000 Euro), and membership payments of 645,000 DKK (86,000 Euro). The running costs are mainly fuel (139,000 DKK, 19,000 Euro), while miscellaneous costs (operation, maintenance, and administration) are in total per annum 83,000 DKK (11,000 Euro).

Technical Description

The heating station includes a 185 kW wood pellet boiler, a 160 kW wood-chip boiler handling up to 40% humidity in wood chips, a Stirling engine of 35 kW electric and 115 kW heat, a 70 cubic meter woodchip storage made to accommodate the tipping of lorry with chips, a 10 cubic meter wood pellet storage made to blow wood pellets into, and an 8 cubic meter heat storage tank (hot water). The distributed heat network is made of pre-insulated double plastic pipes (*see right*), 2 x 50 mm for main lines and 2 x 16-25 mm for connections to individual houses. The energy demand in 2007-08 (one year) was 617 MWh including network losses inside each group of houses. Total network loss was 52 MWh (8%) in the network of the heating cooperative (between house groups).

The energetic centre of the ecovillage: The power station housing the Stirling engine.

Links with National and EU Policies

The Stirling engine is connected to the grid as an independent power producer. We paid only additional connection costs at installation. The Stirling engine will receive a feed-in tariff of 0.75 DKK (0.10 €) per kWh. This is according to Danish legislation that implements the EU Renewable Electricity Directive.

Description from INFORSE-Europe database, see: http://www.inforse. org/europe/success/SU_About.htm

Gunnar is Mechanical Engineer (MSc) and the European Coordinator of the International Network for Sustainable Energy (INFORSE) and energy political coordinator at the Danish Organisation for Sustainable Energy (OVE). Gunnar has lived in Hortshøj eco-community with his family with two children since 1994. He is also Chairman of the Cooperative Energy Association at Hortshøj.

John Vermeulen and Kevin Velasco, from a host-EDE ecovillage project in the Philippines, make an important connection between the availability of alternative technologies and their suitability in regions outside the point of manufacture. They discovered that a gasifier made in California required special considerations when applied to the tropics, while a stove from Italy had more universal applications. In both cases, the authors emphasize the importance of recognizing cultural dimensions when attempting to transfer First World technologies to Third World settings.

Appropriate Technology: Searching for the Right Fit

John Vermeulen and Kevin Velasco – Tuwâ the Laughing Fish, Philippines

Introduction

It is always an intriguing subject when it comes down to energy and the harnessing of it. People have been busy for centuries capturing this life-force of potential in so many different ways. Currently, it seems as if electricity is the most applicable means to get things done. Access is a huge issue in developing countries as they do not have the infrastructure which has been established in First World settings – not to mention the backup services involved. The biggest issue worldwide is the *storage* of the generated energy, since lead-acid batteries and any other type of storage cells are costly to manufacture, have a limited life span, and have a harmful impact on the environment.

So, the question becomes, can a decentralized, small-scale energy system work for people without causing too many challenges?

The emphasis on 'technological solutions' in most of the ideas that have been brought forth to help a rural country or third world state increase development has been very noble; yet there often is a misconception as to what people really need or require. In many cases, we design a product with simple operational needs but the understanding of the equipment might actually be beyond the realm of the user, let alone appropriate to the climate in which it is intended to be applied. In a search for an alternative energy source for the tropical region of the Philippines, the idea was to bring in a gasifier that could run on bamboo, since that is a readily available resource and is carbon neutral.

Gasification Basics

A black-box approach to gasification is essentially the process of turning organic material into usable energy. This of course is nothing particularly new as gasification was used extensively during the Second World War. What gasification does is very different from conventional energy generation mechanisms. Most energy generating involves transferring energy from a specific fuel source into a fluid which carries the energy through a turbine which, in turn, powers a generator. This is true for fossil fuels, natural gas, nuclear, and geothermal energy. Gasification, in contrast, works on the 'operating system' of fire itself.

First, picture a lit matchstick. What you see is a glowing red flame at the end of a stick of wood the size of a toothpick. But there are actually several processes that make up this flame. The visible flame isn't the wood burning but something else. There are four fundamental processes that make up this flame. These are: drying, pyrolysis, combustion, and reduction.

Drying is a rather straightforward process; it is the dehydration of the fuel in question. The material is heated to a particular temperature until water begins to evaporate. In our matchstick system, this is the first process to occur, right there at the tip of the match.

Pyrolysis is an underrated process that is responsible for the visible flame of on your matchstick. Pyrolysis is accelerated decomposition under high temperature. What happens here is that the wood begins to break up into tar and charcoal. Other substances that were in the wood are also released in this process. In the matchstick system, it occurs right below the visible flame. It is the combustion (oxidation) of the released gas, tar, and other volatile substances that is responsible for the visible flame on the matchstick. The combustion of these materials yields carbon dioxide and water vapor.

Reduction is the key process in gasification. During pyrolysis, gas, tar and charcoal are formed, and these are then oxidized. Reduction occurs on the surface of the charcoal that was formed during pyrolysis. The charcoal, at very high temperatures, consists of large amounts of carbon. When the carbon dioxide and water vapor are allowed to react with the charcoal, the carbon in the charcoal takes oxygen atoms from carbon dioxide and water. This leaves carbon monoxide and, our primary concern, hydrogen gas. This latter substance is known as the 'synthesis gas' and is used to power an engine which in turn drives a generator.

There are several types of gasifiers. A gasifier, in general, looks like a cylindrical rocket with openings for fuel and air. One of the simplest forms is an 'updraft gasifier'. Fuel is loaded at the top, air enters from the bottom and synthesis gas is piped out from fittings located at the top. This type of gasifier can be likened to a cigarette. The tip is where combustion occurs followed by the reduction zone, the pyrolysis zone, and then the drying zone. This 'smoker', as a result, breathes in synthesis gas and tar.

Importing the Technology

The gasifier used at Tuwa The Laughing Fish, based in Cabiao, Nueva Ecija, Philippines, is the Gasifier Experimenters Kit (GEK) produced by All Power Labs company based in Berkeley, California. The GEK is a downdraft gasifier. The fuel is inserted at the top, air comes in from nozzles inside the gasifier, and the synthesis gas is piped out from the base. The gas is then used to run a Kohler 26 horsepower engine which drives a 10KVA generator.

The GEK used at Tuwa has incorporated a system designed by All Power Labs called the 'Tower of Total Thermal Integration' (TOTTI). This system makes use of the excess heat generated during the gasification process. In a basic feedback loop, heat from the exhaust released by the engine after combustion and the synthesis gas are used to accelerate the drying and pyrolysis of the fuel. Exhaust from the engine is used to accelerate the pyrolysis while the hot synthesis gas is used to dry the fuel. In some setups, including the one at Tuwa, several components are computer controlled. The GCU, or Gasifier Control Unit, manages the air-to-fuel ratio as well as monitors the temperature and pressure within the GEK.

Localization Challenges

Gasification is an excellent source of alternative energy; however, gasification has several limitations. Gasifiers are very particular when it comes to fuel. Fuels in different locations and altitudes have varying levels of moisture. As we know, the tropical region has a torrential rainy season and this can impose a challenge to keep the feedstock dry, especially when a great bulk of it needs to be stored.

We had certain assumptions regarding fuel materials that were ultimately dispelled when the machine arrived in the Philippines. Gasifiers require that the fuel ideally be processed into two-inch chunks. This is to ensure the complete processing of the material. However, it was only when the machine was being tested that we discovered, due to the long structural strands of the bamboo material, that it is virtually impossible to chip it into the required fuel size for the GEK. If this can be accomplished at all, it is done with heavy equipment which has a huge financial impact.

We also assumed that another suitable fuel material for gasification – wood chips from branches and the bark of trees – would be a readily-available resource because these items can often be found lying on roadsides. These, as we discovered, are being used by people as cooking fuel for stoves; therefore, accessing woody branches is not as easy as we first assumed.

There is also an abundance of rice hulls in our area, which is currently considered an agricultural waste material. If the rice hulls were to be used for the gasifier, they would need to be compacted into briquettes to insure that there is adequate density of the fuel for sufficient burning time – and also to generate sufficient space between the fuel materials since the hulls can be too dense if they are poured straight into the hopper, which results in choking down the draft system.

So, the question becomes, are there any technologies out there that work in a tropical setting and rely on readily-available fuel materials?

More Appropriate Technology

With the natural waste materials such as leaves, bark, woodchips and rice by-products found in this region, the Lucia Stove developed in Italy is an ingenious solution to energy requirements when it comes to cooking. The various fuels can be converted into heat suitable for cooking by means of a double-walled cylinder using the pyrolysis principle. The efficiency is tenfold higher than the conventional open stoves that people are currently using and the system is very easy to build: it requires only a few metal cans or pieces of sheet metal to construct a typical model. The program for the Lucia Stove is designed to empower people to initiate their own livelihoods by manufacturing the stoves and becoming a supplier of fuel and compost.

Besides the large savings of fuel consumed during the heating of a meal, the user has the option of trading the bio-waste for compressed briquettes of fuel. A central collection point is established where a mass of fuel can be brought and exchanged for an equivalent value of briquette. There will always be higher net weight of bio-waste since the energy invested to make the briquette has to be offset. After the burning process, the residue in the rice hull stove becomes a good soil enhancer. This resource can then be exchanged for needed items or saved up for later collection as compost material. The trader or central collection point thus has the option of spreading good organic fertilizer throughout the region. This high quality fertilizer aerates the soil, holds moisture better, and creates homes in the pockets of the material for micro-organisms which are crucial for better soil building.

With this system of local trade, money can be eliminated from the scene. A system of saving and trade is established whereby the buyer of a stove can bring in a large supply of fuel for months or weeks prior to the purchase, thus building up credit and in doing so empowering him or her to be an active part of the local economic system. Many systems have been devised to help impoverished communities rise from their situation but in these systems money usually plays a disproportionate role. With the example of the Lucia Stove, people have the power to move forward on several planes: including saving in fuel costs, enriching their soils to grow better crops, and increasing local self-reliance.

Unfortunately, there is a current trend of ignorance as many valuable resources are lost by burning the 'waste' in piles just to get rid of it. It will take community education programs and the introduction of viable technologies such as the Lucia Stove in this region to help eliminate such unfortunate consequences as air pollution, loss of resources, and the contamination of water bodies due to the dumping of organic and

Appropriate village scale technology: Proud owners of a new batch of Lucia Stoves.

inorganic waste materials which otherwise could have been segregated and used for productive purposes.

Lessons Learned

Oftentimes, it is the economic challenges in the developing world that determine if a technology is readily adaptable and usable for the general public. The downdraft gasifier and the Lucia Stove are both based on the technology of pyrolysis but vary in their application of scale.

Climatic conditions also determine the success of adapting technology to new settings. Most of the fuel material testing for the GEK gasifier was done using walnut shells, peanuts, and wood chips at the Berkeley, California test site. Implicit in the cost of importing the technology is the necessity of determining the suitability of other regional materials as alternative fuel sources. In fact, it was through our test runs in the Philippines that we determined the suitability of available materials and in the process discovered the optimum fuel for this unit. This fuel, created by a local Filipino government unit, is called 'basuling' – a perfect 2 inch sphere made from carbonized solid waste. This material was successfully tested in our trials and offers a potential resource that can close the energy loop process.

The gasifier and the Lucia Stove are both 'open-source' technologies; they offer room for continuous improvement over time by being tested in multiple regional applications, thus providing ongoing back-end technical support. It is these considerations that helped us to see the educational potential of adapting Western technologies to fit a Third World tropical setting. We are now growing our own fuel source for our gasifier to assure a substantial and sustainable supply. Usable materials from our first test plot will be available in two years. We are equally excited about the potential of setting up a pilot project of the Lucia Stove in our home town. This is an example of appropriate technology adapted to real world settings.

John Vermeulen was born in South Africa from Dutch decent and lived in both countries for an extensive time. During his internship as a mechanical engineer for the merchant marines, he sailed around the world twice in a year and was exposed to numerous enlightening cultures. After having worked in the installation and production of logistic systems for several years, he completed his Master studies as an Industrial Designer -Three Dimensional. At the Design Indaba of 2006 held in Cape Town, South Africa, he won the prize for the Most Innovative Design with a tricycle model for a sustainable rural transport project affiliated with SABS. Having been based in the Philippines since 2008, he designed, constructed and completed a 2 year Eco-Homestead, Green Bed & Breakfast Inn & Resilience Center project at Cabiao, Philippines, named Tuwâ the Laughing Fish. He now lives off-grid & promotes a low-carbon lifestyle and is an active EDE facilitator.

Kevin Velasco is a 17 year-old film student at The University of the Philippines Diliman. He is the son of Penelope Reyes and resides at Tuwâ the Laughing Fish. As a child he was raised to think critically. For as long as he can remember, he has had an interest with electricity, electronics and energy. At Tuwâ, he trained with Jim Mason of All Power Labs on gasification, where he worked on the programming of the Gasifier Control Unit (GCU) along with Bear Kaufman.

Existing conversations about appropriate technology within a sustainable community setting generally overlook the important arena of communications technology – perhaps because we've all become so accustomed to the Internet we take it for granted. According to Dr. Jonathan Scherch, the Internet is a fragile, energy intensive system that could easily become unreliable in any number of possible future scenarios. For that reason, Jonathan lays out his rationale for installing 'amateur radio' stations – decentralized, repairable, community scale technology with global outreach – as part of comprehensive permaculture design. Tips for setting up your own system follow.

Getting the Word Out on Sustainability Innovations – via Amateur Radio Communications

Jonathan Scherch, Ph.D. – Antioch University, Seattle, USA

Introduction

Increasingly, the beneficial impacts of local-through-global sustainability efforts originating from communities of permaculture design (PD) practitioners are gaining visibility and popularity. Around the world, people are engaging in local efforts at improving food, water, and energy systems, building healthy homes and community relationships and, essentially, demonstrating acts of sustainable living.

And yet, much needs to be done to advance ways of expanding visions, sharing insights and building collaborations across our communities. The tools deployed to do so often include training courses and workshops, printed materials and/or internet resources and require various physical, technological and financial inputs to support them. How about adding a new tool to our collection, one which can add resilience, flexibility, and community engagement at once? I propose that we enlist the global amateur radio (AR) community in service of our global sustainability.

I am a Professor within the Environment & Community Program at Antioch University Seattle (AUS) and have taught regional and international courses on social work, social change and permaculture design (PD) for over 20 years, and recently launched at AUS the Sustainable Food Systems & Permaculture Design concentration. Within my courses, I have complemented the standard 72-hour PD course content with a new dimension not typically covered among most PD courses (or topical textbooks on sustainable living, urban/rural homesteading, etc.) – an orientation to amateur 'ham' radio communication systems and related community service benefits. As such, I have come to recognize the prospective value and importance of AR to individual, neighborhood, community, regional and global efforts at sustainability.

I have been a licensed AR operator since 1990, and currently hold the top U.S. Amateur Extra Class license. My home radio station is comprised of both older and new equipment and powered by a solar photovoltaic system I designed and installed to provide a redundant (and clean) energy source. I am an accredited Volunteer Examiner (VE) to support testing sessions for licensing new AR operators and co-direct *Seattle Amateur Radio Training* courses. I also volunteer for the *Auxiliary Communications Service* within the City of Seattle Department of Emergency Management and am affiliated with many radio clubs and organizations.

Over the years, I have met AR operators from all over the world and have learned much from them about their cultures, communities and shared interests in sustainability and appropriate technologies – typically over fantastic meals! So, along with the fun of the hobby, the advancement of technical knowledge and the contributions to emergency services and preparedness, new roles are emerging for the approximately four million international AR operators and their skills. With scalable investments in equipment and depending on license class (which defines privileges for access to bands and modes of transmission), AR operators communicate with others around the world (and around their local communities) using voice, Morse code, and/or other modes of digital data including teletype, fax, slow-scan TV and others.

Why Amateur Radio when we have the Internet and Cell Phones?

Amateur radio is a world-wide service like no other. Generations of radio operators have been demonstrating leadership in creating relationships, organizations and actual prototypes underpinning today's common communication systems. The term 'amateur' should not imply second rate; the skills, services and technological developments of volunteer AR operators are often equal to those expected of paid professionals. Their early creations have included now-common tools as email and internet systems, cell phone systems, computer and digital data technologies, among others.

Also, AR operators do not 'broadcast' to anonymous audiences (like commercial radio stations); rather, they transmit person-to-person to other licensed operators identified by their unique call signs. AR operators hold on-air educational and public service nets, discuss science, culture, weather and so on, but do not play music, conduct business or other activities as a commercial broadcast station might. So, why should we consider amateur radio for advancing sustainability when so many other communication tools exist?

AR can be usefully deployed in service of timely *Transition Town* (Hopkins, 2008) efforts, where community sustainability programs are coordinated for post-peak oil resiliency. Establishing reliable, decentralized

Dr. Scherch's HAM radio station in Seattle.

and renewably-energized communication systems can provide and support a host of related benefits. For example, in times of emergency, Ward Silver, N0AX, (2004) notes that 'because of their numbers and reliance on uncomplicated infrastructure, hams are able to bounce back quickly when a natural disaster or other emergency makes communications over normal channels impossible' (p.13). Amateur radio systems can provide affordable, locally-maintained, life-long communication alternatives or complements to purchased commercial and corporate systems.

Moreover, internet and cell phone systems are actually quite fragile, expensive and energy-intensive. Comprised of many types of hardware and software technologies, and representing myriad natural resource uses and origins, these networks perform well when all is going well, where redundant systems of hardware, routine back-ups and security systems among other features have created a reliable, high-performance, high-technology experience. Yet, in face of economic distress, energy transitions and global climate change impacts, these complex operations require increasingly tenuous financial and energy inputs to meet expectations and demands.

Also, the fast-paced evolution and obsolescence of many technologies like phones, modems, computers, peripherals and the like, create tremendous volumes of new and abandoned equipment. We all participate in the whole-system, life-cycle impacts of modern technology (ideally from cradle to cradle) so current use and convenience should be calibrated by anticipated burdens for future generations.

Thirdly, disruptions of service due to energy outages, hardware failures and long replacement supply-chains, and/or emergencies prompting the need of government services to assume control of vital communication systems can interfere with if not curtail normal operational use. AR systems are not the panacea to these and other issues, though they can potentially afford benefits in the following ways:

- Reduced costs of equipment, building of "homebrew" equipment using available local materials, and developing cooperative financial support systems and bulk purchases through community organizations and clubs to distribute costs and minimize individual burdens;
- Reduced(renewable) energy usage in operation and using durable, repairable equipment longer;
- Communication systems designed via permaculture principles – single communication elements perform multiple functions and multiple elements form resilient "communication guilds", allowing for system integrity to sustain in face of disruptions or critical need.

Revealing a Long History of Community Service

In 2012, the AR community will celebrate 100-years of contributions to international relations, communications, technological innovation and community service. Amateur radio's roots with topics of sustainable living and community resilience are not new. In the 1970s through the early '80s, Copthorne McDonald, VY2CM, wrote the popular series on *New Radio Directions* in *Mother Earth News*. And, around the same time, residents of The Farm near Summertown, Tennessee published books on radio communications and used AR to connect with others around the world as part of their PLENTY international development and restoration projects.

This occurred because radio hams operate on many bands, facilitating connections that can span a few miles or a few thousand miles, across local communities, regions, countries and around the world. Utilizing tools for 'line of sight' communications and atmospheric 'skip' effects, operators learn when and how to use their radio systems for optimal performance and benefit.

From my home in West Seattle, Washington, I recently made contacts with AR operators in Tokyo, Japan; Kona, Hawaii; Portland, Oregon; and Palmer, Alaska – as well as with folks around Puget Sound.

This also allows for operators to engage in important public service activities around the world, including international disaster relief efforts following earthquakes, hurricanes, floods, and other emergencies. To do so, they train continuously and learn how to effectively establish and maintain emergency communication (EMCOMM) systems with local, regional and national community leaders, health and medical professionals and others.

Getting Started

Blending old technologies with new, AR operators are well positioned to join permaculture designers in building durable and resilient communication systems in service of sustainable communities. Indeed, one of the hallmarks of AR operators (like most permaculture designers) is their savvy at deploying inexpensive, reliable stations. By understanding the types of radios, antennas, and accessories which comprise their stations, operators can minimize expenses while optimizing performance, whether in an urban apartment or rural farm setting.

To begin, prospective radio operators would need to become oriented to the rules and regulations, technologies, science and cultures of amateur radio. Most people access local ham clubs and/or utilize the variety of training classes and study materials to support their learning and preparation.

Although particular rules and regulations for amateur radio operations differ from country to country, all government licensing frameworks are sanctioned by the International Amateur Radio Union (IARU) and so have a similar breadth and depth of radio theory and skill requirements. In the US, the *Federal Communications Commission (FCC)* oversees licensing of amateur radio stations, allocation of unique call signs, and the maintenance and enforcement of regulations as stipulated within the Part 97 rule book.

Licensing – Getting your 'Ticket'

Each amateur radio operator must pass an entry-level examination to acquire an amateur radio station license. Around the world, radio clubs and groups offer a variety of training programs to support radio education. Many materials exist to meet learning styles and lend to the fun and creativity of learning the skills of competent amateur radio service.

Upon successful completion of an examination, each operator receives a unique call sign depending on their country of origin (in the U.S., every license begins with either the letter A, K, N or W). By identifying themselves via their call signs, if by voice using an internationally-recognized phonetic alphabet, radio operators communicate in English at first, and then switch to other languages as they wish.

Call signs often reflect one's earned license class and, by extension, one's on-air privileges as determined by the associated government licensing authority. While licensing schemes vary somewhat from country to country, they do typically share an incentive licensing scheme which encourages operators to advance their knowledge and skills in order to expand their range of privileges. The chart below, produced by the *American Radio Relay League (ARRL)*, portrays the distribution of bands and respective privileges for U.S. license classes – Technician, General, Advanced and Amateur Extra.

This band plan is a handy reference for operators to ensure that they are operating within their respective privileges. And they can do so using various modes of transmission in a coordinated manner to avoid interference and ease on-air connections.

See You on the Air!

Moving forward, the local-through-global initiatives to achieve sustainable living and community development expectations will benefit from expanding the opportunities for people and organizations to share information about them. AR can provide a timely, useful and inclusive suite of tools to support such communications. These could include:

- Ecovillage and intentional community development updates, initiatives, efforts, etc.;
- Interdisciplinary skill sharing;
- Food system and farming practices such as information on organic crop methods, seasonal performance and results, seed saving and sharing of abundances;
- Cross-cultural and cross-climate collaborations;
- Farmstead-to-farmstead networking and coordination of WWOOF'ers (Willing Workers on Organic Farms);
- Tool, technology and knowledge sharing, training and educational opportunities, etc.

I hope that I have been able to convey a few of the many possibilities of amateur radio in service of our sustainable futures. Please feel free to contact me. I hope to see you on the air

References

American Radio Relay League (2007). *U.S. Amateur Radio Bands*. Newington, CT: ARRL Publishing.
Hopkins, R. (2008). *The Transition Handbook: From Oil Dependency to Local Resilience*. White River Junction, NH: Chelsea Green Publishers.
Silver, W (2004). *Ham Radio for Dummies*. Hoboken, NJ: Wiley Publishing, Inc.
West, G. (2010). *Gordon West's Technician Class 2010-2014*. Niles, IL: Master Publishing, Inc.

Dr. Jonathan Scherch is a member of the Western Washington DX Club (WWDXC), the West Seattle Amateur Radio Club (WSARC) and co-Director of Seattle Amateur Radio Training. He regularly monitors HF, VHF and UHF bands. For more information, visit his website at **www. designtrek.net**. Jonathan is also core faculty of the Environment and Community Program at Antioch Unversity Seattle, where he has guided ecovillage enthusiasts in the creation of Master's degrees.

There are many ways to approach Module 3. One approach that needs to be considered in any EDE course is the technology of 'constructed wetlands' – handled expertly here by Michael Shaw, who is based at Findhorn. Michael treats the subject as a true engineer and here describes the construction process step-by-step, providing the biological and ecological background to justify the design decisions that are made. While available open space is a consideration, there is no doubt that the constructed wetland is appropriate technology at the scale of the ecovillage.

Wetlands for the Ecovillage

Michael Shaw –
Biomatrix Water Technology, LLP, Scotland

Out of their loneliness for each other
two reeds, or maybe two shadows, lurch
forward and become suddenly a life
lifted from dawn or the rain. It is
the wilderness come back again, a lagoon
with our city reflected in its eye.
We live by faith in such presences.

It is a test for us, that thin
but real, undulating figure that promises,
"If you keep faith I will exist
at the edge, where your vision joins
the sunlight and the rain: heads in the light,
feet that go down in the mud where the truth is."

'Spirit of Place: Great Blue Heron'
from *Even in Quiet Places* BY WILLIAM STAFFORD

What is a Constructed Wetland?

Constructed wetlands treat sewage by passing the polluted water through a bed of gravel about 70 centimetres deep in which plants are growing. The gravel is installed over a liner or a bed of clay. The sewage is fed into the wetland at one end and takes several days to pass to the other, where it is collected and discharged. A septic tank is installed ahead of the wetland to collect plastics and other non-organic material and provide anaerobic treatment of the sewage, i.e. without oxygen. The concentration of suspended solids (TSS) is reduced as well as pollution measured as Biochemical Oxygen Demand (BOD). BOD is an index of the amount of organic pollution in the influent water from the ecovillage.

There are two types of constructed wetland – surface flow and sub-surface flow. The former allows wastewater to flow horizontally past and through plant stems growing in soil, flooded with wastewater. While less expensive to build, there are disadvantages associated with open water, such as danger to children and animals and breeding of mosquitoes. For sewage treatment in ecovillages, sub-surface flow constructed wetlands are recommended. In this type of wetland, plant roots and gravel provide substrate for bacterial films and the water flows about 10 centimetres below the gravel surface, which provides a safer system with no odours from the wetland and no mosquitoes, as there is no surface water.

The main advantages of constructed wetlands are that they provide passive treatment; construction is relatively simple and operations minimal. However they take significant amounts of land and need a level site. Wastewater treatment is often a trade-off between energy and land. Operation and maintenance is principally around maintaining the planted ecology in good condition and ensuring ancillary mechanical equipment performs. Wetlands have among the lowest wastewater treatment carbon footprints for operations. Embedded energy and construction carbon footprint can also be low where bulk materials, such as gravel, can be sourced locally. In Ecovillage Design Education trainings, this technology is often used as the basic system for the design and construction of a natural systems sewage treatment plant.

Designing and Building a Constructed Wetland

The size of the wetland will depend on the number of people it serves plus any extra wastewater from other ecovillage sources, such as food processing. Water for washing dishes and food preparation, baths and showers and toilet flushing is included in the person count. The low winter water temperature is relevant as the warmer the water up to 30°C, the smaller the size of the wetland. Although the treatment slows down at cold-water temperatures, wetlands can continue to operate at air temperatures below freezing, provided there is some influent each day of water from the built environment. The plants die back and fall on the wetland surface as insulating mulch. A blanket of snow adds to the thermal insulation.

The following is a typical chart for sizing a constructed wetland for between 100 and 1,000 people for effluent BOD of 15 mg/l at various water temperatures.

The wetland is sized for winter conditions, when microbial life is at its slowest. The size is the treatment area at full depth within the wetland. Allow 30% extra land for sloping sides in the wetland, berming and access. The length should be no more than twice the width. The reason for this

Sizing of SSFCWs to Treat BOB to 15mg/l after septic tank pre-treatment.

Volume 2001/pe 5 pe = 1m³	BOD in mg/l	TSS in mg/l	NH4 in mg/l	Winter Temp ºC	Estimate Person Area/pe	Area m² /m³ of sewage	HRT in days	BOD out mg/l	TSS out mg/l	NH3 out mg/l
1m³	160	100	35	10	4.0	20.1	5.8	15.0	11.1	9.3
1m³	160	100	35	15	3.0	15.0	4.3	15.0	11.2	13.2
1m³	160	100	35	18	2.5	12.5	3.6	15.0	11.4	31.4
1m³	160	100	35	20	2.3	11.2	3.2	15.0	11.5	13.6

The numbers are approximate. Add 30% for gross footprint plus septic tank area.

is to ensure that the influent does not overload the narrower front of the wetland with incoming suspended solids that might cause clogging. It is recommended that the sizing and material specifications for the proposed wetland are checked by a qualified engineer before building starts.

Typically the land is excavated with earth taken out from the excavation used to create berms as shown in the sketch below. Enough freeboard should be allowed above the gravel to take a large storm event. When this happens, the wetland will flood and gradually drain out as the storm subsides.

A liner will prevent the polluted water contaminating the groundwater. This is typically made from 1 mm thick high-density polyethylene (HDPE). This material will normally come in rolls 5 metres wide. Joining sheets will require specialised welding equipment and is best carried out by a qualified contractor. Geotextile, such as 1 mm or 1.5 mm polypropylene, should be installed below and above the liner to protect it from penetration from sharp rocks and gravel.

The influent pipe from the septic tank will pass through the liner using a boot, which again should be installed by an HDPE contractor. This influent is connected to a manifold with cleanouts. This manifold has many holes along its length to distribute the influent across the width of the wetland. A similar effluent manifold is installed at the far end of the wetland. Over each manifold, rocks of around 75 mm are used to help distribute the incoming sewage across the width of the wetland cell. In between, 25 mm gravel is installed to a depth of 70 centimetres. A 5 centimetres layer of 10 mm pea gravel can be laid on top of the 25 mm gravel to facilitate planting.

It is important to protect the liner from sunlight at the edges, as it will degrade slowly with ultra-violet light. The liner can be covered where it comes out of the gravel with the outer layer of geotextile and the geotextile covered with rocks.

A level adjust sump needs to be installed inside the wetland or in the effluent pipe as it leaves the wetland cell. This device allows the water level to be set. If the septic tank or tanks are below ground they will have effluent pumps to feed the wetland. If the septic tank is above the ground, the level adjust sump will control the level from the septic tank through the wetland.

The cell can then be flooded, preferably all or partly with river or lake water, which will come with living aquatic life. Wetland plants are installed

at a density of around 5 plants per square metre. Cattails (*Typha*), reeds (*Phragmites*), bulrush (*Scirpus*), rushes (*Juncus*), and sedges (*Carex*) are usually the preferred species. Use locally grown and adapted plants whenever possible. Look for wetland perennials with deep, dense, fibrous root systems and winter tolerance. It is often possible to collect the plants from local rivers, ponds and ditches. Otherwise they can be grown in pots while the wetland is being constructed. Flowering plants, such as Cana Lilies, can be installed round the edge of the wetland to add colour while harvesting cut flowers is an added bonus. As the plants grow, it is generally good to lower the water level in the wetland gradually using the level adjust sump. This will encourage the plant roots to chase the water and grow deeply into the cell.

Gravel being installed over geotextile and rocks of manifold.

Slowly introduce the sewage so that it replaces the river water over a week or two. It will take up to three months in summer for the system to reach steady state at full load and longer in winter. However, the technology will give many years' treatment at a low operating cost. If species not planted take over the wetland, weeding may be necessary; however, wetland species are quite dominant, especially phragmites. If trees self seed, take them out because the roots of large trees can penetrate the liner.

Treated effluent can be recycled for landscape irrigation, particularly trees. Using treated effluent on vegetables is not recommended. Drip irrigation systems are economical and can be installed without disinfecting the treated effluent. If disinfection is required for recycling to toilets for example, ultra-violet equipment provides a chemical-free and relatively low impact solution.

It is good to monitor the performance of the system on a regular basis. At a basic level this can be by testing the influent and effluent with pH and ammonia strip testers. If a dissolved oxygen meter is available, measurements can be taken in the level-adjust sump and the manifold cleanouts. Constructed wetlands are robust as they have considerable 'biological momentum' because of the relatively long hydraulic retention times. It is important to be aware of the indicators and effects that sudden changes can have on the treatment performance and what appropriate action might be needed.

One of the most common operating issues occasionally encountered is shock loading, which is a sudden and large increase or decrease in BOD and/or ammonia concentration or hydraulic flow. For constructed wetlands, a short to medium-term decrease in influent loading is rarely a problem. Some of the indicators of a shock-loading event include:

- Change in pH from normal;
- Increased odours;
- Decreased dissolved oxygen levels in the level-adjust sump from normal;
- Increased BOD, COD, NH3 and/or TSS concentrations.

The effluent should be recycled to the front end of the wetland during a shock event. Recirculation of organisms from the end of the process increases the recoverability of the entire system.

Normal influent pH values should fall within the range of 6.5 to 8.0. Most aquatic organisms in the system will thrive within this range and more acidic or alkaline conditions will adversely affect the organisms. If changes in pH are gradual, normally there will not be any serious change in the process until the pH reaches the outer limits of what is required for microbial growth. An example of a gradual change in pH is the depression of pH due to the nitrification process.

Biological nitrification is an aerobic process that converts the organic and ammonia forms of nitrogen to nitrate. The extent of nitrification that occurs during treatment is dependent on the extent to which nitrifying microorganisms are present. Biological nitrification consumes alkalinity and produces acid. If the pH is greater than 6, it is likely that residual alkalinity remains. The alkalinity of the wastewater can also be checked by strip tester and if the effluent pH is lower than 6, the addition of alkalinity may be required in the form a calcium carbonate (CaCO3 – lime). A sharp drop in pH accompanied by loss of nitrification is almost certainly caused by the consumption of alkalinity.

Sudden or abrupt pH changes due to spills into the wastewater system are the most damaging and may result in destruction of some or all of the microorganisms in the system. Isolation and recycling of water within the wetland and dilution with fresh water are the best procedures for dealing with this problem.

Under stable operation, the constructed wetland should not release odours. The proper odour is similar to healthy garden soil. Temporary unpleasant odours generally result from anaerobic activity in locations intended for aerobic treatment. The most likely sources are the septic tank

Bolivian wetland.

and influent pumping sumps, which will be anaerobic/anoxic. Sump lids should be kept securely sealed.

If the power fails, storage in the septic tank and the wetland itself allows for short-term operation without power. Within the treatment system, storage space is provided in the wetland freeboard. Although water may surface in the wetland, these levels will be reduced once power is restored.

A key motivation for using constructed wetlands is relatively low capital cost, the small requirement for external energy, ease of sludge handling by pumping the septic tank every few years and minimal labour needed for operations. This results in a low life-cycle cost.

How and Why do Constructed Wetlands Work?

Naturally occurring wetlands purify and filter the Earth's fresh water all over the world. Wetlands are one of the principle ecosystems on the planet for recycling the essential elements of life (carbon, hydrogen, oxygen, nitrogen and phosphorous), as well as micronutrients. Aquatic habitats found in wetlands support a high level of biodiversity that is well adapted and specialized to absorb excess nutrients and breakdown solids and pathogens. The treatment is mainly a breakdown rather than an uptake process. Although the plants take up some nutrients and metals, the main process is the microbial breakdown of organic pollutants. Biofilms, which are colonies of bacteria, form on the roots of plants and on the surfaces of gravel and it is these biofilms that are the treatment engine of this "attached growth" treatment process. The root zones of the higher plants play a central role in this process and provide some of the endogenous sources of carbon that support microbial life. Hollow stemmed plants, such as bulrushes and cattails, transport oxygen to their roots, providing an aerobic environment on the root hairs for aerobic bacteria. Plants also provide a mechanical function by constantly forming new routes for water to flow through the wetlands.

Constructed wetlands rely on the complex ecologies of the pond, marsh, and meadow to convert carbon and nitrogen to gaseous forms (CO_2, CH_4, N_2) and to redistribute the C, H, O, N, and P into more publicly acceptable forms such as plant biomass (e.g. planted landscape and woodlands) or animals (e.g. micro-animals and fish) rather than sludge.

Sewage contains ammonia, which is toxic to plants and is treated by processes called nitrification and denitrification. The nitrifying bacteria, *Nitrosomonas* and *Nitrobacter*, are responsible for the microbial conversion of ammonia to nitrite and nitrite to nitrate. These bacteria will occur naturally in the wetland once it reaches a steady state condition. The final step in removing nitrogen is denitrification, which is the biological conversion of nitrate to nitrogen gas.

Constructed wetlands have a large number of pathways, which is self-organising, self-repairing, self-reproducing and with a great ability to adapt to changes in influent conditions. Their benefits make constructed wetlands an excellent sewage treatment system for ecovillages.

Michael Shaw is a founding member of The Ecovillage Institute at Findhorn and is a resident trustee of the Findhorn Foundation. He pioneered the Ten Stones ecovillage and cohousing community with others in Vermont, USA. An engineer by training, he has been involved in all phases of the development and implementation of natural wastewater treatment and bioremediation systems, including Restorers since 1989 with Ocean Arks International (OAI). With Dr. John Todd, founder of OAI, he is the author of two wastewater treatment patents.

In this introduction to village-scale renewable energy systems design, independent consultant Jeff Clearwater encapsulates 32 years worth of experience. Jeff implores us, "Begin with conservation!" He then discusses the pros and cons of the five basic renewable sources: solar, wind, hydro, geothermal, and waste heat. Finally, these sources are integrated in a whole systems package that is sure to shed light on all that is actually involved in the powering of an ecovillage. Jeff recommends seeking the advice of an experienced practitioner before engaging this complex task. By doing so, you will prevent many future problems and will make your efforts as cost-effective as possible.

Renewable Energy & Electric Systems Design for Ecovillages

Jeff Clearwater – Village Power Design, Oregon, USA

Introduction

When we think of whole systems design in the context of ecovillages, we seek to create the ideal human habitat that integrates seamlessly with Nature. For many, ecovillage living equates to 'simple living' or 'getting back to Nature'; and so, in turn, we tend to think of 'simple tools' to accomplish this human-nature integration. However, for most of us, the life we seek to create – in what Albert Bates calls *Civilization 2* – hopefully includes some of the not so simple creations of Civilization 1, creations like lighting, stereos, cameras, computers, toasters, blenders, phones, and the Internet. Providing a renewable and sustainable electricity supply for ecovillages to power these loads is no simple matter. What I hope to do in this short essay is to distill the essential design wisdom of 32 years of designing and installing village-sized renewable energy systems, or at least introduce you to the terrain.

Appropriate Technology

The primary design driver for a renewable electric energy system is the culture that people want to create. It is essential that the designer explore with the community what 'appropriate technology' means to them by asking some basic questions: Appropriate in what way? How does the electrically driven 'tools' we use serve our mission and values? What is essential? How else can we accomplish any given need? Who will service the system? What percentage of our resources do we devote to what level of electric service? Do we believe in or should we rely on the utility grid? Should we phase out of using it? Get answers to these questions before proceeding with the design. Mutual community understanding of these issues and a clear short-term and long-term plan will greatly help!

On-Grid or Off-Grid?

Assuming you have access to the electrical utility grid, the first major design decision is whether you use it, phase out of using it, use it only as backup, or fully embrace it. For many, the term 'off-grid' equates to all that is good and 'the grid' to all that is bad or unsustainable. First let me inform both views. Off-grid systems usually rely on lead-acid batteries which must be replaced periodically. Until the new non-toxic batteries based on Lithium come down in price, off-grid living now equates to using a ton or so of lead for a typical sized community. Lead is a highly toxic industry – and even the manufacture of solar panels and inverters involves toxic metals and practices. So, 'off-grid' is not exactly ecologically benign.

Present-day on-grid electricity is highly unsustainable, ecologically destructive and one of the major contributors to global warming. The vast majority of grid power comes from coal, natural gas and nuclear; however, there is a growing movement to 'green' the grid with distributed sources of solar, wind, waste heat, and micro-hydro. It will take some time but it is happening. Tying into the grid with your community's renewable power system can contribute to this 'greening-the-grid' movement.

Off-grid living demands a careful and frugal approach to electricity use, much more so than most of us are accustomed to. For existing communities that started off-grid, this frugal use is second-nature by now. For those communities that built their infrastructure *on*-grid, chances are converting to off-grid will require further significant investment in super energy efficient appliances, practices and lifestyle.

If you are designing a new community with access to the grid, I highly recommend that you design your electrical loads as if you were off-grid and plan for as much renewable generation as possible. Assuming you can afford it, efficiency rules! But as in most whole systems design, good design can reduce or eliminate much of the extra cost. You can then use the grid only as backup or to provide a bridge to the sustainable future you want to create.

How to do it?

End Uses & Efficiency

First we need to look at which end uses must be met with electricity and which are best met in other ways. Conservation is everything. For every dollar you spend on energy efficiency you'll save four-five dollars on your renewable energy production system. So let's start there in earnest!

The highest energy users in any community are space heating and cooling, water heating, refrigeration, water pumping and cooking – usually in that order. Designing to meet these needs in passive and sustainable ways that perhaps won't even need electricity is your number one priority. So, first you'll need green buildings that are super-insulated and use passive heating and cooling systems. Super-insulate your existing buildings and look for ways to retrofit passive heating and cooling approaches. Retrofitting, however, only goes so far. Sometimes you'll just need to build new buildings. The art of super-efficient building design is now producing zero-net-energy (ZNE) buildings. These buildings, with a modicum of input from solar or other renewable sources, need no further energy from outside sources.

You'll also need to install solar water heating throughout the community. It's highly cost-effective – both economically and ecologically. Unless you have abundant on-site hydro, there is no better way to heat water for domestic use. And don't forget the conservation end: install low flow showerheads, etc. Save water in the first place!

If you are on-grid and have no other alternatives, then burning propane or natural gas to heat water or space directly (at 85% to 92% efficiency) makes more ecological sense than using electricity that was made in a hydrocarbon-based power plant (at 35% efficiency). And if you are forced to burn hydrocarbons or wood on site then do it through the new Stirling engine combined power and heat system to maximize efficiency – you'll get electricity, space-heat and hot water all from one unit.[1]

Refrigeration? Passive and other non-electric approaches do exist and have been used for thousands of years. In colder climates, simple thermostatically controlled louvers on exposed insulated cold boxes are making a comeback. There are direct solar to refrigeration systems (absorption and adsorption) and even passive refrigerant loops that store winter coolth into the summer. Making large amounts of ice in the winter that are stored and used throughout the summer is another time-tested approach. One can also use agriculturally sourced hydrocarbon or hydrogen gas in propane refrigerators. Short of these more innovative approaches, super-efficient refrigerators are a must if you are going to use electricity for refrigeration.

In all the above design scenarios, remember to think Conservation First! Reduce the need for water, heat, and energy in general – then you won't need to generate so much electricity in the first place.

Renewable Sources

Presently there are five renewable energy sources that an ecovillage should systematically consider when designing a renewable energy electric system:

Solar

Solar is by far the most universally available resource. Even in the most cloudy climes, solar thermal (as in solar hot water) and solar electric (as in solar photovoltaic (PV) work well. It's a common misconception that cloudy climates don't have enough sun to use solar.

Solar thermal energy is the most cost effective and should be used to offset the need for electric generation whenever possible. Solar PV is not

cheap; but PV panels can last 50-100 years and pay for themselves many times over (it takes three years for a solar PV panel to pay back the electricity used to make it). Solar panels are virtually maintenance-free, lightweight and easy to install. One kilowatt (kW) of solar PV panels will produce on average from 60 - 130 kilowatt-hours (kWh) of power per month depending on how sunny a climate you have.

Wind

Wind is an excellent source of power; however it is highly dependent on local conditions and on the micro-climate of your exact area. Your neighbor may have good wind and you may not.

With present technology, you'll need a minimum average wind speed of about 4.5 meters/second (10 mph) for wind to be cost-effective. You can use slower winds to pump water or grind grain. If you have an average speed of 4.5 m/s you can expect about 40 - 60 kWh/month per rated kW of installed capacity. A few more meters/second and the output can be as high as 150 kWh/ month per installed kW. The power goes up as the cube of the average wind speed so professional monitoring of your site is crucial for planning purposes.

Wind can be noisy, so you might want to locate it some distance from social gatherings and sacred places. And be prepared for regular maintenance costs: wind systems break down and need bearings replaced regularly. Finding a good wind generator manufacturer and installer is also a challenge. The industry is in the current situation of not having enough market to produce high quality machines at a reasonable price, so there are not enough of these available. Europe is perhaps the best source. Africa and Asia are starting to produce some good machines. The USA lags behind.

Micro Hydro

Small hydro can be the absolute best renewable energy source for an ecovillage. And you may be surprised how little water it takes to produce significant power. The advantages of hydro are many: For a modest investment you get power 24 hours per day and in many cases 365 days per year. It can be a great source of power even if your flow is seasonal, providing power during rainy months when your solar harvest decreases. If you are looking for land for a new ecovillage, it's worth making a viable hydro resource part of your land search criteria.

One kW of hydro can be produced from roughly 6.3 liters/second (100 gpm) falling 30 meters (100 feet). This would be considered 'high-head' hydro and would use a pelton wheel turbine. Or you can pass 10 times as much water through a 'low-head' turbine with one-tenth the elevation change and produce the same 1kW of power.

The economics of hydro can be fabulous. Let's say you have that 1 kW of hydro potential. One-thousand watts (1 kW) running 24 hours/day for a full month = 720 kWh/month. Not bad for a system that could cost less than U.S. $6,000 installed! A wind system producing an equal amount could cost you 3-4 times that and an equivalent solar system could be 6-8 times that cost.

Geothermal

There are two kinds of geothermal energy. One is the latent heat in the earth or water table that can be harvested with a heat pump. Heat pumps can be 2-4 times more efficient than using a direct electrical heating element but involve more hardware and complexity, with associated maintenance costs. The other kind of 'geothermal' refers to hot springs. If you are lucky enough to have a sufficient source of this energy, you can power your whole ecovillage.

Waste Heat

With the advent of practical, affordable Stirling engines, waste heat now becomes a source of renewable electricity for on- and off-grid living. A free-piston Stirling engine can transform the waste heat of a woodstove, furnace, exhaust stack – or even a fermentation process – into useable electricity. Recently available units burn natural gas or propane and produce all the heat, hot water, and electricity a community may need.

Backup Sources

Even the best renewable energy system design usually requires some backup, even if only for a few weeks a year or few hours a day. The grid can be this 'backup' but the temptation to use it more as a primary source can compromise good, super-efficient design. On the other hand, it makes no sense to invest in a lot of lead-acid batteries to be 'off-grid' and then use the grid as an intermittent backup. Better to install robust 'grid-tie' solar, wind, hydro, and/or Stirling systems and use the grid as your 'battery'.

If you are fully off-grid, when your renewable sources are not meeting your needs or when your batteries are empty, the use of a backup generator becomes essential. You can use a relatively silent natural gas or propane powered Stirling generator or your can use an internal combustion generator running on natural gas, propane, agriculturally produced green gas, hydrogen, or biodiesel.

Whole System Design

Okay, so now it's time to put it all together into an integrated design package. Again, it's best to consult a professional – but the more homework and design practice you do yourself, the easier the process will be for everyone.

Energy Budget

For all buildings and sources you'll need an energy budget. How many kWhs per day, per month, and per year will each building require? This is a critical figure and often one of the most difficult to obtain – but do it! There is no substitute for this accounting; without it you are guessing on design. Use a detailed "load spreadsheet" that lists just about every light bulb and end-use you have, determining the watt-hours per day and hence per month of each. Do this for Winter and for Summer. You won't regret it.

Also characterize your source potentials in detail: solar surveys, hydro surveys, waste-heat and wind surveys. How many kWhs/day or month can you rely on from these sources? Don't skimp on this process either. Quantify it!

Location of Sources and Uses

Map the location of your community's buildings and other power-users as well as all your potential source sites. Critical design decisions in terms of distance and degree of centralization depend on it. Characterize the sources and loads on the map so you know how much power comes from each and goes to where. Which buildings could hold solar panels? Is there a place for a ground- or pole-mount solar system? For hydro or wind, where are optimum turbine sites? And don't forget to mark future expansion possibilities on the map.

Decentralize or Centralize?

Creating your own electrical 'mini-grid' with a central meter may be a better alternative than allowing the local power company to bring power to each building. Depending on your local utility's policies, this may result in more control over the power you generate plus it can make backing-up when the grid goes down much easier.

If you are off-grid, this ecovillage-wide mini-grid may be far superior to an independent system for each building. If your layout plan is in three or four major 'pods', separated by some distance, then maybe three or four sub-systems would be best. The ideal degree of centralization depends on the amount of power each building is using and/or generating

Installation at Rocky Hill Cohousing in Florence, Massachusetts, USA. That's my crew finishing an installation there.

and on the distances between them. It also depends on how many renewable source-sites you have.

In general, I've found that except for very large ecovillages of more than one-hundred people, or where distances between settlements are more than a kilometer, centralizing your renewable energy resources will pay in the long run. That doesn't mean that every little existing off-grid cabin system or every building needs to be on this centralized 'grid'; but generally, you will leverage your sources as well as your backup and renewable energy equipment resources more with a centralized system. This can be achieved even if you are now operating separate stand-alone systems.

Systems Integration

The ultimate in integrating multiple sources of renewable energy – be it solar, wind, hydro and/or Stirling – is to create a 'backbone' of utility-grade power throughout your community. This mini-grid allows you to add loads or renewable sources anywhere rather than having to bring all source inputs to one central location.

If you are on-grid, this mini-grid simply becomes a 'campus' electrical customer to the utility grid with a centralized meter. If the utility requires individual building metering then you can still create this backbone for backup and/or phasing off the grid. If you are building a new ecovillage, it means running conduit between all buildings, and this is well worth it. With this approach, grid-tie renewable energy inputs can be used to turn the central meter backwards by feeding anywhere into the mini-grid with grid-tie solar, wind, hydro or Stirling inverters.

If you are off-grid then this mini-grid becomes a very sweet way to leverage renewable resources. One company, SMA from Germany, offers an integrated grid-tie/off-grid set of inverters that allow you to feed solar,

The Common House at Sirius Community in Shutesbury, Massachusetts, USA employs a passive solar greenhouse, solar hot water, as well as triangular solar electric modules on the octagon roof.

wind, hydro and/or Stirling power from any building or location directly into the mini-grid, thus allowing for a centralized battery pack and generator. In this way, any one renewable input is available to the whole community. For more information on this "ultimate" solution, see the Sunny Island/Sunny Boy system from SMA. Other inverter companies are working on similar mini-grid systems.

Summary

Designing an ecovillage-wide energy or electrical system is no small task. You will need to give it just as much attention and passion as you do your consensus process or child-rearing practices, your food production or green building practices, in order to achieve true sustainability. Energy systems design is a major piece that needs significant community input and process as well as professional consultation and design. It can suffer from the ill-effects of incremental design as much as any aspect of ecovillage living. If facilitated well, it can be an integral part of the very fulfilling endeavor that ecovillages represent and can become a shining example for the new world we are creating. Welcome to Civilization 2!

Notes

1 For more on the Stirling engine, see Gunnar Olesen's article in this Module.

Jeff Clearwater has enjoyed a 32-year career in the renewable energy field as engineer, designer, contractor, consultant, advocate, and teacher. Jeff received a degree in Solar Engineering in 1979 and has owned six renewable energy businesses and served on the Board of seven energy related non-profits. Jeff has provided consulting, design and installation of solar, wind, microhydro, integrated systems, and electric vehicles for businesses, governments and organizations all over the world from North America to Nepal, Sri Lanka, Turkey, Guatemala, Costa Rica, Colombia, Brazil and Mexico. Jeff helped found the Ecovillage Network of the Americas and his real love is working and playing in community and working toward a peaceful, ecologically sustainable, and culturally creative world. Jeff can be reached at **jeffc@ic.org** and his work and play seen at **http://www.visionarycommons.org**

Imagine a Solar Village, a research, training and experimental site where 'tinkerers, inventors and masterminds' of all kinds come together to collaborate in the creation of the low energy-intensive, low capital-investment, high need technologies of the future. This is the Tamera independent peace journalist Leila Dregger paints in this poetic essay. Of course, that's because she was writing for Module 3 of the EDE. Another writing application would have been cause to paint a different picture, for Tamera is a multi-faceted global peace village and prototype healing biotope.

The SolarVillage of Tamera: Technical and Ecological Knowledge for Peace Villages Worldwide

Leila Dregger – Tamera Biotope, Portugal

Introduction

Alentejo, southern Portugal, in August…

Behind a beautiful coastline, brown and grey hills are rolling endlessly. No rivers. No creeks. No forests. In many villages half of the houses have turned into ruins. The extensive cork oak plantations – once the pride of the region – are being replaced by eucalyptus for big paper corporations. Black hills with thousands of tree skeletons covered with ashes are what remains after one of the many forest fires.

Watching humus turning into dust and being blown away by warm winds, one can easily imagine that the Sahara is growing North, that it has extended over Gibraltar and is slowly entering the Iberian Peninsula. This land is crying, and its tears are made of dust.

Desertification is not only a Portuguese tragedy. The Peloponnesus, southern France, southern Italy, Andalusia – regions which used to feed the whole continent – nowadays import 80% of their food. What will we eat and drink when southern Europe has turned into a desert? Local strategies are urgently needed, solutions which can be applied in many places, with the knowledge and experience for local communities to provide themselves with the most basic needs and become independent from the big supply systems.

The peace research center Tamera, located in the hottest part of the Alentejo, has started the SolarVillage project, an experimental village for the autonomous supply of energy, food, and clean water, using easy-to-build technologies which can be constructed in regional workshops. Tamera,

Tamera villagers join hands to encircle the constructed lake: An act of sacralizing a vital energy point in the landscape.

an intentional community with 180 coworkers and students, is a training and research center for the development of peace villages worldwide. Started in 1995 by the German activists and writers Sabine Lichtenfels and Dieter Duhm, it runs peace projects worldwide and a training program for nonviolence and for creating community. The core of Tamera's work and research is the science of 'trust' – reconciliation and cooperation with nature and among human beings, truth, transparency, and love free of fear. This article however focuses on the work in the Ecological Dimension, and technology in particular.

The Permaculture Water Landscape of Tamera: Water is Life

When visitors enter the Tamera site in Summer, they quickly see the effects of cooperation with Nature. Even in August there are green berry bushes, fruit trees and lush gardens. A naturally-shaped lake lies at the entrance – the permaculture water landscape of Tamera, or 'lakescape'. On its terraces and shores, sunflowers, corn, beans and lettuce grow in abundance. A flock of ducks and geese is sleeping on a tiny beach; and on a closer look one can see colorful fish in the lake.

"Water is Life," Bernd Mueller states, a member of the ecology team. "In winter we have an abundance of rain; in summer it is too dry for anything to grow. Due to the wrong ways of cultivation in the last decades, the soil lost its ability to store water. In order to bring back life, we had to keep the water of the winter rain on the site. The water retention basins fill the dry soil through capillary pressure and thus bring back the fertility. The principle is clear, but it took a visionary from the outside to fully see the possibilities."

In March 2007, the community invited the Austrian mountain farmer and permaculture specialist Sepp Holzer to Tamera and asked him, "If this were your land, what would you do with it?" His answer came easily, "I would build a water landscape. In fact, I see it already, right before my inner eyes."

Tamera followed Sepp's vision. 10,000 tons of soil were moved. It took months of heavy work with big machines and many helpers, one and a half winter rains, and a lot of expertise. Knowledge about soil and how to make a lake bed without plastic sheets or concrete, as well as knowledge about wind, water, animals and plants, stones and temperatures was needed to create an aquatic system of self-purification and fertility. Different small climate zones for different biotopes were created – places for nurseries, vegetables, and recreation. Big natural marble stones keep the heat and help create tropical gardens. Sepp states, "If it looks natural, then it is done right." Four to five times a year, he gives seminars about permaculture in Tamera.

Sepp Holzer demonstrating the edible landscape.

Bernd adds, "After two years of its existence, neighbors, school classes, university members and farmers come to see our lakescape. It is not only a good example for organic farming, it is also an acupuncture point for the healing of the landscape."

On 1 August 2009, the Tamera community invited neighbors and friends, and 500 people then 'embraced the lake' – a welcoming ceremony to life and water at the site.

Energy Abundance and Sun Harvest

Maybe the children of the future will be shocked to hear in their history lessons that once upon a time wars were started about energy resources. "But why did they do that?" they will ask. "The sun radiates 50,000 times more energy to the planet than we use. Everybody who needs energy can just harvest it." Those children will probably live in communities that provide their energy needs autonomously. No big industry, no state will be able to monopolize energy resources once we have learned how to produce energy locally – be it by sun, water, wind, tides, or the movements of the tree tops.

Barbara Kovats, coordinator of the SolarVillage team in Tamera, explains, "We are working on decentralized energy systems, using mainly solar technology that can be built independently of big industry."

The SolarVillage Test Field is a village of little houses made from local materials like clay and wood. Fifty coworkers and community members can live together here. Through daily use they can continually improve the

Solar Greenhouse, with Sunpulse Water and Scheffler Mirror, Jurgen Kleinwachter on the nozzle.

energy technologies: solar cookers, heaters, water pumps, and electricity production.

In the middle of the test village there is a shaded square, for which Tamera architect Martin Pietsch developed a large material canopy. The interplay of the canopy and the ecological design of fruit trees and little gardens create various large and small meeting places for the social life in the Test Field. In the middle of the village is a fountain. Four water spouts are pulsating steadily and feed a little artificial creek which runs through the village, into a tiny forest, and back to the lake.

"This fountain shows the work of one of our major technologies," says Paul Gisler, the technical leader of the SolarVillage team. It is the so-called 'Sunpulse Water', a module of the SolarVillage. The robust and round machine stands next to the pond and sounds like a soft beating heart. How does it work? Paul Gisler explains, "The air inside the Sunpulse is alternating between hot and cold, so it expands and contracts. The resulting pressure changes move a working piston that is fixed to a membrane and transmits the power to pump water, generate electricity, absorb oxygen, or other useful applications."

The Sunpulse can be reproduced in any medium-sized European metal workshop. The only energy it needs is direct sunlight, which is abundant in Portugal. "Very quickly we had the vision to get this Sunpulse machine ready for production and economically affordable," Paul continues. "This is one of the things we are working on now."

The Sunpulse and most of the other solar systems were developed by the German inventor Jürgen Kleinwächter, a physicist who has dedicated his work to inventing technologies which make the life of the poorest people in the world easier. "Many women of African villages have to walk 20 or 30 km per day to find firewood," Jürgen says. "For them I developed solar systems which can be built with local means and can be used for the most urgent needs, like producing heat for cooking, energy to pump and clean water, and electricity."

The SolarVillage team in Tamera works closely together with Jürgen to further develop his inventions under real-life conditions. Jürgen adds, "In this way practical solutions will emerge that are suitable for the future while simultaneously improving the quality of life". The core of the SolarVillage is a 25m-long energy greenhouse. Under its roof, lines of transparent lenses are mounted – Fresnel lenses which focus sunlight onto a tube. Through this tube plant oil flows, heated by the sun to more than 200°C. The hot oil is then stored in a tank and can be used for cooking day and night. Called the 'Sunpulse Hot Oil', it can also be used to provide electricity (1.5 kW) from the thermal energy.

In addition, the community kitchen of the SolarVillage uses SK 14 parabolic reflectors, cooking cases, and the Scheffler Reflector. Large, impressive, and shining, the Scheffler Mirror is a 10m² parabola – a sun reflector with a fixed focus, meaning that the sunlight is focused on a fixed point that is the cooker. It is designed in such a way that the burning point remains fixed and does not wander by constantly adjusting the mirror's position to the sun. The German Wolfgang Scheffler invented this adjustment mechanism based on the principles of a mechanical clock, made from parts of bicycles. On a sunny day the fixed focus for a solar oven, for instance, can be run without needing any manual adjustment. Through this fixed focus of the Scheffler Mirror, the construction of solar kitchens is possible, since the mirror supplies continual condensed light energy.

The basic idea which led to the development of the Scheffler Mirror was the desire to make solar cooking as comfortable as possible and available indoors. Depending on the season of the year, the output of a reflector with a surface of 10m² varies from between 2.2 kW during summer and 3.3 kW during winter with a sunbeam input of 700 Watt per m².

Another solar system in Tamera, which is mainly used during the harvest times, is the solar dryer. A roof of plastic is mounted over a grid where tomatoes, apples, herbs and oranges are drying. A fan run by solar energy keeps the air dry and clean and prevents molding. "The solar dryer was built in a very short time out of literally nothing," Barbara Kovats states, "Now it provides us with dry fruit all year long. It allows us to preserve the abundance of the summer. For a village this could be a small business."

For Paul Gisler, these easy-to-build developments are merely the beginning. "I am dreaming of a future lab, a creative playground for developing high tech systems for the future, places where international technologists, tinkerers, inventors, and masterminds of all kinds come together, share their knowledge and develop their visions in a cooperative way – especially pioneers who were never accepted into the universities and corporations. Tamera is helping with its human knowledge and community experience, and together we will come up with the most unexpected results."

The plan is to create a 'TTT' – a Technology, Training and Transfer platform for a decentralized community based on high tech research. Already some very unusual and innovative inventions are being tested. Words like 'hot lake', 'vortex research', 'oxygen-enriched burning' give us just a taste of the future possibilities.

What is Tamera?

The Healing Biotope 1 Tamera in Southern Portugal is an international training and experimental site for the development of peace research villages and healing biotopes worldwide. Under the motto 'Think Locally, Act Globally', approximately 180 people live, work and study in Tamera. Tamera's aim is to develop an example of a model for a nonviolent co-existence of people and between people and nature. The main tasks of Tamera are: the education of young people within the Monte Cerro peace study, the building of a village model called 'Solar Village' which produces its own food and solar energy, and global networking under the name of GRACE.

Notes

SolarVillage, Tamera, Monte do Cerro, 7630 Colos, Portugal
solarvillage@tamera.org
www.tamera.org and www.solarpowervillage.info (video)

Leila Dregger is an independent journalist based in Tamera, following the inspiration of peace journalism. Her dream is to establish a school for peace journalism in Tamera and the Middle East.

*Isn't it interesting that some of the basic principles of permaculture, ecological design, and ecovillage design can be substantiated scientifically? The concept of EMERGY is one such example. EMERGY is a common denominator that can be applied to all forms of available energy. David Holmgren found it worthwhile to include a section on EMERGY in his book **Permaculture: Principles and Pathways beyond Sustainability**. The present article is included in the Ecological Key to give EDE students an expanded understanding of energy when approaching their designs. This is an all-important consideration, for, as both the physicist and the meditator would say, 'Energy is fundamental'.*

EMERGY and Ecovillage

E. Christopher Mare – Village Design Institute, Cascadia, USA

Introduction

In this article, I wish to introduce students to the important concept of 'EMERGY' as formulated by Howard T. Odum at the University of Florida. EMERGY (spelled with an 'm') can be considered as 'energetic memory' or the total amount of energy – both environmental and human – introduced into and utilized by a system over time. If we think of the ecovillage as a whole system, then some of these energy inputs would be sun, wind, rain, money, goods and services from the global economy, knowledge imported from other ecovillages, the genetic inheritance of plants, etc. The question becomes, "How do we possibly compare the value of all these inputs when they use different kinds of measurements?" Odum solved this problem with his EMERGY analysis: EMERGY uses a common denominator, the EMJOULE, which can be translated into a common value, the EMDOLLAR. Says Odum, "By selecting choices that maximize EMERGY production and use, policies and judgments can favor those environmental alternatives that maximize real wealth, the whole economy, and the public benefit" (1996, p.1).[1]

Pictured overleaf is an example of an EMERGY analysis. In this case the system under consideration is a typical salt marsh. Since this is a 'systems diagram', the first thing we do is create a boundary around the system being observed. Then we note the environmental energy inputs originating from outside the system – 'tide', 'sun, wind', and 'rain, river'. These supply energy to the *primary producer* 'marsh processes'. The primary producer stores embodied energy in the *storage tanks* 'channel form' and 'peaty soils'. The primary producer also feeds directly the *consumer* 'small animals' and this consumer in turn feeds a secondary consumer 'fishes'. There is an *interaction gate* where 'fishes' interacts with a further external source 'fishing' to finally

EMERGY analysis
for a typical salt
marsh.

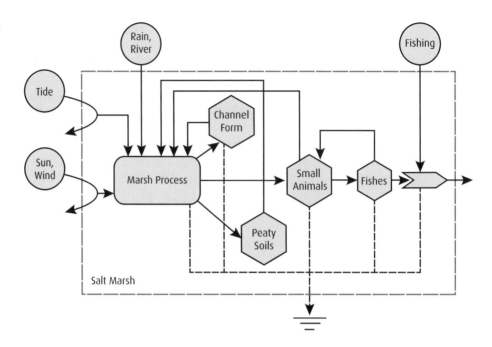

produce an energetic output leaving the window. As per the Second Law
of Thermodynamics, all components in the system, in the process of doing
work, channel degraded energy to a *heat sink*, or ground. This systems
overview illustrates clearly the interrelationship between all the parts and
between the parts and the whole. It would be possible from here to add
specific energetic calculations, in EMJOULES, to each of the components
and processes so as to arrive at a total economic value for this salt marsh in
EMDOLLARS.

Take special note of the arrows in the systems diagram. These
graphically display the *interconnections* being made between components
in the system. These arrows represent pathways or *lines of influence*. Of
particular importance are the arrows that are moving backwards. These
represent *feedback loops*. A feedback loop shows how some of the energy
of a component in the system is returned back to its source. In such a
situation, the energy that is being returned helps to reinforce or augment the
performance of that component. Later we will see how feedback loops can
be *designed* into a system to increase total performance – and this is done all
the time without people actually thinking of it in these terms.

One more feature of the systems diagram needs to be explained before
moving on to playing with these concepts in the design of an ecovillage.
In all systems diagrams, high-quality, renewable environmental sources –
such as sun, wind, rain, geologic heat, etc. – are depicted on the *left* side of
the window, as primary energy inputs. Their gradual, eventual degradation
over time in the course of economic work, both environmental and human,
is accounted for in the symbols and pathways that move to the *right* of
the diagram. In EMERGY terms, this energetic degradation is called

transformity. All energetic processes on Earth ultimately originate with the initial pure solar input; this is fundamental. The solar input is utilized by bio-geophysical processes at successive steps along the economic pathways until it is eventually consumed; but at each step the initial solar input (available energy) does work of some kind for the system as a whole. Transformity, then, is a measure of the stage of solar degradation, and subsequently, almost paradoxically, energetic investment. "Goods and services that have required the most work to make and have the least energy have the highest transformities" (Odum, p.10). To the left of the systems diagram is high potential energy but low transformity and to the right of the diagram, after successive stages of use, is low consumed energy but high transformity. EMERGY is a calculation of the *total energy* used in the process, and does not degrade or diminish, but accumulates.

Do you see how this idea could be useful when determining the value of energy inputs to an ecovillage? Think about this book you are reading. It embodies *extremely* high transformity but relatively low energy. How many decades of accumulated study and experience did it take for all the contributing authors to finally get their words down on paper? How many meals did the authors consume during all those years? How many individual plants were cultivated and harvested to make those meals? What, then, was the *total solar energy input* that went into producing this book – even before it went into the energy consumption phase of designing, printing, and distributing? While a market economy may assign this book the equivalent value of, say, ten meals and fifty harvested plants, the actual value – what Odum terms *real wealth* – is much, much higher. As another example, what is the real wealth – in terms of total solar energy input – of the genetic inheritance of plants that took *millennia* to adapt to a specific niche? Do you see what I'm getting at? A *sustainable* economy, one that is not subsidized by fossil fuels, will need to start paying attention to these energy transformities. A sustainable ecovillage will prioritize the preservation and enhancement of those energy inputs that benefit the ecovillage over the longest term.

Another way of looking at this is in the language of the energetics of the fundamentals of ecology: "Terrestrial energy in any form ultimately originates from the Sun. Plants, as primary producers, collect this energy and utilize it in their metabolism, photosynthesis, creating sugars and expelling degraded energy. Humans and herbivores then absorb plants for their own metabolism, and in turn expel degraded energy into the environment as waste material that can be utilized by bacteria and other decomposers. The bacteria and decomposers then convert this waste material back into a form that can be utilized by plants. The original pure solar input is eventually lost, however, so the plants need a continual supply of incoming solar energy to keep the whole process alive. This is a simplified version of the primary energy cycle of Life on Earth – it all begins with the Sun. The continual, inevitable degradation of incoming solar energy to less usable forms is termed 'entropy' (heat loss to the environment). A viable economy – which ultimately means the process by which Life sustains *Itself* – will be modeled upon this primary energy cycle. Its goal will be to arrest the flow of entropy and enhance the utility of the solar input at each stage. This is the essence of sustainable settlement economics" (Mare, 1997).

Now that the basic principles have been introduced, it is possible to apply them to the design of ecovillages. Here is an example of a systems diagram for an 'idealized' ecovillage, the outcome of a project I undertook in 2002:

Systems diagram for an idealised ecovillage.

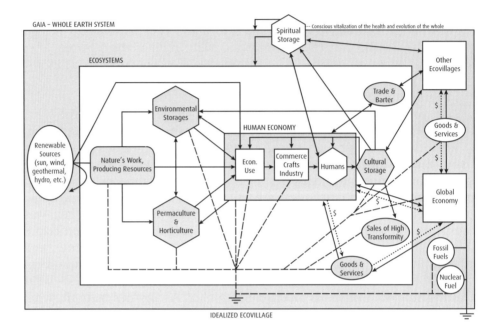

Here, in true systems fashion, I've chosen to place the window of the 'human economy' of the ecovillage within the window of the 'ecosystem' within which the ecovillage is embedded. This is like saying that the human economy is a *subset* of the ecosystem. The ecosystem, in turn, is placed within the total Gaian system, recognizing that ecosystems don't exist in isolation but are part of larger *supra*-systems. Multiple 'renewable sources' are the energetic inputs for 'Nature's work', and this primary producer feeds generic 'storages' and 'consumers' of the ecosystem as well as directly the 'human economy' of the ecovillage. The 'human economy' itself interfaces with two external windows: 'other ecovillages' and 'global economy'. Note that all these relationships, as they are depicted, are *reciprocal* energy exchanges, and in the case of the two external economies are characterized by very different qualities of interaction. I've also chosen to add two additional storage tanks: 'spiritual storage' and 'cultural storage', influences not considered by Odum. 'Cultural storage' is in a position of high transformity, and has feedback loops to all the components of the human economy as well as to the storages of the ecosystem, symbolizing a cultural appreciation for maintaining high stocks of environmental services. While this systems diagram is theoretical, it has the value of displaying in symbolic form a very complex situation. One merely has to meditate upon the various levels of relationship to get a grasp for the essential interconnections in a sustainable ecovillage as a whole. A systems diagram for a 'mega-city' would look much different!

Now it might be a good idea to begin wrapping up by encapsulating all these EMERGY concepts into a useful set of design criteria. These criteria will be based upon the proposition that optimal use of available energy is the *essential* characteristic of a sustainable settlement. The goal here is not to wantonly reduce energy throughput, as if that was some kind of moral imperative, but rather to broaden the concept of energy to its EMERGY counterpart, thus optimizing the use factor of *all* available energy. This will take a lot more thinking than the crude strategy of simply maximizing throughput of crude oil!

Here are the proposed criteria:

1. Diversify and maximize EMERGY *sources*. Since these originate from locally occurring environmental sources, this means a thorough evaluation and inventory of intrinsic environmental energetic inputs, depending in character on the qualities of the particular ecosystem to which the ecovillage is coupled, and including in various proportions: sun, wind, rain, tides, geothermal, hydro, gravity, ecological succession, evaporation, chemical processes, uncaptured flows and surges, temperature differentials, etc. In whatever capacity these sources are available, each needs to be exploited and maximized to its fullest extent. These are 'free' and renewable sources and so amount to a virtually inexhaustible supply of potential energy, limited only by the imagination. Spiritual sources need further contemplation here as energetic inputs. Is conflict a source of energy? Then don't shy away from it, harvest it! What about sexual energy? I believe the matriarchal cultures portrayed by Riane Eisler (1988) cultivated this. Love? Prana? Kunalini?

2. Diversify and maximize EMERGY *storages*. Applying the concept of transformities, these storages can take on a multitude of forms. For a partial listing: Net Primary Production;[2] biomass fuels such as methane and alcohol; species and thus genetic diversity; productive soils; water storages of all kinds including wetlands, dams, and ponds; tools and tool-making technologies; stored and reusable heat; electric potential stored in batteries; credit unions; useful knowledge and memory in all their forms, including writing, stories, and mythologies; vernacular cultural traditions specific to a place; artwork, including music; seed banks; goodwill and good deeds; etc. In sum, *diversify and maximize the storages of natural, social, economic,* and *spiritual capital.* These storages need to be conserved and multiplied wherever possible entirely within the confines of the ecovillage; they are the real wealth of the community.

3. Given a flow of maximized, diversified EMERGY sources and given a supply of maximized, diversified EMERGY storages, abundant creativity can then be applied to *productively channel and direct the storages into positive reinforcing feedback loops to qualitatively amplify and enhance the productivity of the initial sources*. This takes settlement design to a whole new level; the applications are virtually inexhaustible. A simple example is the use of compost, where crop residues are fed back into the soil from whence they came to enhance agricultural productivity. Another example is when profits from a business are fed back into its infrastructure to make the business more profitable. A familiar example from Permaculture demonstrates how *multiple* storages can be employed as positive reinforcing feedback loops: Take a dwelling in a temperate climate that is to be heated by passive solar. The amount of solar insolation falling on the dwelling is fairly constant; yet through good feedback design this steady rate can be amplified. First, situate the dwelling with the long axis running east-west so there is more surface area facing the Sun. Then place a glasshouse on the sun-side to serve as a storage of warm air. Further, place dark-colored barrels full of water in the glasshouse to serve as more heat storage. Place a pond storage in front of the glasshouse to increase solar gain with its reflection. Inside the dwelling, use dark-colored building materials with dense mass as walls in locations where the Sun can shine directly on them. Then, plant a semi-circle or U-shape of tall evergreen trees around the dwelling, open end facing the Sun, to create a favorable microclimate for further trapping and storing heat and deflecting cold polar winds. Each of these design applications uses storages as positive feedback to amplify and multiply the source – the heating effect of the initial solar input. Combined, they can produce a comfortable dwelling in cold weather without the need for heating fuels.

4. Within and among the feedback designs, actively promote complex network configurations for the purpose of creating interconnecting, mutually-beneficial interrelationships. These relationships can support one another in their amplification functions and can serve as a) a string of multipliers when arranged in series, or b) as a multi-pronged power block when constructed in parallel. This principle can be paraphrased by the permaculture aphorism, "Each function is supported by many elements, and each element has many functions". An example of this principle applied to an ecovillage setting would be the cultivation of a wide diversity of companion-planted food crops, many perennial, instead of relying on simple monoculture. Another example would be the rotation of tasks and responsibilities within the ecovillage so that many people can become familiar with them, instead of having individuals always laboring at the same task.

This principle can further include (perhaps can even be restated as) the deliberate establishment of multi-purpose, mutually-beneficial, interconnecting communication networks, of all kinds. What happens when we begin maximizing the cross-dimensional interconnections, in parallel and/or series, between available stocks of natural, social, economic, and spiritual capital? This is EMERGY in action; once again, the possibilities are limited only by the imagination.

Prevailing systems are those whose designs maximize EMPOWER by reinforcing resource intake at the *optimum* efficiency [emphasis added]…This statement includes the maximizing of the resource intake *and* the operation at the optimum efficiency for maximum power…In other words, both *intake* and its best *use* are maximized.

ODUM, p.26

Whereas *power* is generally defined as "energy flow per unit time," EMPOWER makes the subtle distinction between *maximizing* sources and *optimizing* usage. "In the competition between sustainable and unsustainable settlements, those that maximize EMPOWER will prevail" (Mare, 2002, p.43). This principle can be applied, for example, to the management of a woodlot adjacent to an ecovillage. Eco-commonsense would say, "Let it grow to its climax stage". An understanding of ecological energetics, however, would insist on keeping the woodlot at 50% NPP – this is the level where EMPOWER is maximized, where the curve begins to move from concave to convex. Can we apply these principles to our daily affairs?

References

1 Don't worry if this all sounds way too technical at the moment. My purpose here is to introduce some basic concepts so that later we can apply them to the design of ecovillages.
2 NPP is the amount of carbon sequestered in an ecosystem from atmospheric carbon dioxide.

Eisler, R. (1988) *The Chalice and the Blade: Our History, Our Future.* HarperSanFrancisco
Mare, E.C. (1997) *A Pattern Language for Ecovillages.* Village Design Institute; Bellingham, WA
Mare, E.C. (2002) *Sustainable Settlement Energetics: EMERGY and Ecovillage.* Village Design Institute; Bellingham, WA
Odum, H.T. (1971) *Environment, Power, and Society,* John Wiley & Sons, Inc.; New York
Odum, H.T. (1996) *Environmental Accounting: EMERGY and Environmental Decision Making.* John Wiley & Sons, Inc.; New York

E. Christopher Mare has been a full-time student since 1994. He has been given the luxury of self-designed programs in which he gets to organize his own studies. The general progression of interest over the years has been: Permaculture to Ecovillage to Urban Village to Traditional Village to Design for Consciousness. In 2002, Mare founded an educational non-profit – Village Design Institute – which will one day secure a land-base for the purpose of setting up a combination 1) research, training, and demonstration site; 2) Academy of Village Design; and 3) community of contemplative scholars. This project most likely will be called an 'ecovillage'.

MODULE 4
Restoring Nature

Contents

Omsunisa Jamwiset, from Wongsanit Ashram in Thailand, provides an ethnographic account of life in Soblan village of the Karen hilltribe on the Thai-Burmese border. The Karen have developed lifeways deeply integrated with the forest ecology of their home. Omsunisa describes how the villagers of Soblan have developed daily life patterns full of ritual designed to maintain respectful relations with Nature. As a real bonus to ecovillage designers, a description is given of how the forest is divided into functional zones and how the social life of the village itself is focused on the fire-pit of the most respected elder. This article is a real lesson in deep sustainability.

Designing with Deep Respect: Deep Ecology in a Karen Village

Omsunisa Jamwiset – Wongsanit Ashram, Thailand

Background

Soblan is a village of the Karen [Ka – *ren*] hilltribe in the hills amidst the forest in Samoeng District, Chaingmai province, northern Thailand.

> Karens are the biggest hilltribe in Thailand. They traditionally live in the forest along the Thai – Burmese border. There are four subtribes of Karen. They speak slightly different languages but their lives are based on the same basic beliefs and worldview.

Soblan is a village of *Skaw,* a subtribe of Karen, with about 30 families living together. Their main occupations are shifting cultivation, hunting and gathering. They are now twelve generations, since the first families came to live on this mountain nearly 300 years ago. Like all traditional Karen, the people of Soblan live intimately with Nature, with a deep respect that comes from their animist worldview.

The Karen believe in spirits of Nature. Every single element in Nature has a spirit that is responsible to that element. Spirit of the Water is responsible for the water, Spirit of the Forest responsible for the forest, Spirit of the Fire, Spirit of the Land, Spirit of the Mountain, Spirit of the Road, and so on. The ancestor spirits are responsible to the family. As for the people, they believe everyone has souls that live in the body parts, to ensure the healthy life of the person. The souls of each person can be influenced by the spirits of Nature. Spirits of Nature will give penalties to people if they disrespect Nature. The penalty can be sickness, an accident, a small harvest, an environmental disaster or unhealthy life. It is important, for a healthy life, to have a respectful and mindful relationship with Nature. Taking more than what is needed and unmindful or wasteful consumption are considered disrespectful activities among the Karen. Based on their worldview that Nature has a spirit or a soul of its own, they could never 'own' Nature. They communicate with the spirits of Nature for their very survival.

Ritual is a way of communicating with the spirits of Nature. During any given year they will have many rituals in the village – communal rituals, family rituals and personal rituals. The message to communicate is to ask for blessings, to give thanks for the blessings, or to apologize for unmindful or disrespectful behaviors.

Integrated Design

Soblan is organized with the village and community living amid the forest, surrounded by agriculture lands.

Forest Zoning

The forest is divided into three zones, which are:

1. **Reserve Forest**: source of the headspring, abundant with diversity of species. In this area it is forbidden to hunt, cut wood, farm or garden, though gathering is allowed.

2. **Sacred Forest:** this forest is zoned for sacred ritual or spiritual energy. It is divided into semi-zones which are the *Tha – De – Do* forest, the area between two hills which is Spirit's path; the *De – Mhue – Berh* forest, the headspring forest by the river that looks like an island where the Spirit of the Water lives; the *Burial* forest for burial of dead bodies, including the *Ta – Vi – Do* forest for burying dead babies under the banyan tree so the baby may have milk from the tree; the *De – Pho* forest or *umbilical cord* forest to connect the babies' souls with the trees by hanging their umbilical cords on the trees. The tree will then support the baby for a healthy life until he/she dies. If the tree is harmed, it will affect the baby. Gathering is allowed in the Sacred Forest, especially of medicines.

3. **People Forest**: the forest closest to the village and agricultural fields. Here it is acceptable to hunt and cut wood as needed.

Agriculture Zoning

From an economic perspective, the Karen sense of ownership is very limited. They traditionally don't own the land – for how can you own a piece of Nature? Their main occupation is shifting cultivation on the highland fields (hillsides). They plant the seeds of upland rice together with many other kinds of vegetables, grains, taro, and potatoes. While the rice is growing

Karen villager cultivating a hillside. To most Western observers, this hillside would look 'wild' and 'overgrown.'

they can already pick some vegetables in the field, and after rice harvesting some vegetables still remain for one to two years for both human and animal consumption.

Every year each family looks for a 'land-field' for their shifting cultivation, which has to be a piece of land that was used six to seven years ago so that fertility may have been restored. They cannot just choose any spot of land they like, but have to ask the Spirit of the Land first, to get permission. According to this ritual, one family may not receive the signs to use the land while another family may be allowed. The land use is rotated in this way.

Some families also have low-land plots for rice cultivation, which entail differences in the cultivating process compared to upland varieties. The main reason that families need low land to grow rice is because the harvest from the shifting cultivation on the hills may not be enough when the family gets bigger (meaning that someone in the family got married and continues to live with their parents). If they have to expand the field of their shifting cultivation it will be too much work. The shifting cultivation process is much more difficult and complicated than low-land rice cultivation.

In a culture of shifting cultivation, people must support each other. The members of a single family are not enough to completely work the land; they need help from their neighbors. From the very beginning of the process, clearing the land, they need labor support. Also during the process of burning the brush after clearing, each family needs support from the whole village to make a fire break and secure it. They also need some help with the planting, harvesting, and transporting of the harvest. They take turns supporting each other at each step of the process. Collaboratively working together in the hills has become the basis of their culture. When they are in the fields working together, they have traditions to enjoy each other and celebrate life. They play music, dance, sing, and share poems. There is courtship among the young people. Because their traditions and culture emerge from their shifting cultivation relationship with the land, they say 'the Karen soul is in the field'.

The people will build a small hut in the field at the entrance to their land, where they can control the energy flow in and out. The hut is also designed to store the harvest while waiting for transportation to the barn in the village. Since their plantations are small, and for subsistence only, not for retail, the people don't need advanced technology, only a few hoes and baskets. They also don't need to build big storage sheds to keep their tools and harvest. Some families build a hut on stilts to use the open space underneath for their animals.

During every step of their cultivation, the people make rituals to communicate with the spirits of Nature, especially the Spirit of Rice. These rituals take place on the land and in the hut until the end of the harvest. The rituals remind the people to remain aware, and to take care at every single step of the production process.

Village Zoning

The village lies at the very heart of the agriculture and forest zones. The center is an open space surrounded by houses on the hillsides. An open space with a fire set in front of each cluster of houses is the meeting point for each neighbor group. The open space and fire set in front of the elder's house is the meeting point for the community as a whole.

In Soblan, Uncle Daeng is the elder who is most highly respected. He is not a political leader, but a story teller. People of all ages in the village like to come and spend time around his house. Every morning in winter, Uncle Daeng lights a fire in front of his house. His neighbors join him around the fire shortly after sunrise to warm themselves before heading for the fields. Almost the entire village will come to the fire at night for story-telling and poems about the Karens, Spirits, and Nature. When a leader wants to call villagers for a meeting, Uncle Daeng lights the fire and blows the horn to call the people. They all sit around the fire for the meeting.

Uncle Daeng's house is situated at the entrance of the village. As people are leaving, they like to stop at this meeting point and converse with friends. They also like to stop here when they come back, to share news from outside before returning to their homes. (It's not easy to travel between the village and the main town, which is 18 kilometers distant over many hills, so there is always lots of news to share when somebody does make the trip.) Outsiders who visit the village will meet first with the elders gathering around Uncle Daeng's house before they are permitted to walk freely around the village.

As far as house design, Karen traditional style is a modest, one-room structure. They build the roof low to harmonize with the mountain winds. In the single room, they have a hearth for cooking and warming. The

Construction of building materials using local resources: the body as a tool.

Through the practice of a natural form of Deep Ecology, the Karen hilltribes retain vast stores of knowledge concerning quality of life.

hearth is where the ancestor spirit lives. Above the hearth is a set of shelves for storing grains and seeds. The smoke from the fire keeps the insects away. In this way, they can keep the grains till next year's planting season. They don't put the fire at the very center of the room but nearer to a wall because they like to sleep close to the wall since it's warmer that way. They leave the bigger space open for cooking, some kitchen utensils, and to welcome guests. Above the sleeping place is where they worship the Spirit of the House, the ancestors, and the Spirits of Nature in the new-year, mid-year and harvest-time celebrations. For these celebrations, people come to witness and support each family's ceremony in their house. The whole village comes together in this way; everyone's house is open. With less individual ownership, the design is for more sharing. More sharing brings greater intimacy. If you come to visit, you will get to share with them in their single-room houses also.

Among ecovillage people, we often hear talk about respecting Nature. Respect seems to be a prelude for change. In this regard, it is interesting to contemplate further – what exactly do we mean by RESPECT? Soblan is an eminent example that teaches us a kind of respect that is mindful about the relationships and interconnections between human beings and Nature. With this respect, the people of Soblan over the ages have designed a form of gracious simple living that brings intimacy and sacredness into their lives.

However, though the people of Soblan live far away in the forest, it's still not far enough to be unaffected by globalization and so-called 'development' by the government in the name of modernization. The Karen people in general have resisted this development since they regard it to be threatening to their way of life. For example, when the government registered their forest as a National Park, it resulted in limitations on the movement of the hilltribes, who in their shifting cultivation rely on freedom of movement attuned with the cycles of Nature. The elders of the villages are well aware that if their way of life is moved off of the land, they will lose everything – culture, wisdom, dignity, grace – because 'the soul of the Karen is in the field'.

As a result of issues such as this, over the last 20 years the people of Soblan have been fighting for their right to maintain their culture and lifestyle centered upon a deep respect for Nature. As a compromise, they have redesigned certain aspects of their village to conform to the pressures to modernize. They have built stronger houses made of modern materials and a community school. In this school, along with the government's curriculum, they try to educate their children about the Karen lifeways and raise awareness about the effects of consumerism from the outside world. With the help of NGOs, the school is becoming a center for opening the village as a Life University for Sustainability for outside learners.

Traditional villages such as Soblan are valuable reservoirs of genuine sustainable culture. They have a lot to teach us about sustainable community design – which here means designing with a deep respect for Nature.

Omsunisa Jamwiset was born into a farmer's family in a genuine small village, Nongkhai province, by the Mae Khong River, northeastern Thailand. She graduated with a Bachelor's degree in Social Development Management, Faculty of Humanity and Social Science, Khonkhaen University. After graduation, she worked as assistant researcher for rural community research, a project of collaboration between Khonkhaen University and Japanese universities. She decided to quit the job after one year to start her spiritual journey – that brought her to Wongsanit Ashram, an intentional community of activists with spiritually-based practices. She is representative of NextGen Thailand and part of the Thai teaching team for EDE courses hold at Wongsanit Ashram each year, where she is introducing Participatory Action Research (PAR) into the curriculum.

Auroville is an astounding story; and Marti Mueller tells the tale with all the familiarity of a close friend. Started as a 'cluster of ecovillages', it has grown into a 'model green township' with over 3,000 permanent residents. Seeing the lush green forests that surround the township today, it's hard to believe that just 40 years ago the settlement began on a parched, red-earth desert plain. Auroville is a shining success story in restoring nature, so much so that her Forest Group is enlisted to consult on restoration projects around the world. If there were a motto to Marti's tale, it would be: "It can be done."

Environmental Restoration in Auroville

Marti Mueller – Auroville, India

Introduction

Auroville is a multi-cultural community in South India founded on the principles of human unity. It is regarded as a 'living laboratory of evolution' and has long been a contributor to globally replicable environmental aims. Auroville's work in environmental restoration is a precedent-setting example of how a small community can transform severely degraded land into beautiful forests full of a wide range of birds and wildlife species. The community has done pilot work in species diversity and has proven that the land can be restored, even if at considerable effort. The ancient plateau near Pondicherry was once a dry red eroded desert; today it is lush green forest – and that's just the beginning.

The first community settlers arrived on the arid coastal plateau some 40 years ago. There were a few isolated villages, a dozen lone palmera trees, and a vast wasteland that stretched for miles in all directions. The original dry tropical scrub forests had all been destroyed during the colonial era. Today, Auroville boasts more than three million trees, an impressive reforestation program, a botanical garden – the first of its kind in south India – a heritage seed saving program, several environmental research centers, pilot medicinal training projects, a green outreach program, water harvesting, organic farms, and an environmental education unit that produces books on the environment for children and adults throughout the world.

Reforestation

The early Aurovillian settlers experimented with local and exotic tree species and contour 'bunding' to loosen up the hard soil and get the necessary ground cover for indigenous species to reappear through spontaneous regeneration. Interestingly, the only areas where they had any clues about what was indigenous were near temple groves, where the people had never dared to cut the vegetation. Gradually the forests came back with a rigorous program of watering trees by hand during the hot season and mulching and bunding to prevent water runoff during the heavy monsoons. Keeping the goats and cattle away from the young seedlings was another challenge and required hiring watchmen to keep an eye on the young trees until they were four to five years old. Funding came from the Indian Government's Department of the Environment as the project proved interesting for its replicability factors. Indeed, Auroville Forest Group members became planting consultants on projects in other parts of India, the Tibetan settlements, and in Cambodia.

Land Regeneration

The Pitchandiculum Resource Center did early work in identifying the medicinal value of indigenous species and held conferences in which local tribal plant experts came to share their knowledge. The Center also did pioneer work in kitchen gardens to help locals to be more self-sufficient in vegetables by using household and kitchen waste to provide compost for vegetables in small garden plots adjacent to village homes. At present, the Center has a village educational unit and is working to regenerate a watery wasteland swamp in the center of Chennai. Here they are creating a teaching park for city inhabitants in collaboration with the Tamil Nadu State Government and the City of Chennai.

Revelation bridge canyon.

Heritage Seed-saving

The Anadana Seed Saving project, which is a component part of the Auroville Biological Garden, is modeled on the work that the French organization, Kokopelli, has done to conserve heritage seeds. Anadana is creating a significant seed base for India, as well as for South East Asia.

Species are carefully planted under nets to assure that heritage plant varieties are not adulterated by genetically-modified plants.

The Botanical Garden

Auroville has initiated a botanical garden and, with help from the European Community, is experimenting with many varieties of trees and plants indigenous to our area. It has a teaching component and serves as a nursery to help regenerate areas of Tamil Nadu with beautiful plants, including planting around villages and doing hotel landscaping as an income earner.

Farms

Auroville has more than a dozen farms. Most are organic; one even practices some of the farming techniques taught by the Japanese natural farming pioneer, Masanobu Fukuoka, who came to visit Auroville some years ago. Most of the farms are part of a well-organized agricultural cooperative called 'Food Link' that was set up to assure distribution of organic products to the Auroville community. Food Link has its own quality label: 'Made in Auroville' that assures consumers that the food has been grown in a healthy and tasty way.

Environmental Education

The award-winning Children and Trees project was set up to provide books and teaching materials to ordinary people on the importance of trees, land contouring, the dangers of pesticides, and the role that women can play in protecting the environment. Teaching materials also deal with the problem of human overpopulation and the importance of limiting human numbers to allow greater diversity for other species as well. The Children and Trees project received a Rolex citation and has been replicated in other parts of India, Kenya, Chile, China, and Malaysia. One of the books – *What is a Tree* – has been reproduced in forty different languages and is used all over India, as well as abroad.

Water Harvest

Auroville's Water Harvest unit has done a study of the bioregion and works to establish water features in the landscape through large-scale land contouring. Goals are to assure that monsoon runoff is reduced and that lakes remain around villages to provide more water in the hot season. The Harvest team helps local villages to de-silt traditional water tanks and to restore ancient irrigation systems.

Sadana Forest

A more recent project, Sadana Forest, was set up to re-vegetate a barren water catchment area in a region adjacent to Auroville. Sadana has experimented with drip irrigation systems that actually allow water to run uphill, on a gradual slope. They are also working on new bunding techniques and appropriate energy technologies, including a cycling machine which allows three cyclists hooked into a stationary bar, with their pedals turning a magneto in a generator, to create enough energy for lighting. The Sadana Forest team plans to go soon to Senegal to reforest one of the most degraded sub-Saharan deserts to prove that it can be done.

Appropriate Energy

Awarded the coveted Green Prize by England's Prince Charles for electrifying small villages with clean energy, AuroRE produces micro-water generators for small inaccessible villages and works at creating solar products. Auroville products include large and small solar panel installations, solar lamps, bicycles, electric scooters, and solar hot water heaters. Through its Centre for Scientific Research (CSR), Auroville has done work in windmill production and has installed windmills in different parts of India, Bhutan, and the Tibetan settlements.

Samriddhi hut.

Auroville Earth Architecture

This unit holds the UNESCO South East Asian Chair in Natural Building. The Mine Houses, a system for using earth blocks to create emergency housing within a matter of nine to 25 hours, were demonstrated at the United Nations Habitat II Conference in Istanbul. They were used for housing-relief programs after the devastating earthquake in Gudjurat. The technology also has been extended to building temples in India and mosques in Saudi Arabia.

Success Sanctuary

Auroville has delineated certain specific areas as sanctuaries for birds and wildlife. Expanding on the concept that green wildlife corridors can interlace city settlements, the community has set up the Success Sanctuary to demonstrate that indigenous subtropical forest species can be integrated into selected folds of the community fabric of Auroville. This is particularly important because the region of Pondicherry is growing rapidly and human incursions into forested areas are becoming more frequent. Sanctuary outreach work has gone so far as aiding the set-up of wildlife sanctuary areas in Terra del Fuego on the Chilean-Argentinean border in South America.

A Green Township Model

If Auroville started as a small cluster of ecovillages, today it is a burgeoning eco-township, with a stable population of about 3,000 people and nearly 2,000 guests a day. Students from many universities throughout the world come to study sustainability, while visitors abound to learn about *community* in one of the oldest cultures in the world. Today, our primary preoccupation is building a 'model green township', with systems of cluster-houses, parks, green corridors and agricultural areas that can distinguish Auroville as a model community in a new kind of world, where preserving and enhancing the environment become the most critical of concerns. We've come a long way from those early days of planting trees and simply praying that they would survive.

TREE

I am a tree

I stand tall and majestic. I silently listen to life moving all around me.
Born of a small seed, I push into the earth, take root and begin my long silent journey into cool moist layers of earth and stones. My roots form a dense web that steadies the soil and sucks water from pools deep in the Earth.

I am home to many creatures. Squirrels live in holes in my trunk.

Cats stalk prey from my sturdy branches. Spiders hang between my leaves. Birds nest in my leafy crown. Monkeys swing from shoots that bend like reeds. Winged travelers rest on me.

My roots are planted firmly in the earth. My trunk and branches stretch towards the sun's warm rays. I feel the might force of the sky's great winds. I call out to clouds and catch moisture from rain and snow. My leaves dance. Tiny golden sunbeams make them translucent green.

I give refuge: shade from the hot sun and shelter from the rain.
I am wood for the fire and company beside the rushing stream.
I am gentle witness to life's many changes. I stand silent and listen to the Earth's deep inner pulse.

I am a tree.

from Marti's book of prayers, This Earth of Ours

Marti has lived in Auroville for more than 20 years. She is a photographer and writer who has been instrumental in creating sanctuaries throughout the world. She is Chair of the International Advisory Council (IAC) of the Global Ecovillage Network (GEN) and is a United Nations ECOSOC representative to Geneva.

Sajini Pathiraja, from Sarvodaya, the largest NGO in Sri Lanka, describes the efforts undertaken to establish a model ecovillage for survivors of the 2004 tsunami. Using a strategy of 'moral education for environmental protection', future residents of the ecovillage underwent extensive preparation in a participatory process to lay down the social infrastructure that would become the foundation for the physical infrastructure. The project has proven to be a tremendous success in that the environmentally friendly, economically self-reliant, socially and spiritually inclusive lifestyle of the residents has become a model that is spreading throughout the region and attracting national and international visitors as well.

Damniyamgama EcoVillage: Sustainable Development for Tsunami Restoration

Sajini Pathiraja – Sarvodaya, Sri Lanka

Introduction

The Lanka Jathika Sarvodaya Shramadana Sangamaya movement – or the *Sarvodaya* for short – is the largest non-governmental organisation (NGO) in Sri Lanka, with a unique philosophy and strategy for development. Dr. A. T. Ariyaratne founded the movement in 1958, when he was a school teacher in Colombo. From early beginnings in a rural village it has grown to encompass more than 15,000 villages throughout the island (Sarvodaya, http://www.sarvodaya.org/about).

The Sarvodaya movement seeks a no-poverty/no-affluence society based on the sharing of resources. The Sarvodaya movement is a people's development organisation that embodies an integrated strategy which includes the development of social, cultural, moral, spiritual, economic *and* political dimensions. It works *with* people, encouraging them to come together and share their resources to address the needs of the community, emphasizing self-reliance not just for individuals but more importantly for the communities of which they are a part.

> Sarvodaya is a movement which promotes human development.
> The uniqueness of the Sarvodaya lies in the fact that it promotes inter-connection between people and communities, which we call spirituality, which is the glue that keeps this holistic approach together.
>
> Executive Director, Sarvodaya Shramadana Movement

Beginning a series of meetings that would become the social infrastructure underlying the physical structure of the new ecovillage.

Sarvodaya villages operate within the framework of a model of 'moral education for environmental protection'. This is based on traditional Asian cultural values and differs from material-oriented, isolating development models. The Sarvodaya model emphasizes balanced sustainable agriculture based on eco-friendly farming practices; further, it promotes practices conducive to sustainable natural resource management.

Development Objectives of Damniyamgama Ecovillage

Sarvodaya implemented the Damniyamgama Ecovillage Development Project under its overall Tsunami Reconstruction Programme. The overall development objective of the recently constructed ecovillage was to test an innovative model that is environmentally friendly, operationalises participatory planning at village-scale, and empowers communities to effectively make their own decisions – thus leading to environmentally self-sustainable development and education.

Through training, education, information sharing, courses, and community interaction the Sarvodaya organisation worked diligently on development of a *social* infrastructure that was to become the underlying foundation for the *physical* infrastructure.

To achieve the above objective, several programmes were conducted by the Sarvodaya before resettling the community. Environmental awareness programmes were undertaken by the bio-diversity unit and included topics such as the concept of an ecovillage, environmental degradation and organic farming. The social empowerment division undertook programmes to develop peoples' positive attitudes toward their social relationships. Trainings were undertaken on topics such as 'conflict resolution' and 'leadership'. The objective of the social empowerment and capacity building was to develop the necessary institutional and human resource competencies of the village Shramadana society so as to empower them to plan, implement and manage village development activities in an efficient, equitable and sustainable manner. Spiritual development programmes were also undertaken. The early childhood development unit undertook education programmes particularly relating to young children. The community health unit undertook programmes regarding the development of community health. The women's movement conducted training programmes for starting self-employment; for example, training in handicraft production and food-processing. The legal division took a major role in providing birth certificates and identity-cards for people who lost these important documents in the tsunami. Such programmes created a dynamically positive impact by actively involving the community in the early stages. This active involvement leads to senses of ownership and empowerment – essential qualities for eventual self-management of the Village.

Infrastructure and Development

The Damniyamgama Ecovillage presently hosts 220 people in 55 families. All are tsunami survivors in the Kalutara district of south-western Sri Lanka. The village is designed as a model of 'participatory development towards environmental sustainability'. Placed on a five-acre plot provided by the Sri Lankan government, the village features fifty-five eco-friendly houses, a playground with volleyball court, a central meeting area, a comprehensive road network, expansive green areas, and a multi-purpose community centre. The houses and the community centre are equipped with solar panels for electricity. They receive an ample supply of water through five drinking wells and fourteen rainwater harvesting tanks, with overflow into drainage canals. The village also incorporates a sub-terra system, a natural method for waste-water treatment, and a recycling facility for solid waste materials. Each household consists of two bedrooms, a living room, a kitchen, and sanitation facilities that altogether encompass a space of 500 square feet. Housing design considered drainage and slope of land, access to sunlight and ventilation. Around 20% of the property is 'common property' to be shared and managed by the community as a whole.

Permaculture Practices in Damniyamgama

Permaculture is the thoughtful design of integrated systems of plants, animals, energy flows, natural resources, infrastructure, information, etc. to provide food, energy, shelter, and other material and non-material needs in a sustainable manner.

> Permaculture is a system design of integrating good housing, landscaping, organic farming, minimisation of waste and maximisation of recycling and

conservation of natural resources. Within the Damniyamgama we have integrated those things in the best possible ways.

Sarvodaya Director

The village has five drinking-water wells to fulfil the drinking water requirements of the community. All drinking-water wells have a water purification system to ensure safety. Drinking-water wells are more effective for water conservation than tap-water systems because they minimise water wastage. The waste-water purification system was explained as follows:

A sub-terra system was introduced for waste-water treatment. Black water coming from the toilets flows through the pipe lines to the sub-terra and it then gets filtered through different diameters of sand layers and charcoal layers built underground. After purification, the water is pumped to the surface and used for watering the plants in common areas.

Sarvodaya Engineer

In Damniyamgama, each household engages in compost-making from degradable solid waste. For collection of non-degradable solid waste, separate bins are provided in two corners of the Village. These bins are marked as 'paper', 'plastics', 'glass', and 'metal'. There is a committee in the village which is responsible for proper waste management within the community. The Waste Recycling Agency comes and collects the recyclable waste when the bins are filled. In the initial stages of awareness, it was difficult to implement the compost making and separation of garbage practices. Residents needed to become much more aware of the harmful impact of careless waste management. Many of the residents admitted to throwing their waste on the beach or in the river or road while living in coastal villages. Before the establishment of the ecovillage, none of the residents had attempted compost making, organic gardening or realised the benefits of sorting garbage. They learned the significance of these practices from Sarvodaya officials who worked in the transit camps after the tsunami.

In the initial stages of development, all the households requested to have electricity from the national grid because according to their perception there is less trouble with the national system. Now, when comparing electricity bills, they are much happier using solar panels. Lower cost motivates people to use renewable energy sources. Fluorescent lamps are used for lighting because they consume less electricity. These are the most energy-efficient form of lighting for the households. Although more expensive to buy, they are much cheaper to run and can last up to ten thousand hours. Such lights also produce less heat, helping keep homes cooler in the tropical climate of Sri Lanka.

Each household has its own integrated home garden consisting of tree species, vegetables, and herbs. In the initial stages, Sarvodaya had to assist residents in establishing their gardens, since the people did not have any

Typical house in the new ecovillage, with garden plot out front.

interest in or experience with gardening. After tasting food from their own plots, however, the residents soon developed a real passion for growing and consuming the harvest of their own hands.

Management by Sub-committee

Various sub-committees were established for the operation, maintenance and management of different aspects of the Village. Such organisation has been very important for capacity building and local self-empowerment.

An Environmental Committee is responsible for the landscaping, water and soil conservation, and waste management. The aim of this Committee is to establish and maintain standards to protect and enhance the environmental quality, visual beauty, and property investment-value of the ecovillage. Other responsibilities include: promoting maximum energy independence and processing requests for specific architectural and/or environmental design changes throughout the village.

A Multi-purpose Centre Committee oversees the uses of the Centre, manages it, and makes sure that the building is always orderly, clean and inviting.

The objectives of the Economic Development Committee are to facilitate the improvement of livelihood of the community members and to develop sustainable, micro-finance institutions at the community level, thus enabling villagers to meet their needs for savings and credit services and to assist them in taking up a wide range of income generating activities. The Committee links with the Sarvodaya Economic Empowerment Division (SEED) at headquarters and district level to implement training programmes and micro-finance schemes according to community interests and needs.

Overall responsibility for the function and management of the village lies with an Executive Committee of the Sarvodaya society. This committee oversees the work of other sub-committees. It also deals with maintenance of inventories, preventive maintenance, repair, and security of buildings and equipment held centrally. It provides community waste pick-up and promotes well-maintained residential exteriors. The Executive Committee is committed to improving residents' ongoing understanding and knowledge related to ecovillage goals and objectives, and to promoting positive relations with the wider world beyond the village. The committee organises activities such as tree planting and events such as village concerts.

Socialization

Damniyamgama Ecovillage has a large eye-catching Community Centre which is the venue for Society meetings, seminars, short workshops, awareness and training programmes, meetings of sub-groups such as the youth group and mothers' group and society executive committee meetings. The Centre, in addition to being an architecturally pleasing building, is designed for thermal comfort. It hosts the library, information technology centre, a cooperative bank and a pre-school. Programmes held here attract participation from a number of villages in the surrounding area. Recently a cultural centre also was established with dance and music lessons for young people from Damniyamgama and ten other villages. This was considered necessary to improve cultural and aesthetic awareness and to build a mentality that values peace and harmony – both with nature and with the rest of society.

Community events and socialising regularly occur and are essential in promoting senses of common ownership and harmony. An example of such an event at Damniyamgama is the New Year festival, traditionally held in April. Children, youth and adults actively engage in the activities and this helps to forge very strong relationships within the community. Another example is Wesak, which is the religious festival when people make wesak lanterns to celebrate the Lord Buddha's birth, enlightenment and passing away. A competition for wesak lantern-making was held within the village. Then, on some full moon poya days, the community gets together and organises alms-giving and perahera festivals (Perahera is a Buddhist festival consisting of dances and richly-decorated elephants. There are fire-dances, Kandian dances and various other cultural dances). All of these festive occasions greatly improve the spiritual attitudes and morale within the community.

Environmental Education

Even the youngest children in kindergarten in Damniyamgama undertake environmental education programmes. They engage in educational activities such as tree planting. Beyond the village itself, Damniyamgama plays an all important role in environmental education on a wider scale. In other words, the educational function extends far beyond the village. Nearby neighbourhoods become involved in programmes. Also, national and international visitors come to the village to learn about eco-concepts and to see how a good, well-designed ecovillage may function. Government officers and officers of other NGOs visit the project to gain knowledge about implementing the eco-concept to a resettlement scheme. Damniyamgama has become a pilot project and something of an experimental ground which will inform the development of future similar settlements. Without doubt, Damniyamgama may be regarded as a model village for demonstrating environmental sustainability, community-based development, and education to other development agencies and donors.

Conclusion

Out of tsunami destruction and despair, a 'model' of good practice in ecovillage sustainable development has been established by Sarvodaya. So far, it may be deemed a tremendous success – both from the point of view of the quality of life for the people who inhabit it and also because of its highly successful role in the education of residents and observers about living in an environmentally friendly and sustainable fashion. It is an excellent example of community-based environmental education that impacts upon people of all ages within the village and policy makers beyond it.

Sajini Pathiraja was born in Sri Lanka in 1980. She completed her BSc. Degree in Agriculture at the University of Ruhuna in 2005. Shortly afterwards, she joined the Sarvodaya movement – the largest Non-Governmental Organization in Sri Lanka – doing community service work all over the country. As part of her work at Sarvodaya, she was given the responsibility of implementing the ecovillage development project for tsunami affected families. In 2007, she entered Durham University in the United Kingdom and completed a Master's degree in Education. After that, she continued her work with Sarvodaya, specializing in community services with respect to implementing environmental conservation projects with community participation. She has practical experience with disaster management and community education as well.

Claudia Menendez writes on behalf of Trees, Water & People, recipient of the prestigious Alcan Prize for Sustainability in 2008. TWP has been establishing reforestation projects throughout Central America, educating rural populations on the necessity of maintaining intact arboreal ecosystems, as well as providing these populations with efficient cookstoves to reduce the demand for fuel wood. Claudia describes the disastrous conundrum whereby rural populations are absolutely dependent on forest resources for their very survival yet the combination of economic and population pressures have forced them to denude these very same resources. There are valuable lessons here about the inescapable interpenetration of the social, economic, cultural, and ecological dimensions of sustainability.

Rebuilding Family and Environmental Health in Central America & the Caribbean

Claudia Menendez – Trees, Water & People, Colorado, USA

In the Central American country of Honduras, the capital city Tegucigalpa is located in a valley surrounded by bare, rolling hills. Decades ago these hillsides were covered with diverse vegetation including splendid oak and pine trees. Since then, the majority of trees have been cut down to make room for new communities, build homes, or simply for cooking fuel. Some of these peri-urban communities are located on the highest hilltops making them difficult to access. They often exist without running water, sewage, electricity, or telephone lines. Aside from lacking these basic services these communities are also threatened by landslides during the rainy season, as the slopes are denuded of all vegetation.

In the early morning, smoke filters from between the boards of Dona Gabriela's small kitchen. Inside and out, the walls are blackened from years of soot build-up. The kitchen is filled with smoke and the thick smell of burning wood as she lights the stove to prepare for a day's work, making tortillas. Doña Gabriela is a single mother of four girls ages 25, 22, 13, and one, and also has three grandchildren. The family of eight lives on the hillside community of Buena Vista (Spanish for 'nice view'), in a simple two-room wooden house covered by a tin roof held down by rocks. To make a living, Doña Gabriela and her oldest daughter devote their time to making tortillas, a regional flatbread made from corn flour, a staple of the Honduran diet.

In the morning, one of the youngest daughters balances a large pail of boiled corn kernels on her head as she walks to the mill, where it will be ground into dough. The other daughter pushes a cart to buy bark stripped from pine trees and sawmill remnants. While the wood burns easily it doesn't hold a good flame, so Doña Gabriela has to feed her barrel stove continuously. The smoke released by this resin-heavy pine is black and toxic. It fills the room and lungs and irritates the eyes of the women working and the small children tugging at their skirts.

Introduction

Latin America and the Caribbean are tropical climates with exotic animals, lush rainforests, volcanoes, and fertile lands. However, there is an unromantic reality to this part of the world that is only now becoming evident. Guatemala, El Salvador, Honduras, Nicaragua, and Haiti are all facing grave ecological challenges, afflicting community wellbeing and development. Vital forest cover and watersheds have been degraded extensively to satisfy growing demands for firewood and charcoal for cooking, timber for building, and precious hardwoods for export.

Most rural families living in the five nations in which Trees, Water & People has been working for the past decade are highly dependent on forests for income and survival. Natural resources are abundant in the tropics, but replenishing what is harvested is not a common practice. There is insufficient government involvement in promoting environmental awareness, education, and stewardship to help communities take responsibility and ownership of natural resource management. Instead, government efforts are generally concentrated in the crowded urban centers where rural folk have migrated in search of economic gain. Neglecting the needs and traditions of rural populations has led to the severe overcrowding of urban centers. Encouraging rural families to revive their traditional way of life is the first step to rebuilding the communities and landscapes, as well as curbing urban migration.

Trees, Water & People (TWP) collaborates with local partners to protect and manage the natural resources upon which a community's long-term wellbeing depends. Our international projects revolve around the protection of forests and watersheds in five Central American nations and Haiti. They help marginalized communities learn about environmental stewardship to improve economic livelihoods while protecting natural resources. TWP introduces eco-friendly technology, such as fuel-efficient cookstoves, to reduce the demand for wood from native forests. Primary benefits from TWP reforestation and stove programs include:

1. Improved indoor air quality by removing toxic smoke and particulates from the kitchen

2. Reduction of time and/or money spent collecting firewood

3. Increase in forest cover through tree planting and lower demand for wood fuel

4. Climate change mitigation

Smiling beneficiaries of the work of Claudia Menendez and Trees, Water & People.

Saving the Forests

Forests provide numerous environmental services vital to our survival. The resources we derive from them propel our local and global economies. These intricate living systems produce the oxygen we breathe and provide a bounty of biodiversity. Their complex root systems filter water and connect microorganisms and fungi that recycle leaves into rich fertile soil. Forest canopies remove toxins from the air by absorbing tons of CO_2 and feeding moisture into cloud condensation nuclei to create dense clouds that reflect sunlight, moderating global temperatures.

Flora and fauna thrive in healthy, well-managed forests allowing the harvesting of non-timber forest products (NTFPs) such as fruits, nuts, resins, medicinal plants and flowers. The traditional use of wood for furniture and firewood for cooking provides livelihoods for many. Furthermore, protecting carbon-rich ecosystems remains essential to any effort to limit global climate change. Every day, we learn more about our reliance on forests and how they can supply continual abundance if respectfully managed. It is our duty to transfer this understanding to those in less fortunate circumstances so that we can rebuild the integrity of global ecosystems.

For many families living in rural or peri-urban areas, the ability to harvest forest products is integral to maintaining current levels of subsistence and preventing the household from falling into poverty. Forest-based income-earning activities generate mostly very low returns, but can often be the most viable work activity for households with limited options. This need can lead to rapid over-exploitation of forest resources with neither time nor energy allotted for replanting or replenishing.

As these resources are depleted, income sources destabilize and families and communities can easily fall into precarious economic situations. Graph 1 depicts the ratio of rural population to national forest cover or forest resources available, and clearly illustrates that population numbers exceed natural resource supply.

Graph 1

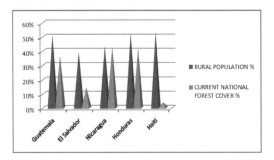

When we consider that the survival of rural populations in these nations depends on consumption of primary resources, many of which come from forest ecosystems and surroundings, the relationship depicted in the graph is disquieting. This rings alarms in El Salvador where forest cover is quickly disappearing and especially in Haiti where it is nearly gone.

The growing demand for cooking firewood in

Central America and charcoal in Haiti, plus the increased need for agricultural lands to provide food for a burgeoning population, are overwhelming for the forest reserves of these countries. In fact, all five nations have less than 50% of their forest cover remaining. The standing forests, unless already recognized by the government as a protected area or national park, most likely have had their best trees harvested (legally or illegally), and what remains are secondary growth forests no more than two to three decades old. These forests are not guaranteed to survive unless communities and institutions are educated about the importance of replenishing what has been taken and conserving what remains.

Community Forestry

Trees, Water & People has established long-term community-based partnerships with passionate groups dedicated to educating and inspiring land owners, communities, schools, church groups, local non-governmental organizations (NGOs), and municipalities to recover their forest ecosystems. Our programs in El Salvador, Guatemala, and Nicaragua each maintain two or three tree nurseries producing 40,000 seedlings in El Salvador and Guatemala, and 500,000 seedlings in Nicaragua. In 2009, the nurseries produced various medicinal plants, fruit trees, hard woods, and trees for firewood from seeds and cuttings collected from the forests or purchased from national forest associations.

In El Salvador, the smallest nation in Central America, TWP partner *Arboles y Agua para el Pueblo (AAP)* has worked to stabilize the forests of 'La Magdalena.' This 776 hectare area has seven types of forest and is the source of 24 springs that provide water to five townships and 25,000 people. AAP has managed to recover 65 hectares of land within the park and continues to supply nearby residents with tree seedlings to plant in and around their homes to reduce the demand on park resources.

AAP works with Pedro Medina, who from the age of six developed a deep respect for La Magdalena. He has led community initiatives to maintain the integrity of the park and its valuable water resources. Pedro claims that since the population became active in caring for the natural area, paying for forest rangers and planting trees within their household space, the park looks fuller and greener, the breeze is cooler, and wildlife has returned.

Conservation Methods

TWP and AAP have been working diligently to create a buffer zone between agricultural lands and the limits of the park. House sites in and around the Magdalena Protected Area are planted with trees that will grow into maturity and continuously cycle carbon, release oxygen, create soil, and provide animal habitat, shade and fodder for livestock, and fruit and firewood for personal consumption. Sensitizing the farmers and their families and workers of the area has been quintessential to ensuring that these trees reach maturity. Prior to commencing a project, AAP meets with farmers to educate them about the importance of reforestation in relation to their present and future economic and social wellbeing. They teach agro-forestry methods that combine farming, proper animal grazing, and forestry to help both practices thrive, and monitoring visits encourage them to observe and maintain growing trees. AAP strives to instill a sense of pride and ownership in these projects so participants feel invested in ensuring long-term success by being part of the solution.

Fuel-Efficient Stoves: Saving Forests and Changing Lives

Mother Nature's force is felt with great intensity. The small Central America isthmus bears 29 volcanoes in five countries and braces itself annually against destructive tropical storms and hurricanes. In 1998, Hurricane Mitch pummeled Central America, especially Nicaragua and Honduras, with over 1900mm of rain over five days. Communities living on vulnerable, deforested hillsides were some of the most afflicted, losing their humble homes to massive landslides. In the wake of Hurricane Mitch, it became evident that deforestation needed to be curbed and forest systems replenished.

Reforestation is one method that contributes to regaining ecosystem balance. However, more action is needed in places like Honduras, where it is commonly estimated that more than 75% of the population still cooks over open flames on U-shaped, rammed-earth stoves or large oil barrels, consuming an enormous amount of firewood. Trees, Water & People partnered with the Aprovecho Research Center in Oregon, the Honduran Association for Development (AHDESA), and Rotary International to take on the dual challenge of developing a fuel-efficient, wood-burning stove that would be accepted and readily used by Honduran women.

Doña Justa smiling proudly next to her fuel efficient stove.

Working with well-loved community leader Doña Justa Nuñez, TWP and Aprovecho stove engineers created the Justa stove (named in her honor), which combines principles of clean combustion and insulation. The unique L-shaped clay elbow or chamber sends heat upwards at a high velocity. Insulation traps the heat and forces it up against the pot or cooking surface above the elbow. The goal was to create a stove acceptable to Honduran women, especially for making tortillas, yet reduce the amount of firewood used in their everyday cooking to help protect the valuable forests and water resources.

Since 1999, TWP has built over 35,000 fuel-efficient stoves throughout Central America and Haiti with the help of Aprovecho, Rotary International, various foundations, regional NGOs, and dedicated community members.

Healthy Stoves

The inefficient burning of open fires has a number of negative repercussions for families. There is significant time and money invested in gathering or buying firewood and the physical toll of carrying heavy loads of wood, as well as the respiratory illnesses caused by inhalation of toxic gases from cooking over an open fire.

AAP community work meeting.

The World Health Organization states that over 1.6 million people, mainly women and children, die each year due to indoor air pollution caused by traditional open fire cooking methods. The millennia-old tradition of three stone fires used in spaces with no ventilation has caused families to inhale noxious fumes on a daily basis that are blamed for Acute and eventually Chronic Respiratory ailments *(Graph 2)*. Furthermore, the World Bank has listed indoor air pollution as one of the four largest environmental problems facing the developing world today.

In 2005, TWP and health practitioners from Colorado State University visited Honduras to study the effect of traditional open flame stoves on women's health. Women were given a fuel-efficient stove and re-tested six months later. Graph 2 positively shows the correlation between use of an improved TWP cookstove and better health conditions. Improved health also means less spending on doctor visits and medication, not to mention longer, healthier lives.

Graph 2

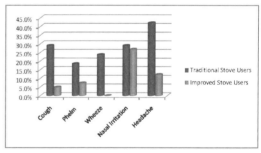

People-centred Approach

Trees, Water & People's reforestation and improved stoves effectively confront some of the serious environmental and economic issues shouldered by marginalized communities in Latin America. Furthermore, we pride our work on people-centered projects that take a holistic approach, replenishing ecosystems and building communities. We not only teach the importance of natural resource management and economics, but also the intrinsic value of healthy, harmonious living with nature for overall wellbeing. Through our projects, TWP builds vested interest and commitment in partner communities which we feel is pivotal to the success and longevity of our programs.

All it takes is a little bit of funding for local villagers to greatly increase quality of life.

Claudia Menendez, International Program Consultant for Trees, Water & People (TWP), has enjoyed living and working in Honduras, El Salvador, Nicaragua, and Cuba over the past four years. She has been an International Project Coordinator with the Canadian Environmental NGO Falls Brook Centre since 2005, implementing ecological programs that improve communities' relationships with and management of the natural resources that surround them through focused environmental education and the development of locally appropriate technologies. In 2009, Claudia worked with International Lifeline Fund in Lira, Uganda on the strategic planning of the marketing and community components of their stove and environmental programs. She earned a BA in Latin American Studies and International Development from the University of Calgary. Claudia assists with TWP's international fuel-efficient stove and reforestation programs in Central America and Haiti.

A recurring theme throughout Module 4 is the interconnections between social, cultural, and political influences in any environmental restoration effort. Erian Ozorio, co-organizer of EDEs in Rio de Janeiro, highlights these connections in her report about restoration of the mangrove ecosystems surrounding Guanabara Bay. Another recurring theme is the necessity of ongoing education with local populations who may not be aware of the larger consequences of their immediate actions. Erian instructs on this point as well. Fortunately, one other recurring theme is that given the will, it can be done – thanks to the devoted commitment of people like Erian Ozorio and countless others like her working in NGOs all over the world (and organizing EDEs in their spare time!).

Impact, Recovery & Conservation of Coastal Ecosystems in Brasil

Antonia Erian Ozório da Silva – Foundation Ondazul, Brasil

Introduction

In Brasil, it is estimated that the amount of degraded soil exceeds 200 million hectares. Coastal biomes (*Caatinga*), open fields (*Cerrado*), Amazon Forest, and Atlantic Forest (*Pantanal*) are all directly affected by actions such as deforestation, mining, construction of roads and railways, dumping of waste material, introduction of exotic species, inappropriate farming methods, construction of dams, and placement of industrial areas among other actions that result in immediate impact on soil fertility.

There are various techniques to restore vegetation in degraded areas. For each biome, there are proper techniques that accelerate the recovery process, even in places where the soil has been exposed. Universities and research institutions have been studying feasible and cost-effective methods for these purposes.

The continuous interference of human activities on Brasil's continental aquatic systems has had direct and indirect consequences, causing impact on water quality, aquatic *biota* and the operation of lakes, rivers and dams.

Brasil's vast water resources are of great ecological, economic and social significance. The management, conservation and restoration of these ecosystems have repercussions on the economy, the use of aquatic systems and society as a whole. This management is very complex due to significant geomorphological, ecological and anthropological differences in the various latitudes of Brasil, thus emphasizing the importance of a compatible scientific database to support the restoration activities.

Regarding the degradation of coastal ecosystems, restoration is an activity that has been increasingly employed in Brasil, though little discussed. In addition to identifying the factors that challenge the third sector entities active in environmental recovery, this paper addresses, in particular, the recovery of the mangrove ecosystem – one of the most endangered in the world. This example demonstrates the capacity to restore large areas and highlights the turning point of social change that occurs when the environment is restored. Furthermore, it stresses the need to seriously consider the social, economic, cultural *and* political reintegration of the recovered areas into the social life of the affected communities.

Degradation of Coastal Ecosystems – Guanabara Bay Mangroves

Mangrove is a coastal ecosystem that occurs in the inter-tidal areas in tropical and subtropical regions of the world. It is characterized by typical woody vegetation adapted to the limiting conditions of salinity, unconsolidated substrate, poor oxygenation and constant tidal submergence (Soares, 1997). It is associated with the edge of bays, inlets, bars, river mouths, lagoons and coastal indentations, where the water from rivers and sea meet, or are directly exposed to the shoreline.

Geographical Distribution of Mangroves on the Globe

In Brasil, mangroves are found virtually along the entire coast. They are among the ecosystems that have suffered the most coverage rate loss, leading to the fragmentation of former contiguous sectors along the Brasilian coast. Nowadays, despite the various forms of protection, this pressure has not been reduced since approximately 70% of the Brasilian population is concentrated in the coastal region.

Due to its strategic position and protected waters, the Guanabara Bay had an important historical and economic role in the development of the State of Rio de Janeiro. Guanabara Bay always impressed its visitors with the beauty of its geography, fauna and surrounding vegetation. Despite the lovely postcards coming from Rio de Janeiro, it is one of the most degraded environments, both environmentally and socially, in the country.

These associated ecosystems have been strongly affected by increased industrial activity over the last 20 years. Over 50% of the mangrove areas were deforested giving rise to civil construction and installation of industries in the vicinity. Oil pollution in the bay has been a major cause of destruction. There is only one large area protected by the Environmental Protection Area (APA) Guapimirim.

Social Importance of Mangrove Ecosystem

Nowadays, it is known that the mangrove is a key ecosystem for the survival of the whole coastal *biota* and various terrestrial species. Fish, whales and dolphins, shrimps, crabs and many other invertebrates live in the mangrove waters. It serves as a source of food, shelter, and nursery for many other marine species, as well as landing and feeding grounds for migrating birds.

Village people who settled in the country's remaining mangrove areas earn a living from extractive activities in this ecosystem. As for social benefits, mangroves provide a singular culture and organization for the harvest, process and sale of crab. There is still some fishing, and previously larger scale shrimp harvesting.

The mangroves' 'prohibition law' – prohibiting harvest during breeding periods – has created serious social problems because of marginalizing, periodically, the activity of crab catchers. The enforcement of environmental protection ultimately encourages the appearance of an illegal market. This relationship between environmental and social issues needs to be solved by educating about the handling of species, so as to ensure permanent economic activity for the social groups involved in the use of the products originating in the mangroves.

Initiatives for the Recovery of Highly Degraded Guanabara Bay Areas

Many environmental recovery projects in Brasil have been initiated due to the urgency of addressing economic developments that have adversely impacted the environment. An example was a major accident that took place in the Guanabara Bay in January of the year 2000. The accident occurred within a pipeline of the Petrobras oil refinery. This accident was a leak coming out of the pipes of REDUC, more precisely from the dark products duct (PE-II) that deposited nearly 1,293 million liters of oil *in natura* into the Guanabara Bay waters, resulting in severe damage to ecosystems.

To mitigate these effects, in partnership with other non-governmental organizations (NGOs), the NGO 'Foundation Ondazul' began the restoration work of highly degraded areas in the city of Mage, the area most affected by the oil leak. An area of 120,000 m^2 has already been recovered from a total of 640,000m^2.

Environmental awareness is raised in the western world via non-profit organizations that disseminate and report problems that severely affect the environment. The problems start with the lack of action by governments not fulfilling their role. Insufficient technical staff hinders the execution of projects for the recovery of degraded areas. Governmental bodies are far from meeting the need for regulating enterprises that cause adverse impact.

Ondazul Foundation has shown that it is not difficult to recover large areas, but it takes many years of ongoing work to fully restore the habitat of various birds, crustaceans, mammals and reptiles. The greatest challenge, however, for the sustainability of such projects is educating the population as to the importance of these ecosystems.

Soil preparation before reforestation in November 2001.

Aerial photo of the reforested area in February 2009.

Stages of Environmental Recovery

The environmental recovery of an area of 120,000m² included the characterization and diagnosis of the involved areas, soil preparation, planting the predominant species in the region (*Laguncularia racemosa* and *Rhizophora mangle*), monitoring and maintenance.

Fishermen and people who live in the region were hired for the execution of these activities. There were many difficulties during the first stage (2001-2003). One of the techniques used was to transplant seedlings; but this showed little effectiveness, resulting in a very high loss. Only 1,500 from 18,000 replanted seedlings survived.

A   B   C

Steps enclosure for containment of solid waste. (A) beginning of the process, (B) fencing completed, and (C) result of the enclosure.

It was only from 2004 on that the first positive results appeared, thanks to finding the proper mix of native plants, *Spartina alterniflora*, *Hibiscus permambucensis*, *Schinus terebinthifolius*, *Bacopa* sp., and including some fruit trees. This successful mix attracted birds, crustaceans and some mammals, which also contributed to the strengthening of the system. The areas are fully restored in 2010 with trees ranging from 1m to 5m in height.

An important part of the restoration of the environment is the contribution of NGOs in educating against depredation actions. Main goals of this education are relaying understanding of the historic, cultural, social and economic recovery that will accrue to the community. Positive results of environmental restoration, in this regard, are transforming the minds of the population and the surrounding community, who still consider the mangroves a proper place for domestic and industrial dumping.

An interesting fact is that around the year 2005, schools in the region started assisting in the re-planting operations. This was when Foundation Ondazul began a new program promoting joint efforts among schools, businesses, and universities, inspiring a community process of environmental recovery.

The current stage of recovery is a scientific production, with studies of genetic variability among plants, studies of economic valuation of the ecosystem, the distribution of crustaceans, among other interdisciplinary studies. The goal is to increase knowledge of the recovery of degraded ecosystems to highlight that areas originally devastated can restore their biodiversity, allowing subsistence activities to return in a sustainable manner, thus improving the quality of life in the region.

Conclusion

Mobilizing communities through awareness and clarification programs about the importance of the mangrove ecosystem is crucial, especially in respect to the projection of future developments like the proposed Petrochemical Plant of Rio de Janeiro, the largest enterprise yet envisioned. Just as happened in Guanabara Bay, the projected scenario is of increased pollution, contamination and destruction of ecosystems. Despite the attention that the enterprise has received regarding technologies for containment of the contamination caused by industrial waste, it is possible that the biggest problem will be the increase in population in the vicinity of the petrochemical plant, since more than 100,000 new work posts will be created.

It is most likely that infrastructure issues in relation to the increased population, such as sanitation systems, may be delayed or postponed, leading to an increase in the sewage dump in the neighboring Guanabara Bay. Furthermore, with the projected population increase, the likelihood of illegal occupation of the remaining fragments of mangrove will further reduce the area of this ecosystem. Thus, actions aimed at awareness and mitigation of tensors of degradation, coupled with actions in collaboration with city governments in the region, will help ensure that the conservation of coastal ecosystems moves alongside the economic development of the region.

References

AMADOR, E.S. 1997. Baía de Guanabara e ecossistemas periféricos: homem e natureza.
  Tese de Doutorado, Instituto de Geociências, Universidade Federal do Rio de Janeiro, 539p.
RODRIGUES, F.O., LAMPARELLI, C.C., MOURA, D. O. Indicadores de Qualidade Ambiental
  – Padrões ambientais para manguezais impactados: efeitos de derramamento de óleo em áreas de
  manguezal. São Paulo. CETESB, 1990. 21p. (Relatório do setor de bentos e manguezais).
SCHAEFFER-NOVELLI, Y. 1991. Ecossistema Manguezal e suas comunidades. Curso de Difusão
  Cultural, Depto.Ecologia USP. 3 a 7/6/91.
SCHAEFFER-NOVELLI, Y.1995. Manguezal: ecossistema entre a terra e o mar. São Paulo,
  Caribbean Ecological Research, 64p
SORRENTINO, M. ONGs e meio ambiente: análise das ONGs ambientalistas e de seus human
  resources. Sócio-environmental debates. Year III, No. 10, Jul / Oct 1998
Águas Doces no Brasil - Capital Ecológico, Uso e Conservação. 2.° Edição Revisada e Ampliada.
  Escrituras. São Paulo - 2002. Organização e Coordenação Científica: Aldo da C. Rebouças;
  Benedito Braga. Capítulo 06 - Limnologia de Águas Interiores. Impactos, Conservação e
  Recuperação de Ecossistemas Aquáticos. José Galizia Tundisi, Takako Matsumura Tundisi e Odete
  Rocha. Páginas 205 - 221.

Antonia Erian Ozório da Silva – Economist, graduated at the Federal Rural University of Rio de Janeiro, Expert in Biodiversity Management at the Botanical Garden of Rio de Janeiro and the Federal University of Rio de Janeiro, Expert in Management of Social Programs at FESP-RJ, serves as Coordinator for Projects of Recovery of Coastal Ecosystems – Mangrove Guanabara Bay – Rio de Janeiro for Ondazul Foundation and takes part in the organization group for Educational Course Gaia – Sustainability Design for NGO Terra UNA.

In this definitive collaboration, Zaida Amaral and Loralee Makela broaden the concept of design to adding unseen earth energies. This is an aspect usually overlooked in design courses; yet, from a deeper perspective, it could be considered fundamental, the very first layer in a comprehensive site design. The authors also introduce the concept of 'geomancy', or divining with earth energies. Admittedly, a certain sensitivity needs to be cultivated before becoming astute in this terra-art; yet, the authors demonstrate through case studies that ongoing practice and an openness and responsiveness to the world as it is will reveal numerous clues capable of adding a palpable sense of magic to any design.

Incorporating Earth Energy into the Design: 'Conscious Design & the Designer as Geomancer'

Zaida Amaral – Ecovila Cunha, Brasil and Loralee Makela – Makela Feng Shui, New Mexico

Introduction

In this article, we propose a 'new', inclusive way to reach the vision of good ecological design – one that encourages us to open up our senses and our curiosity toward the realm of previously unseen forces operating within our environment. This vision and the ensuing processes – already applied in the designs of many traditional cultures and some of the most successful communities in the world – are keys to developing what we call "conscious design", thus unfolding the awakened role of the 'designer as geomancer'.[1] The designer as geomancer becomes aware of and takes into account other-sensory sources of information, and creates physical structures that support the fulfillment of a new paradigm. This is a designer capable of re-linking ancient wisdom design principles with permaculture – reflecting the explosion of environmental consciousness and whole systems thinking over the last 30 years.

Broadening the Concept of Design

Learning to create an ongoing dialogue with our planet, the 'designer as geomancer' can effectively program designs to produce a certain effect, goal or vision.

As form and shape determine our sense of place, built or natural, it follows that certain arrangements and shapes of mountains, rivers, buildings, pathways, vegetation and light will determine the personality of each settlement; even predicting its destiny. Modern designers create programs that take into account people and future outcomes such as beauty, ease, happiness, health and prosperity. We propose that the designer as geomancer is in total alignment with that goal – she just uses a few additional tools in order to achieve it.

We realize that the act (or art) of predicting one's destiny is shrouded in mystery and universally invalidated by the 'real sciences'. But if we broaden our concept of 'science' to what Stephan Harding calls 'holistic science',[2] then we arrive at a place where it becomes entirely valid, even imperative, to use our direct apprehension of the world around us in a conscious design process. Holistic Science is:

> a direct apprehension of the things around us through the medium of our physical bodies... weaving together the empirical and the archetypal aspects of the mind so that they work together as equal partners in a quest that aims not at a complete understanding and mastery of nature, but rather strives for a genuine participation with nature.
>
> STEPHEN HARDING

Earth Energies – Destiny and Design

We are born into the Earth

The Earth consists of the planet and its biosphere. She is influenced by the solar system in which she lives. The solar system is influenced by the galaxy, and the galaxy by the universe. We are composed of the same elemental matter as the Earth and the Stars. We know the Earth's language at a visceral, unconscious level.

Becoming a competent geomancer is more a process of remembering and unlearning than gathering more knowledge or information. That said, and because we have traditionally been trained to learn by thinking, there are a few design modalities that can be helpful in expanding our conscious design process. Concepts such as vaastu, feng shui, shamanism, whole body perception, meditation, sacred geometry, geobiology, bio-geometry, radesthesa and bio-mimicry can assist the designer with shortcuts, guidelines and a common language for the design process. The designer may use one or more of these design concepts, depending on the needs of the project.

Interestingly, many of these concepts overlap and support each other at their most fundamental levels even though they span many different cultures and times. When appropriately executed, they are a gift for the village designer/geomancer's toolbox and, more importantly, are a rich compilation of centuries' worth of data based on careful observation of the physical environment and its effect on peoples' destiny. Our combined journey has taught us the importance of integrating these concepts with our ultimate goal of sensing the Earth, interacting with Gaia as a conscious collaborator in the design process.

The Design Process

Most design processes emphasize technology, necessity and utility. As an example of a more holistic, earth-based design process we refer here to the outline used in the Ecovillage Design Education Training 2007 – New Mexico, USA: "Unseen Structures Checklist for Land Planning" – *Values and Concepts for the Ecological Dimension:*

- What level of ecological restoration are you willing to accomplish?
- How does the natural shape of your land define your design concept?
- What structures can you incorporate using local resources and local skills?
- Is there a space in your planning for food growing, energy production and resilience?
- What building technologies have been chosen and how appropriate are they for the climate, culture and specifics of your site location?
- How can you export these elements (technology + knowledge) to your local community?
- How does your planning integrate living systems theory with restoring nature?

We propose to answer these and other design questions by adding extra-sensory practices to the existing methods. These can be considered 'meta-processes' that utilize our full capacity of perception, generating 'new' data that emerges from within.

Case Studies

> We create our environments and then our environments create us.
>
> WINSTON CHURCHILL

We present here two personal case studies which illustrate different ways of integrating earth energies into the design process and the effect it has had on the outcomes of each project, from the decision point of buying a piece of land to a final acknowledgement of what we have to "live with" and evolve from. We hope to show how our designs shape us as we shape them at the levels of both individual and community.

Case Study 1

Holistic Land Planning for Ecovila Cunha, Sao Paulo, Brazil
Conscious Design Steps – Zaida Amaral

Map your Mind

In the search for land, the group gathered and visited five different prospective sites. Main goals: ecological restoration, educational center, place to live closer to Nature, food for the soul. Guidance: find the land that "calls to us".

Sensing

The entrance of the chosen land spoke to the newcomers. A sense of vital energy and purpose was felt from beginning to end of the first visit. It was time to identify the vocation of the land and determine what matched our goals and/or how to adapt our intentions.

Perceiving

As the enclosing canopies of forest would suggest, the land 'proposed' hosting more introspective work rather than large open conferences or educational gatherings. The idea of a Retreat and Renewal Center for "soul restoration" was then added to the vision.

This logo came from a vision of a winged dragon, sensed as the 'Deva of the Land' by Zaida on the first visit after purchase. The logo designer, also a member, captured the 'healing relationships' aspect of the vision and multiplied the dragons into eight pairs of healing partners, face to face. This aspect was reinforced by the feng shui orientation of the main entrance road onto the property, located in the Relationship/SW compass sector. This indicates a "call" for the relationship aspects of life unfolding. The well-received logo design happened without meetings or need for group decisions; perception and trust were the guides.

Identifying and Mapping

Natural design patterns such as water flow, large boulders, vegetation, and prominent natural spots – considered as living elements of the land, also known as Earth and Water Dragons in feng shui – were placed on one layer of the planning maps. The natural flow of chi, or life energy, was identified and linked to natural courses of rivers and pathways, and then mapped as a layer. The sources of earth energies were zoned and mapped on a land resource layer. A separate map layer for the location of dwellings was then created.

Feng Shui Overlay

The diagram of feng shui compass orientation, called BaGua or Eight Gates of Energy, was then located over the topological map of the land and over the main areas of land use. This provided information about predicted influences on the life of the land users, on the definition of pathways and the location of dwellings.

All the waters run to a point located toward the south-southwest, further emphasizing a strong focus on recognition and relationships.

Integrating

The maps and overlays were discussed by the core group members and were essential in directing the next steps of strategic planning. A final composite map was then created, using permaculture zoning and sectoring, with proposed areas for locating structures. A special intuitive map design – channeled by Zaida after spending some days in quiet connection with the land – is now in the process of being implemented.

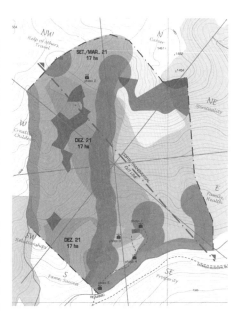

Case Study 2

Edgewood, New Mexico, USA
Designer as Geomancer – Living Design – Loralee Makela

I include here my most recent, more personal example of a design process still unfolding. It has become a pulse-like conversation between my inner self and the outer environment of pinion-juniper forest that surrounds me, punctuated by long pauses and surprising events. It has not always been a comfortable journey, but one that I could have not made without the conscious collaboration of Gaia herself.

Background

Summer of 2008, I was living downtown Albuquerque, NM, in a live-work townhouse, feng shui consulting and working at an interior design firm whose primary client was a large multinational corporation who apparently saw the writing on the wall way before the official 'crash'. From one day to the next, all design work was put on hold and I was out of a job. My decision was to either: ramp-up my consulting business and get more involved with my clients doing urban re-development; or drastically scale down, get simple, be closer to nature, learn to grow food and create community. I began the requisite business evaluation and started meditating for guidance.

Ecovillagers at Cunha in the midst of their site design process.

Decision

Within a month a large raven, a belly dancing class, an old friend with a casita, a Japanese garden, and a desperate drug addict collaborated to guide me toward the decision to downsize and move from busy downtown into the quiet mountains East of Albuquerque.

The Move

Viewing the casita (little house), my new home, with feng shui eyes, I could immediately see there were challenges with the positioning and chi flow; there was a certain undefined energy about it and the other nearby home. My position was that I could 'fix' just about anything but I certainly did not expect what an interesting journey I was embarking upon.

The surrounding land however was alive with possibility including healthy trees, winding paths, a personal healing vortex, water harvesting, open fields, edible forest, abundant wild life, new greenhouse and 2,000 sq.ft. of garden space – a dream come true.

Experience

Re-reading my personal journals from that time, I see that the challenges with the site made themselves evident within the first month. There were difficulties organizing into such a small space, confusion and misunderstanding arose quickly between my friend and I, much loneliness and isolation prevailed. My solace was walking the land with my feline friend and travel companion of 11 years, Shakti; learning to sense and revel in this wild, new environment through her animal nature.

Many times I thought to move away but whenever I did shining heart rocks would appear on my walks. I viscerally felt these love messages from Gaia telling me to stay put. This was not a time to leave, it was a time to go within, open up, listen and learn.

Animal Guides

Often there are bluebird feathers in the healing vortex. I learned to go to it when out of balance and immediately my energy would shift into a more peaceful state. Problems would be solved and the cat, outside too long after dusk, would be found and taken to the safety of home.

One afternoon, there were two large raven feathers on either side of the laughing Buddha statue nestled at the base of a juniper. So deliberate was the placement, I was sure my friend had put them there; but no, it was not him: simply another sign from my raven friends playfully encouraging me to stay with the unfolding.

Animals began to show no fear: raven circling me in the garden, hummingbird bathing in my hand-held sprinkler, snake and lizard within inches of me... unmoving, rabbit dancing on the path, bird nesting in the garden, bee and wasp without aggression. I began to feel they accepted me as one of them – 'natural, wild and free'.[3]

Part of the unfolding has been learning to flow with the seasons and nuances of the weather. I am less impatient, more able to take the long view. Peaceful.

I began to use a unique blend of esoteric arts in healing my little energy efficient, passive solar home – which, I discovered, was constructed on an old garbage dump from timbers salvaged from a burned house on a nearby Indian Reservation. (In the native culture, these kind of homes were often abandoned as sites for spirits). The casita is constructed on a plane higher than my friend's (dominating), on a rise with little support at the back or either side (instability, insecurity) and with an entry door directly in line with a service road, exactly opposite the back door (adversely affecting prosperity, opportunity and grounding). There was a distinct lack of comfortable outdoor space for people to gather and commune with each other and with Nature.

There turned out to be very little opportunity or willingness to construct external forms to stabilize the casita's configuration. I found myself resonating with the isolation and a weak energy field. Something had to be done.

It became my mission to discover alternate ways to achieve the stability and harmony I desperately needed within some fairly narrow constraints.

Designer as Geomancer

The following list chronicles some of the tools and processes used over the last two years. I have been guided toward ways to address each one of the initial challenges without major construction, the details of which are too long for this article.

- Day and night property walks using full body perception.
- Ceremony with friends and colleagues for the purpose of gathering data and guidance.
- Painting, planting, cleaning and clearing.
- Asking. Following guidance. Taking appropriate action.
- Feng Shui, geomancy, dowsing, bio-geometry and visualization.
- Interior architecture redesign.
- Creation of healing exterior forms, spaces and gardens with food and medicinal crops.
- Meditation, surrender, acknowledgement, gratitude and service.

Where I am now...?

A wise person once said that if you want to know the result of your intention and actions, notice what is happening around you. My circle of family and friends has grown and is flourishing. My soul continues to be nurtured by the earth, the sky and all things in between. The gardens flourish. Last evening, my friend invited me to a spontaneous celebration at a newly created fire pit whose rocks had been on the property for many years. In this beautiful new gathering space, sitting together on the circle of stones, he dedicated the exquisite 'small fire' to, among other things, a new phase in our relationship, celebrating a new way of relating and working together on this beautiful piece of Gaia's sacred creation.

"And in the end....."[4]

What Joana Macy[5] calls the 'Time of the Great Turning' presents us with a chance to 'change' by turning back to restore our deepest connection with the Earth. She asks us to see the process of design as a complete interrelated system between observer and object of observation; one that includes our relationship with the earth, the cosmos and nature as a whole, including our own inner nature.

We wonder about the role of earth changes in the awakening process of our evolving consciousness and the awakened role of the conscious designer as geomancer – the designer who operates within a higher source of information, creating structures, forms and shapes that link to the foundation of a new paradigm of living, thinking and being.

It is our hope that the concepts outlined here will emerge as a parallel force for the successful development of intentional communities, ecovillages, restorative towns and resilient cities, recalling the wise settlements of the old times, now and in the future to come.

Notes

1 Geomancy: to divine, or predict, using earth energies.
2 Stephen Harding: *Animate Earth: Science, Intuition and Gaia.*
3 Aldo Leopold. "A Sand County Almanac".
4 From the song "The End" by Lennon/McCartney, performed by the Beatles. " And in the end, the love you take is equal to the love you make."
5 Joanna Macy, co-philosopher Ph.D., scholar of Buddhism, general systems theory, and deep ecology.

Zaida Amaral is principal of Ecovillage Design Southwest and Resonance Design, consulting and educating on ecovillage design, integrated feng shui and the development of sustainable sacred spaces. With a degree in architecture and urban planning from her native Brazil, and ecovillage design certification from Findhorn Foundation in Scotland, she coordinated the first Ecovillage Design Education course in the US. She is co-founder of Ecovila Cunha (Brazil) and is a certified trainer for the international Transition movement, facilitating trainings towards resilient communities in the US and Brazil. **www.sustainablesacredspaces.com**

Loralee Makela, lives in Edgewood, New Mexico, USA learning the deep ecology of high-desert forest and how to grow food. Principal of Makela Feng Shui... just add water!, consultant, speaker, teacher and author. Provides customized consulting services to architects, interior designers, developers, business and homeowners. Classical Feng Shui practitioner since 1989, specializing in Water Dragon Placement, Graduate of The American Feng Shui Institute, Bachelor of Science in Business & Management.

Her second published work *Your Step-By-Step Feng Shui Workbook* provides a proven, practical process for a comprehensive Feng Shui analysis of your home or office. **www.diyfengshui.com**

*Nala Walla has long been spearheading a growing recognition that 'place' begins in our own bodies; therefore, restoring Nature is merely a consequence of restoring this vital connection that is our most immediate sensing of Nature – we **are** Nature. Nala uses well-chosen words to put this into perspective and introduces strategically meaningful terms such as 'ecosomatics', 're-indigenization', and 'the embodied arts'. She then weaves these terms into a new language that reveals just how woefully disconnected we've become from our primary home – body. Nala's writing embodies a profound evolution of consciousness whose integration could be considered the first step in competent ecovillage designing.*

Body as Place: A Somatic Guide to Re-Indigenization

Nala Walla – BCollective, Cascadia, USA

Introduction

Today, many millions of people are part of a growing worldwide diaspora which may never know precisely where its ancestors lived, or what practices they used to maintain respectful connections to the land. This same concept of diaspora – a dispersion from place – applies to those of us who do not feel at home even in our own skin, who feel somehow estranged from our own bodies. Countless modern people are currently wondering: how do we create a true sense of home, an ecologically relevant sense of *place* instead of a mere *space* where we extract what we need, and dump toxic waste when we're done?

Since our bodies are indeed our primary home, any endeavors to create a sense of place must include strategies for getting to know our bodies more deeply. Here, developing awareness of our own felt-experience can be a beneficial practice which connects us inevitably back to Earth via our own flesh. Thus a reinhabiting of our own bodies is an essential step towards *re-indigenization* – behaving in an ecologically respectful and culturally sustainable manner which truly honors 'home'. The embodied arts are designed to help us to do exactly this.

Zone Zero: Localism Begins with the Body

For those of us in green movements seeking a deeper sense of home and respectful relationship to place, it can be very helpful to recognize that, as infants, our sensation of gravity provides our very first experience of a sense of 'place'. Our relationship with Earth is primary, forming the basis for development of every other movement we make.

When we add permaculture terminology to our discussion of 'home' and 'place', we notice that the body likewise forms the basis of the concept of *zone zero* – the natural center from which all activity radiates. Accordingly, any sound ecological habitat design will plan to optimize bodily health and strive to take basic bodily patterns into careful consideration. Our bodies are the first units of *localism* from which homes, villages and communities are built. By serving the health of body and community, the embodied arts are very useful tools to placemakers, to cultural regenerators, and to village designers.

ECOSOMATICS: A Working (and playing!) Definition

Ecosomatics is an emerging interdisciplinary field which connects movement education, improvisation, healing arts, psychology, ritual, performing arts, and good old-fashioned play with ecological consciousness. The practice of ecosomatics heals the separation between mind, body and Earth by encouraging direct sensory perception of one's body both *in* the natural environment, and *as* the natural environment.[1]

In order to understand ecosomatics, we must first grasp the distinction between *soma* and *body*:

When you look at me, you can see that I have a body. What you cannot see is my 'proprioceptive', or felt-sense, of my own body – my *soma*. In 1976, Thomas Hanna coined the term *somatics* to distinguish this subtle 'inner body' from the outer, gross body. This term is based on the holistic Greek concept of *soma*, which refers to the entire mind-body-spirit system.

Thus, *somatics* refers to the art and practice of sensing the *soma*, or 'the body as experienced from within'. The somatic sense is a veritable sixth sense, as it cannot be adequately explained by any of the other five categories: taste, touch, hearing, sight, or smell. In an age where experts and professionals in the human health field often provide conflicting diagnoses and ineffective treatments, *somatics* is an empowering concept that affirms our innate knowledge of our own body, and encourages us to participate deeply in our own healing.

By tuning-in to our direct sensory experience, we can learn to release habitual tension and pain, instead optimizing for ease, efficiency and enjoyment. Any movement – sacred or mundane – can be re-patterned in this way, from dancing and singing, to simply getting in and out of a chair.

We can also apply these sensing and repatterning skills to activities which restore a sustainable relationship to Earth, such as planting trees, harvesting food, or creating a community ritual. Noticing the analogies between patterns in Nature and those we sense in our bodies helps us create effective ecological design. When we do this, we venture into the realm of *ecosomatics*.

e•co•so•*ma*•tics

1- The art of sensing the 'inner body' as a way to connect to the greater social and planetary (Gaiac) bodies. 2- The view of somatics as inseparable from ecological health and sustainability. 3- The practice of using somatic principles to facilitate and enhance sustainable work in the landscape (i.e. gardens, farms, village building).

Re-Indigenization: Creating a Sense of Place

> Okanagans teach that the body is Earth itself. Our flesh, blood and bones are Earth-body; in all cycles in which Earth moves, so does our body. As Okanagans we say the body is sacred. It is the core of our being, which permits the rest of the self to be. Our word for body literally means 'the land-dreaming capacity'.

JEANETTE ARMSTRONG, Okanagan Teacher, Activist, Traditional Council

The word *ecosomatics* has recently evolved to describe a gateway to the greater 'Earth-body' via our individual bodies. It expresses the fluid nature of the Self, and a world of boundaries which are at once distinct and permeable. And though the term comes from a scientific language that the modern human – steeped for generations in a rational worldview – can comprehend, the concept is as old as humanity itself, and well understood by indigenous cultures.

Because we are microcosms of earthly patterns, practicing respect for our bodies demonstrates respect for the Earth, both of which are characteristic of sustainable, indigenous cultures. Members of the diaspora may never be indigenous in the same way native peoples who have resided in a particular place or region for thousands of years; however, we can (indeed, we must) learn to behave with the same respect of place which is exemplified by indigenous culture.

A key step towards *re-indigenization* is a 'coming home' to our own bodies, a deep 'rooting' into Earth through our own flesh, a return to the sense of connectedness which is ever-present in sensation. There are many simple somatic practices that can help us access sensation any time we are feeling 'out of body'.

Art as Technology, not Luxury

At this crucial time in human evolution, we are wise to uproot the foolish notion that The Arts are only for the 'talented', for 'professionals', or that they are a luxury that the average person cannot afford. The embodied arts are far more than frivolities for the privileged few. These systems were evolved over eons by the grassroots, and are better regarded as potent and sustainable 'soft' technologies in the truest sense of the word. (*Technology* comes from the Greek word *tekhne*, meaning *skill* or *art*.)

Jobsite contact.

In direct contrast with 'hard' technologies (automobiles, computers, etc.) which commonly pollute and consume vast resource supplies, the body-based arts depend only on resources within *ourselves*. Considering the dangerous imbalance and over-reliance upon hard-tech in industrialized societies, a refocusing upon the soft technologies is actually an intelligent survival strategy.

Technologies of the social realm like dance, ritual, storytelling, and song (the original software!) have always served as communication methods, social exchange and conflict resolution strategies, information transmission schema, knowledge banks, and efficient energy utilization patterns. And, as anyone involved in ecological and activist groups can attest, it is primarily social conflict that impedes our progress and creates burnout, not lack of hard-tech. The Arts have always served as grease for the social wheels. Thus, if social dysfunction is the great limiting factor in implementing truly ecological habitats, it is greatly helpful to view them as tools for re-indigenization.

Embodied Activism – Countering Dissociation

As techno-industrial society races along ever more digital and virtual pathways, humans witness the disturbing side-effect of losing touch with our embodied experience. Our modern habit of fouling our own nest is evidence of a people suffering acutely from disconnection and dissociation from *the body* at every level – the personal body (*Soma*), the social body (*Community*), and the greater earthly body (*Gaia*). Dissociation is a serious psychological pathology; yet it is so widespread among modern people that it is unfortunately considered normal and even encouraged by technologies in which we 'inhabit' virtual and cyber 'worlds'.

Since our bodies are quite literally composed *of* and *from* Earth (carbon, nitrogen, hydrogen, oxygen...) a reinhabiting of our bodies amounts to a profound activist strategy for re-association with Earth, and re-indigenization to Place. Aligning with our bodies may seem to be but a small contribution, but since our habitual denial of the body lies at the root of our mistreatment of Earth, these small ripples eventually become a sea change that affects the entire world. Simply by becoming advocates for our own flesh and blood, we initiate an *embodiment of activism,* practicing behaviors which come closer to those of true 'indigeneity'.

By utilizing The Arts, we can facilitate a shift away from slavery paradigms, where we push our bodies beyond their capacity, and learn to honor our needs for proper alignment, rest, and play as essential to community function. Such a body-based philosophy encourages us to dissolve outdated views of manual labor as a chore that is somehow "beneath" us. Instead, *we learn to value earthwork as a privilege*: an enjoyable and healing endeavor where we can express our creativity, breathe fresh air, and exercise our bodies – all the while helping the shift towards sustainability.

Log dance. Whole body awareness becomes the basis of good ecological design.

The Yoga of Earthwork

All of the arts originally evolved within the context of Place and Community. Long before they arrived in the halls of Academia or Broadway, the arts belonged to The Folk, who wisely cast them in valuable healing, therapeutic, and integrative roles. For example, somatic practices such as yoga have developed to tune our body-mind systems to the daily tasks of building and sustaining a village – squatting and reaching to harvest food, flexing arms and legs to carry water or dig a foundation. To learn how best to push a heavy wheelbarrow and build an earthen house without throwing out our backs, becoming bored, or sunburned is indeed a yogic practice.

When we recognize the somatic opportunity in earthwork, we move more slowly and deliberately, checking for proper alignment and breath patterns, and we heed our bodies' requests for a break. By treating our bodies kindly and humanely, by dancing and telling stories in the garden much like our ancestors have always done, the line is blurred between work and play, between action and activism, between life and art. Over the last few years, I have facilitated many earthwork and building projects which integrate dance, song, bodywork, rest and play into the worksite, with results that are both empowering and fun.

Here, I am suggesting that we view embodied arts though a holistic lens. Ours is no armchair movement. We cannot simply sit back while someone else does the 'dirty work' for us. To create ecological habitats, we will need to rid ourselves of the outdated stigmas attached to manual labor, and welcome the sweat on our brow. Thriving, sustainable villages and gardens will not build themselves. Only healthy, vital bodies and communities working cooperatively can achieve the vitality we seek.

The arts are designed and destined to move beyond the bamboo-floored yoga studio or velvet-cushioned theater, where they can be put to practical use – out of doors – in our everyday lives. In true egalitarian fashion, the arts have always offered *anyone* (not just professionals) who practices them deep

Leaf toss. Festivity and play is not an optional add-on but rather is integral to the activities of a sustainable lifestyle.

understanding of Earth's grand cycles and strength of community. The good news is that these tools are still there – all we need do is use them.

The Ecology of the Body

Every time we take a breath, a billion electrochemical reactions occur within our bodies, a billion cells are born, and a billion die. Billions of organisms are right now living synergistically in our guts. Our modern sciences have now provided evidence confirming what indigenous cultures have always known: that universal and ecological patterns are right here, beneath our skin, and beneath the soil-skin of the Earth. These ecosomatic patterns can be experienced and perceived directly within our bodies through embodied arts practices.

It is imperative at this time to invest in the soft technologies – the skills, stories, and arts which connect Earth, Body, and Community. As they have always done, The Arts are helping us to create the respectful, cooperative, sustainable cultures of the future, and thus ought to be widely adopted as best-practices, especially among activists. And as a pleasant side effect, our lives will include more play, and more celebration as we become, once again, indigenous to the places we live.

> Even if I knew that tomorrow the world would go to pieces, I would still plant my apple tree.
>
> DR. MARTIN LUTHER KING

Notes

1 See Susan Bauer's article "Body and Earth as One" in *Conscious Dancer Magazine*, Spring 2008.

Nala Walla is a transdisciplinary artist, educator, and homesteader in Washington State, USA. Nala holds a Master's degree in Integrative Arts and Ecology, and is a founding member and facilitator of the BCollective: an umbrella organization dedicated to creation of healthy and sustainable culture through the embodied arts. The BCollective offers community-building workshops, creates participatory educational performances for kids and adults, and hosts permaculture skill-shares from somatic building to creative mediation. Please visit **www.bcollective.org** for more info, or contact Nala directly: **nala@bcollective.org**

MODULE 5
Integrated Ecological Design

Contents

Maddy Harland leads off Module 5 with an updated review of Permaculture Ethics and Principles. This is an excellent way to begin a study of Integrated Ecological Design. Her approach to the traditional statement of Ethics lends it a more humanitarian, even compassionate tone. For her treatment of Principles, she has chosen to paraphrase David Holmgren's 'List of 12' so that it might be relevant to a larger audience, with a more diverse array of applications. Even experienced permaculturists will find great value in reading Maddy's piece; after all, Permanent Publications is the center of permaculture thinking in Europe (and beyond).

The Ethics & Principles of Permaculture Design

Maddy Harland – Permanent Publications, England

Permaculture is primarily a thinking tool for designing low carbon, highly productive systems. The discipline of permaculture design is based on observing what makes natural systems endure, establishing simple yet effective principles, and using them to mirror nature in whatever we choose to design. This can be gardens, farms, buildings, woodlands, communities, businesses – even towns and cities. Permaculture is essentially about creating beneficial relationships between individual elements and making sure energy is captured in, rather than lost from, a system. Its application is only as limited as our imaginations.

Permaculture is not just a green way of living or a guiding system of ethics, it is a way of designing using nature's principles as a model, 'bending' them as much as possible to create fertile, self-reliant, productive landscapes and communities. Where permaculture stands out as a design system is in its capacity to integrate the intellect with ethics. It can teach us to 'think' with the heart and respond with the head. By combining pragmatism with philosophy, we can create a greater synthesis.

The three ethics are: Earth Care, People Care and Fair Shares or Limits To Growth. They are not exclusive to permaculture and were derived from the commonalities of many worldviews and beliefs. What permaculture does is makes them explicit within a design process.

Earth Care

Imagine the originators of permaculture, Australians Bill Mollison and David Holmgren, in the 1970s, watching the devastating effects of a temperate

European agriculture on the fragile soils of an ancient Antipodean landscape. Like the dust bowls of Oklahoma in the 1930s, an alien agriculture has the capacity to turn a delicately balanced ecology into desert. Their initial response was to design a permanent agriculture with tree crops and other perennials inhabiting all the niches, from the canopy to the ground cover and below. The soil is left untilled to establish its own robust micro-ecology. Key to this is that the land must be biodiverse and stable for future generations.

This ethic of Earth Care was the basis of permaculture design, but the original vision of care for all living and non living things has grown to embrace a deep and comprehensive understanding of Earth Care that involves many decisions, from the clothes we wear and the goods we buy to the materials we use for DIY projects. Though we can't all build our own house or grow all our own food, we can make choices about what and how we consume and conserve. Key to this is the understanding that up to one third of our ecological footprint is taken up by the food we buy, so even growing a small amount in a city allotment or container garden can make a difference.

People Care

Fundamental to permaculture is the concept of Permanent Culture. How can we develop a permaculture if our people are expendable, uncared for, excluded? People Care asks that our basic needs for food, shelter, education, employment and healthy social relationships are met. Genuine People Care cannot be exclusive in a tribal sense; there can be no elites here – no plutocracies or oligarchies – all members of the community must be taken into account.

At the core of People Care is an understanding of the power of community. If we can change our lives as individuals and make incremental differences – think what we can do as a community! The permaculture designers who helped initiate Cuba's post oil urban agriculture are a good example.[1] They mobilised a whole country to become self-reliant.

Fair Shares

The last ethic synthesises the first two. It acknowledges that we only have one earth and we have to share it with all living things and future generations. There is no point in designing a sustainable family unit, community, or nation whilst others languish without clean water, clean air, food, shelter, meaningful employment, and social contact. Since the industrialised North uses the resources of at least three earths, and much of the global South languishes in poverty, Fair Shares is an acknowledgement of this terrible imbalance and a call to limit consumption (especially of natural resources) in the North. Permaculture fundamentally rejects the industrial growth model at the core of its ethics, and aspires to design fairer, more equitable systems that take into account the limits of the planet's resources and the needs of all living beings.

The fertile edge of the river bank.

Whilst these permaculture ethics are more like moral values or codes of behaviour, they are not enough on their own. We need the principles of permaculture to provide a set of universally applicable guidelines that can be used in designing sustainable systems. Otherwise, permaculture becomes merely a lifestyle choice within an existing unsustainable system. These principles can be inherent in any permaculture design, in any climate, and on any scale. They have been derived from the thoughtful observation of nature, and from earlier work by ecologists, landscape designers and environmental science.

Each principle can be thought of as a door that opens into a whole system of thinking, providing a different perspective that can be understood at varying levels of depth and application. David Holmgren, the co-originator of permaculture, redefined permaculture principles in his seminal book, *Permaculture – Principles and Pathways Beyond Sustainability*.[2]

When I started giving talks about permaculture to all sorts of different audiences, I decided to write my own explanations and apply the principle not only to designing gardens and farms but to business, society and culture. Every principle comes with David's 'proverb' and is followed by my explanation.

Observe & Interact

This element of stillness and observation forms the key of permaculture design. In a world of 'fast' everything, having the capacity to observe the seasons, watch the changing microclimates on a patch of land, understand how the patterns of wind, weather and slope affect the frost pockets and plant growth, is an opportunity to begin to learn the deeper aspects of Earth Care. It also makes us more capable of making wise decisions about how we design or eco-renovate our houses and plan our gardens and farms.

Catch & Store Energy

Intimately connected to observation is the art of capturing energy in a design – so that we minimise the need to seek resources from the outside. In a garden this is about avoiding planting tender seedlings in frost pockets in spring or maximising solar gain by siting a greenhouse/ conservatory on the south side of a building so that we can both extend the season and heat a house with passive solar gain. We are attempting to capture water, sunlight, heat, soil, biomass and fertility whenever we can in order to become more self-resilient.

Obtain a Yield

Food can account for as much as one third of our ecological footprint so it makes sense to grow as much as we can, even if this is limited to tasty sprouted grains on the windowsill of a flat. So a permaculture garden is by default an edible landscape with good floral companions to attract beneficial insects, and a building is a potential heat store and structure for solar panels. But the concept of 'yields' is not merely about renewable energy or veggies; a yield can be about social capital; people positively changing their lives, building community and reducing their carbon.

Apply Self-regulation & Accept Feedback

When we burn fossil fuels we release CO_2 into the atmosphere, trapping heat and increasing temperatures. This causes ice to melt which leads to loss of reflective surfaces, leading to more absorption of sunlight and even higher temperatures. We must accept responsibility for our actions.

Use & Value Renewable Resources & Services

Whenever possible, permaculture seeks to use resources that can be renewed. This naturally applies to energy but also to ecological building, coppicing, soil conservation, and the planting of perennial food crops, as well as annuals with seed saving. The danger of relying on non-renewables, technological fixes and speculative money are becoming ever more evident.

Produce No Waste

In the UK, we throw away the equivalent of 24 bags of sugar per household per week: 14.1 kg. That's 29 million tonnes (55% of that is household) per year. I have a favourite saying that the landfill of today will be the 'mine' of tomorrow.

Design from Patterns to Details

When Tim Harland and I designed our house and garden, we read up on permaculture design, forest gardening, renewable energy, eco-architecture and eco-renovation as much as we could. We spent a year observing the land before we started planting and planned how best to make our house a happy, energy efficient place to live in. We observed the seasons, the climatic variations, the weather, the soil patterns, slope and our own human activities on the site as a family. In other words, we started off looking at the bigger picture – the pattern of what sustainable living might be – with examples from other places, and then we refined our exploration into the detail appropriate for our particular site. We didn't make a 'shopping list' of individual items or projects and try to mesh them together in a hotchpotch of what might be regarded as 'green'.

Integrate rather than Segregate

We have a cultural tendency to separate veggie gardens from flower gardens and use hard edges to design our spaces. Companion gardeners will know however that the more integrated the orchard is with the wildflower meadow, or the vegetables are with flowers frequented by beneficial insects, the less pests will prevail. The same is true for people. Cultural diversity yields a robust and fertile culture, whereas a rigid monoculture of politics and religion can bring sterility, even social and political repression.

Use Small & Slow Solutions

Our society currently depends on vast inputs of fossil fuels, whilst our biosphere is over-loaded by their outputs. The more accessible and fixable our technology and chains of supply are, the more robust the system. This principle speaks of hand tools, of appropriate technology that can easily be fixed, and of relocalisation. Currently we have a three day 'just in time' supply chain of supermarkets. If the fuel supply is interrupted, the super-market shelves will empty at an alarming rate. Better to build resilience into our systems by relocalising our essential needs as much as possible and having technological alternatives that we can fix.

Use & Value Diversity

Biodiversity creates healthy ecosystems. Diversity in terms of crops, energy sources, and employment, make for greater sustainability. Valuing diversity amongst people makes for a more peaceful, equitable society. Conflict and wars are the biggest slayers of sustainable development.

Use Edges & Value the Marginal

Examples of 'edge' in nature are: where canopy meets clearing in the woodland, inviting in air and sunshine and a profusion of flowers; where sea and river meet land in the fertile interface of estuaries, full of invertebrates, fish and bird life; where the banks of streams meet the water's edge and fertility is built with deposited mud and sand in flood time, giving life to a riot of plant life; where plains and water meet, flooding and capturing alluvial soils... Edge in nature is all about increasing diversity by the increase of inter-relationship between the elements: earth, air, fire (sun), and water. This phenomenon increases the opportunity for life in all of its marvellous fertility of forms.

   In human society, edge is where we have cultural diversity. It is the place where free thinkers and so-called 'alternative' people thrive, where new ideas are allowed to develop and ageless wisdom is given its rightful respect. Edge is suppressed in non-democratic states and countries that demand theological allegiance to one religion.

Creatively Use & Respond to Change

In nature, there is a process of succession. Bare soil is colonised by weeds that are in turn superseded by brambles. Then pioneers follow, like silver birch, alder and gorse which stabilise the soil in temperate climes. The latter two even fix nitrogen to create an environment that can host slow growing temperate climate species like oak, beech and yew. But nature is dynamic and succession can be interrupted by browsing animals, storms that fell trees and create clearings or a changing climate that is less hospitable for certain climax giants like oak and beech. The challenge of a permaculture designer is to understand how all these factors interact with each other in a landscape or on a particular plot of land, and design accordingly. It is no good restoring coppice without fencing out deer, or planting trees if they will shade out the solar panel in a decade's time.

Equally well, we need to appreciate how climate change will affect our agriculture, with higher summer temperatures, greater volumes of rain in winter and springtime, and more violent storms with higher wind speeds. Hotter summers may allow more vineyards on the gentle southern slopes of the English chalk downland. They may also make English oaks less viable in the south. What then do we plant and how do we design in resilience to our settlements? One example is to plant more shelterbelts for farmland as well as housing estates and forgo building on floodplains.

Hand Spiral.

The principle is deeper than this, however. It invites us to imagine a future world, a world without cheap oil, and a world that necessarily radically reduces its carbon load in the atmosphere. By doing this, we take the first steps towards creating it. We stand on the bedrock of permaculture ethics – Earth Care, People Care and Fair Shares – and are empowered by a set of principles that can inform our planning and actions.

Notes

1 www.communitysolution.org/cuba.html
2 *Permaculture – Principles and Pathways Beyond Sustainability* by David Holmgren, published by Permanent Publications, 2010.

Maddy Harland is the co-founder and editor of Permaculture Magazine **www.permaculture.co.uk** and Permanent Publications **www.permanent-publications.co.uk** She co-founded The Sustainability Centre in Hampshire in 1995, a recycled naval base on 55 acres of the South Downs, now a thriving education centre and community. Maddy is also a founder of Gaia Education. In 2008, Tim and Maddy's company won The Queen's Award for Enterprise for their 'unfettered dedication to promoting sustainability internationally'.

Sean Esbjörn-Hargens and Michael Zimmerman team up to offer here a 'multi-perspectival' approach to ecological design. Integral Ecology is derived from Ken Wilber's Integral Theory; as such, it uses the Four Quadrants to define four separate yet inter-related perspectives from which to view a design challenge: objective, interobjective, subjective, and intersubjective. The authors argue that all too often only one of these perspectives may be used to justify a given solution, which makes that solution inherently incomplete or one-sided. What is needed is understanding the problem from all four quadrants. This parallels perfectly the organization of the EDE curriculum into four dimensions.

Integral Ecology:
Design Principles for Sustainable
Human Habitats

Sean Esbjörn-Hargens Ph.D. and
Michael E. Zimmerman Ph.D. – Integral Institute, Colorado, USA

Introduction

Since its inception in 1866, with Ernst Haeckel's publication of *General Morphology of Organisms,* the field of ecology has multiplied, divided, and morphed into numerous schools and sub-schools. Each such school is an attempt to capture something not included by other approaches. Every knowledge niche seems to have a corresponding school of ecology connecting its insights to the understanding of ecological processes and environmental dynamics. With the emergence of new schools of ecology, as with most disciplines, there is a tendency for the nascent approach – the 'new kid on the block' – to define itself against existing approaches in order to justify its particular position. All too often, fences are built between approaches where bridges are needed, and some approaches pair up with each other to discredit other seemingly misguided approaches. The net result is a fragmented field of various approaches either pitted against each other or in alliance through protective politics.

So what is someone concerned about the environment to do when confronted with the magnitude of variety that currently exists within the field of ecology and environmental studies? How is an activist, scientist, or philosopher expected to be effective in the face of such multiplicity? No wonder the world of ecology is in such disarray – it has grown so big that it no longer knows itself. For instance, all too often practitioners of *landscape ecology* have never heard of *environmental aesthetics*; *environmental philosophers* do not know the difference between *population ecology* and *community ecology*; individuals working in the field of *acoustic ecology* do not know about *linguistic ecology*.

Today there is a bewildering diversity of views on ecology and the environment. With more than 200 distinct and valuable perspectives on the natural world – and with researchers, economists, ethicists, psychologists, and others often taking completely different stances on the issues – how can we come to agreement to solve the toughest environmental problems of the 21st century? We need a framework to help sort through these many approaches and connect them in a pragmatic way that honors their unique insights on their own terms. Integral Ecology provides this framework: a way of integrating multiple approaches to ecology and environmental studies into a complex, multidimensional, meta-disciplinary approach to the natural world and our embeddedness within it. Integral Ecology unites valuable insights from multiple perspectives into a comprehensive theoretical framework, one that is already being put to use around the globe. This framework is the result of over a decade of research exploring the many perspectives on ecology available to us today and their respective methodologies. In short, this framework provides a way of understanding the relationship between *who* is perceiving nature, *how* the perceiver uses different methods, techniques, and practices to disclose nature, and *what* is perceived as nature.

Integral Ecology is a comprehensive framework for characterizing ecological dynamics and resolving environmental problems. It is comprehensive in that it both draws upon and provides a theoretical scheme for showing the relations among a variety of different methods, including those at work in the natural and social sciences, as well as in the arts and humanities. Integral Ecology unites, coordinates, and mutually enriches knowledge generated from different major disciplines and approaches. Integral Ecology can be: a) applied within a discipline (e.g., by integrating various schools of ecology); b) applied as a *multi*disciplinary approach (e.g., by investigating ecological problems from several disciplines); c) applied as an *inter*disciplinary approach (e.g. by using social science methods to shed light on economic or political aspects of environmental values); and d) applied as a *trans*disciplinary approach (e.g. by helping numerous approaches and their methodologies interface through a well grounded meta-framework).

The Integral Ecology framework has promising applications in many areas: outdoor schools, urban planning, wilderness trips, policy development, restoration projects, environmental impact assessments, green business, village design and community development to name a few. In fact, a wide variety of ecologists, environmentalists, urban planners, wilderness guides, and activists recognize the theoretical comprehensiveness and practical efficacy of Integral Ecology and have been using its principles and distinctions successfully in a variety of contexts: community development in El Salvador, marine fisheries in Hawaii, eco-activism in British Columbia, climate change initiatives in Norway, permaculture in Australia, environmental policy in Tasmania, sustainable consumption and waste reduction in Calgary, and urban design in Manitoba.[1] In this article we will be focusing on how aspects of this framework can be used for design initiatives. But first let us introduce one of the key conceptual lens involved with integral ecology and design.

The Four Quadrants

The Integral Ecology framework draws on integral theory as developed by American philosopher Ken Wilber.[2] Integral theory provides a content-neutral framework – the AQAL model – that has been developed over 30 years and is being used in over 35 professional disciplines (e.g., economics, law, medicine, art, religious studies, psychology, and education). According to integral theory, there are at least four irreducible perspectives (objective, interobjective, subjective, and intersubjective) that must be consulted when attempting to understand and remedy environmental problems. These perspectives are represented by four quadrants: the interior and exterior of individual and collective realities. These four quadrants represent the intentional ('I'), cultural ('we'), behavioral ('it'), and social ('its') aspects of ecological issues.

The Four Quadrants of the Integral Theory framework.

	INTERIOR	EXTERIOR
INDIVIDUAL	**UPPER LEFT** I Intentional (subjective)	**UPPER RIGHT** IT Behavioral (objective)
COLLECTIVE	WE Cultural (intersubjective) **LOWER LEFT**	ITS Social (interobjective) **LOWER RIGHT**

Put briefly, the *objective* perspective examines the composition (e.g., physiological and chemical) and exterior behavior of individuals such as humans, bears, salmon, redwoods, or beetles. The *interobjective* perspective examines the systemic structures and exterior behaviors of collectives, ranging from human socio-economic systems to ecosystems. Data generated by methods belonging to objective and interobjective perspectives are valuable, but they neither provide an exhaustive understanding of the problem at hand nor do they necessarily provide motivation for action. Technical information alone cannot persuade people to act. Motivation arises when we experience a given environmental problem through two additional perspectives – *subjective* and *intersubjective*. Academic and public environmental efforts only infrequently approach problems with awareness or appreciation of the role played by these interior perspectives, including aesthetic experience, psychological dynamics, religious meaning, ethical issues, and cultural values.

Integral Ecology labels these four irreducible perspectives as follows: *terrain of experience* (first-person subjectivity), *terrain of culture* (second-person intersubjectivity), *terrain of behavior* (third-person objectivity), and *terrain of systems* (third-person interobjectivity). In other words, Integral Ecology recognizes and draws on first-, second-, and third-person perspectives. The perspectives are irreducible because, for example, a first-person perspective contains important aspects of a situation that are not captured or represented by a third-person perspective. When I say, "I feel devastated as I look at this polluted stream," I am speaking from a first-person perspective. The perspective informing my assertion cannot simply be replaced by a third-person perspective, which would issue forth a statement such as: "That person sees the polluted stream." There is quite a difference between simply 'seeing' the polluted stream and 'feeling devastated' by it. Likewise, the second-person significance of a multi-stakeholder gathering, which brings together culturally divergent and even contentious worldviews, cannot be equated with the third-person function that the meeting may have in socio-economic terms. Each of these terrains highlights a different and essential aspect of reality and are known through different types of methodologies and practices.

The Four Terrains.

INTERIOR   EXTERIOR

Terrain of Experiences   **Terrain of Behaviors**

The subjective realities   The objective realities
of any being at all levels   of any being at all levels
of its perception.   of its organization.

Known by Felt-Experience   *Known by Observation*

I | IT

WE | ITS

Terrain of Cultures   **Terrain of Systems**

The intersubjective realities   The interobjective realities
of any being at all levels   of any being at all levels
of its communion.   of its intersection.

Known by Mutual Resonance   *Known by Systemic Analysis*

INDIVIDUAL

COLLECTIVE

These four perspectives are often used to *look at* an environmental problem or ecological reality, either informally or through formal disciplinary traditions. Following is a simple example of an Integral approach to design provided by the work of Mark DeKay and his colleagues. This section briefly examines some of the principles at play within each of these terrains and the kinds of perspectives that would be included in looking at and addressing a design issue.

Principles of Integral Ecological Design

Mark DeKay is an Associate Professor in the College of Architecture and Design at the University of Tennessee in Knoxville.[1] He has been a leading figure in the emerging new field of Integral Ecological Design.[2] DeKay has been applying integral principles to a variety of design contexts for many years. For example, he recently co-authored a paper with fellow architect Mary Guzowski that presents "A Model for Integral Sustainable Design Explored through Daylighting," for the 2006 American Solar Energy Society Conference (ASES). After presenting an overview of Integral Theory, this article discusses Integral Ecology's four terrains and applies them to sustainable design by asking, "From an integral sustainability perspective, how shall we shape form?".[3]

From the perspective of behaviors, (UR), the design question is, "How shall we shape form to maximize performance?" In this terrain, good form minimizes resource consumption and pollution while maximizing preservation and recycling. From the perspective of systems, (LR), the design question is, "How shall we shape form to guide flow?" In this terrain, good form solves for ecological pattern by creating structure in the built environment that best accommodates ecological process through mimicry of and fitness to the context of natural ecosystems. From the perspective of cultures, (LL), the design question is, "How shall we shape form to manifest meaning?" In this terrain, good form reveals and expresses 'the patterns that connect' in ways that celebrate the beauty of natural order, place inhabitants into relationship with living systems (or the idea of nature), and situate human habitation in bioregional place. From the perspective of experiences, (UL), the design question is, "How shall we shape form to engender experience?" In this terrain, good form orchestrates rich human experiences and creates centering places conducive to self-aware transformation, in which we can become most authentically who we are. Summarizing this in a table (see below), they explain that "This expanded multi-perspectival view can enable designers to more comprehensively address the complexity of today's ecological challenges by including the individual, cultural, and social dimensions that contribute to the creation of a sustainable world".[4]

Building on the "The Four Terrains of Sustainable Design," DeKay and Guzowski present the "Twelve Niches of Daylighting" to illustrate how they "could integrally-inform sustainable design thinking, allowing a designer to move beyond objective physical performance to also consider

	INTERIOR	EXTERIOR
INDIVIDUAL	**TERRAIN OF EXPERIENCES** Shape form to ENGENDER EXPERIENCE • Environmental Phenomenology • Experience of natural cycles, processes, forces • Green design aesthetics	**TERRAIN OF BEHAVIORS** Shape form to MAXIMIZE PERFORMANCE • Energy, water, materials efficiency • Zero energy & emissions buildings • LEED rating system • High performance buildings
COLLECTIVE	**TERRAIN OF CULTURES** Shape form to MANIFEST MEANING • Relationships to Nature • Green design ethics • Green building cultures • Myths & rituals	**TERRAIN OF SYSTEMS** Shape form to GUIDE FLOW • Fitness to site & content • Buildings as ecosystems • Living buildings

The four terrains of sustainable design.

rich experiential, ethical, moral, and social implications of light".[5] After presenting an overview of the Twelve Niches of Daylighting (see figure below) they apply them to daylighting at the United Theological Seminary's Bigelow Chapel in New Brighton, Minnesota.

DeKay is also using integral design principles to guide the Beaver Creek Watershed Green Infrastructure Plan.[6] This project is connected to the Green Vision Studio at the University of Tennessee's College of Architecture and Design. DeKay and his colleague, Tracy Moir-McClean, are the principle investigators. The project is a visionary exercise with the goal of creating a document that can be used by various individuals and institutions to support their decision making process around issues of preservation, conservation, and land use development. According to DeKay, "This is probably the most integrally-informed project we have. Our use of integral theory and integral ecology shows up in various places in the language of the report and in the issues we chose to address and the methods we used to address them. While the integral model is not overt it nevertheless is the guiding framework."[7] While the details of the project extend beyond the scope of this article, the following quadrant chart provides good overview of how DeKay and his colleagues are using the Integral Model in the context of this project:

Conclusion

In summary, there are numerous approaches to the environment and ecological design: philosophical, spiritual, religious, social, political, cultural, behavioral, scientific, and psychological. Each highlights an essential

*The Four Quadrants
and Twelve Niches of
Daylighting.*

INTERIOR   EXTERIOR

TERRAIN OF EXPERIENCES

[L3] Pneuma: *Spiritual Realization*
- Experience of subtle or spiritual aspects of light
- Mystical light & enlightenment
- Experiencing Inner Light

[L2] Psyche: *Psychological Dynamics*
- Environmental psychology of light
- Phenomenology of light
- Aesthetics, beauty, poetics of light

[L1] Soma: *Body Feelings*
- Physical sensations of sunlight and daylight
- Archetypal responses (diurnal, seasonal)
- Experiences of delight, comfort, health & well-being

TERRAIN OF BEHAVIORS

[L3] Skillful-means: *Effective Actions*
- Models for sustainable action
- Designing healing environments
- Building transfiguration (alchemy of light)

[L2] Action: *Intentional Conduct*
- Dynamics modeling & simulation (quantitative & qualitative)
- Technological systems, constructions, codes
- Architectonic systems & spatial order with light

[L1] Movement: *Physical Behaviors*
- Physics of light in buildings
- Biology of vision
- Physiological response to light and visual comfort

INDIVIDUAL

Upper Left (UL)   **I**   **IT**   Upper Right (UR)

Lower Left (LL)   **WE**   **ITS**   Lower Right (LR)

COLLECTIVE

TERRAIN OF CULTURES

[L3] Commonwealth:
Compassionate Perspectives
- Perspectives on nature
- Cosmology & light
- Spiritual / religious symbolism and interpretation

[L2] Community: *Shared Horizons*
- Values for daylight & conservation
- Ethics of light (right-to-light, and healthy places)
- Building cultures & pattern languages of daylight

[L1] Communion: *Shared Cultural Practices*
- Daylight savings time
- Rituals of light (celebrations, seasonal holidays, lighting candles, sunsets, bonfires)
- Meaning of characteristics of light and dark (positive & negative)

TERRAIN OF SYSTEMS

[L3] Matrices: *Subtle Systems*
- Effect of light on subtle energy patterns
- Color properties of Inner Light
- Alexander's Field of Centers

[L2] Institutions: *Social Systems*
- Urban planning for light access, politics
- Education, building & energy codes
- Social activity patterns (work schedules, programming, etc.)

[L1] Interaction: *Natural Systems*
- Ecological impacts and fitness of architectural daylight
- Bioregional & contextual response
- Complex building systems integration

component, but too often remains silent concerning other important dimensions. To overcome this fragmentation, Integral Ecology provides a way of weaving all approaches into an environmental tapestry, an 'ecology of ecologies' that honors not just the physical ecology of systems and behaviors, but includes the cultural and intentional aspects as well – at all levels of organization. Thus, integral ecology is the study of the four terrains of the natural world at different levels of complexity. In addition, Integral Ecology takes into account the multiple worldviews within individuals, communities, and cultures, and their accompanying environmental perspectives – each with its specific forms of mutual understanding. Furthermore, Integral Ecology highlights that the environment and its various aspects are revealed differently depending on the

Green Infrastructure in The Four Quadrants.

INTERIOR   EXTERIOR

UL: EXPERIENCE **Individual-Interior: Self and Consciousness** The invisible subjective interior reality of an individual **Intention:** Rich, full-sensory experiences. Facilitate individual development to higher levels of ecological self. Provide opportunities to relate to nature at each level. **Areas Addressed:** Human experience of landscapes, ecological education, ecological aesthetics, landscape and urban aesthetics, environmental psychology, personal identity, 1st-person phenomenology. **Tools:** Integral aesthetic awareness of the designer, role-taking, design for nearby nature, access to natural recreation, visual impact assessment, view-shed analysis, environmental education, and educational landscapes.	**UR: BEHAVIOR** **Individual-Exterior: Organism and Part** The visible, objective, external reality of an individual **Intention:** Settle the land with minimum impact and maximum health. Conserve resources and reduce flows to environmental sinks. **Areas Addressed:** Resource conservation and efficiency, reducing water and air pollution, habitat conservation, farmland, wetland, and forest preservation. **Tools:** Best Management Practices (BMPs), ecological monitoring, performance standards such as TMDL, conventional engineering, flood zones, stream buffers, slope protection rules, conservation easements, NRCS techniques, urban forestry.
LL: CULTURE **Collective-Interior: Meaning and Worldviews** The invisible, intersubjective, internal realities of groups **Intention:** Come to agreement on how to design and live with nature. Manifest rich symbolic human-ecological relationships. **Areas Addressed:** Civic dialogue, fitness to cultural context, cultural regionalism, sense of place, Genius Loci, historical and cultural landscapes, collective values, meaning of form languages, ideas of and relationships to nature(s). **Tools:** Charettes, community visioning, public input processes. Pattern Languages of the building culture, multiple intelligence communication, visual preference surveys, symbolic design languages, civic design, urban design with nature for community identity, shared knowledge bases.	**LR: SYSTEMS** **Collective-Exterior: Social Systems and Environment** The visible, interobjective, external realities of groups **Intention:** Fit settlement pattern to natural pattern using principles of ecological order Making cities work like nature. **Areas Addressed:** Bio-regionalism, spatial pattern of habitat, ecological restoration, greenway and park networks, ground-surface water system, pedestrian-bicycle networks, building-transit-open space patterns. **Tools:** GIS landscape analysis, urban design, zoning, including special historic, cultural and environmental overlays, comprehensive planning, site review processes, design guidelines, development and building codes. Pattern Languages, land trusts, parks foundations, Low Impact Development (LID), Smart Growth, ecological engineering, science of landscape ecology, contextual thinking, network thinking.

INDIVIDUAL — COLLECTIVE

I / IT — WE / ITS

mode of inquiry or methodology used to investigate it. As a result, Integral Ecology identifies eight methodological families that need to be utilized, on their own terms, for comprehensive knowledge of any given ecological reality. In short, Integral Ecology recognizes that different approaches to ecology and the environment are the result of a spectrum of perspectives ('the who') using a variety of methods ('the how') to explore different aspects of the four terrains of nature ('the what').

Only by becoming increasingly aware of the who, how, and what of environmental issues can we truly integrate the multiple voices calling for a more just and ecologically friendly world. Only in such a world is there the capacity to generate sustainable solutions to complex multidimensional problems, and only in such a world are all the notes of nature's song sung. Integral Ecology is committed to the complexity and multidimensionality of this world in its entire mysterious splendor. Integral Ecology supports us in becoming increasingly reflective of *what* we are looking at, *who* we are as we are doing the looking, and *how* are we looking at it. By becoming deeply reflective individuals, we can hope to reach effectively across the divides that separate us, and foster mutual understanding in service of our blue-green planet.

People who use the Integral Ecology framework recognize that it is not enough to integrate ecosystems and social systems (e.g. economies, laws, education). Nor is it enough to also include objective realities (e.g. behavioral studies, laboratory testing, empirical analysis). Instead, what is needed is to integrate these interobjective and objective realities with subjective (e.g. psychology, art, phenomenology) and intersubjective (e.g. religion, ethics, philosophy) realities. In effect, Integral Ecology unites consciousness, culture, and nature in service of sustainability.

It is our hope that Integral Ecology supports a new kind of ecology – an ecology of perspectives – one that is informed by the strengths of many approaches and methods while at the same time exposing the limits and blind spots of any single approach. Integral Ecology provides one of the most sophisticated applications and extensions of integral theory available today, and as such it serves as a template for any truly integral effort, especially integral design.

References

1 For additional examples, see the seven case studies edited by Sean in a special double issue of *World Futures* and the two dozen examples presented in chapter 11 of our book, *Integral Ecology: Uniting Multiple Perspectives on the Natural World* (2009).
2 Ken Wilber has published over 20 books since 1977 (nearly 10,000 pages of content). Most of this content is found in his *Collected Works* (1999-2000). For an overview of Wilber's philosophy, see Frank Visser's book *Ken Wilber: Thought as Passion* (2003).
3 For a description of all 200 perspectives, see the appendix in our book, *Integral Ecology: Uniting Multiple Perspectives on the Natural World* (2009).
4 *Ibid.*
5 *Ibid*, 4. Note the third level in the presentation of the twelve niches is based on an earlier version than the one presented in the book.
6 For an overview of the project see http://www.knoxvilleparkway.com/bcgitdot.pdf
7 DeKay, personal communication, 7 July 2006.

DeKay, Mark. "Integral Sustainable Design: Re-Integrating What Modernism Differentiated and Post-Modernism Dissociated." *Society of Building Science Educators*. http://www.sbseretreat.lsu.edu/theme.html.
DeKay, Mark, and Mary Guzowski. 2006. "A Model for Integral Sustainable Design Explored through Daylighting." Presented at the American Solar Energy Society Conference, Denver, CO, July 7-13.
Esbjörn-Hargens, Sean, Ed. (2005). Integral Ecology. *World Futures: The Journal of General Evolution, 61,* (1-2).
Esbjörn-Hargens, Sean, & Zimmerman, Michael E. (2009). *Integral ecology: Uniting multiple perspectives on the natural world.* New York: Random House/Integral Books.
Visser, Frank. (2003). *Ken Wilber: Thought as passion.* Albany, NY: SUNY Press.
Wilber, Ken. (1995). *Sex, ecology, spirituality: The spirit of evolution.* Boston, MA: Shambhala.
Wilber, Ken. (1999-2000). *The collected works of Ken Wilber.* Boston, MA: Shambhala.
Wilber, Ken. (2006). Integral Methodological Pluralism. In: *Integral spirituality: A startling new role for religion in the modern and postmodern world.* Boston, MA: Shambhala.

Zimmerman, Michael. (2009). Interiority regained: Integral ecology and environmental ethics. In Donald K. Swearer, Ed., *Ecology and the environment: Perspectives from the humanities* (pp. 65 88). Cambridge, MA: Harvard University Press.

SEAN ESBJÖRN-HARGENS, Ph.D., is associate professor and founding chair of the Department of Integral Theory at John F. Kennedy University in Pleasant Hill, California. A prominent scholar-practitioner in integral theory, he is the founder and executive editor of the *Journal of Integral Theory and Practice* and founding director of the Integral Research Center. He has published extensively on the applications of the integral model in a variety of areas. He is a practitioner within Tibetan Buddhism and the Diamond Approach and lives in Sebastopol, California, on five acres of redwoods with his wife and two daughters. Sean is an integral coach and consultant through Rhizome Designs (**www.rhizomedesigns.org**).

MICHAEL E. ZIMMERMAN, Ph.D., is Director of the Center for Humanities and the Arts, Professor of Philosophy, and a member of Environmental Studies faculty at the University of Colorado, Boulder. He has published nearly 100 scholarly articles and book chapters, and he is the author of four books, including *Integral Ecology: Uniting Multiple Perspectives on the Natural World* (Integral Books, 2009), which he co-authored with Sean Esbjörn-Hargens. Prior to relocating to Boulder in 2006, Zimmerman was co-director of the Environmental Studies program at Tulane University for 10 years.

Everybody knows the permaculture strategy of closely observing a site for a year before beginning the design process. Robyn Francis demonstrates this with the immense value of working as an international permaculture teacher for 40 years before writing a knowledgeable synopsis of integrated design. It's all here: the proper attitude and mindset, the diverse array of considerations, the strategy for putting it all together. Most importantly, Robyn introduces her Eco-Social Matrix methodology, a tool for integrating natural, social, and services catchments into a comprehensive design. While the Eco-Social Matrix can be applied at any scale, it is especially useful for evaluating the catchments of a village scale community.

Macro to Micro: Introducing EcoSocial Matrix as a Tool for Integrated Design

Robyn Francis – Djanbung Gardens, Nimbin, Australia

Overview

I've always striven to achieve what I term an wholistic lifestyle, living in an environment that seamlessly integrates all aspects of my life: social, work, living, personal, community, creative, spiritual, productive and so on. I have consciously used the original English word, 'wholistic', spelt with a 'w', rather than the American-influenced spelling, 'holistic'. Wholistic is derived from 'whole', a state of completion, all encompassing, whereas a 'hole' to my mind infers something still missing, an emptiness waiting to be filled.

In my travels and work with traditional and indigenous societies over four decades, I've been intrigued by how the boundaries between work and play, material and spiritual, function and productivity, individual and community are blurred – how they integrate seamlessly into everyday life. Our contemporary society is quite fractured or dis-integrated in comparison, to the extent that many of these aspects of life are perceived as almost irreconcilable opposites. Through over-specialisation we have separated out and effectively 'mono-cultured' most aspects of society and living, not just our agriculture and land-use systems.

What is integrated design? What are we bringing together? What factors are we integrating? Permaculture Design inherently seeks to develop integrated systems, which can be overwhelming for the beginner as the array of factors and elements to consider very quickly build into a rather complex web of relationships. We can integrate on many different levels, from micro to macro, from details in the design and management through to the bigger picture context.

Most permaculturists are comfortable with integrated design on the individual garden or property level, and this in itself can take several years of observation, research, creative thinking, experimentation and design. Integrated design demands an interdisciplinary approach and systems thinking. One needs to know enough about a lot of different things to see where and how they can interact beneficially.

Permaculture Design methodologies inherently support an integrated approach. Like Sector Planning, which is primarily concerned with harnessing and/or ameliorating the energies of elemental forces of sun, wind and fire; working with the geophysical landform in terms of topography, slope, gradient and soil; plus the diverse interactions and patterning of elemental energies within the landscape in terms of aspect and the mosaics of soil qualities, vegetation and microclimate arising from these interplays.

Then there's the patterning of elements and functions within the site, designing a complex web of beneficial inter-relationships between the various physical elements – plants, structures, animals, technologies – ensuring needs are met in a diversity of ways. Integrating the invisible flows of nutrient cycles and energy, and the movement of water through the system, closing the loops and ensuring no pollution also must be considered. Then, patterning and assembling all these systems and individual components in the design for efficient management through conscious relative placement that integrates the time-space logistics of access, schedules and proximity – this is design for convenience. The Permaculture Design methodology useful in this phase of integration is often referred to as Zonation.

Integrated systems go beyond the design and into the management and maintenance of systems, right down to the daily interactions. I often find students wanting to separate jobs out in rosters: one person to do the garden, another the animals, another the orchards and so on. But the system is designed to integrate these daily actions. Animal green feed is collected by doing five minutes of weeding in the garden; thus through the process of collecting green feed for the animals the garden is maintained, so we don't need to spend a lot of time just simply weeding as a single purpose exercise. Tending the animals is integral to maintaining the plant production systems and visa versa – separate these jobs out and it's not long before management systems begin to collapse.

There are countless excellent permaculture designs within the confines of individual property boundaries, integrating physical elements such as buildings, plants, animals, technology and water systems with energy flows and human interaction. However, many fall short in terms of their integration with neighbours or with the wider landscape and community. A truly integrated design needs to address these surrounding influences and interactions by designing the details within the context of the bigger picture. This lack of integration with neighbourhood and bioregion has also been true of much of the intentional community and ecovillage movement in Australia and the USA. Ultimately it is on this larger community scale that we, as a society, have the greatest capacity to develop self-reliance and resilience in these changing times, particularly in meeting the challenges of climate change and peak oil.

In Australia, there are big challenges with isolation and motor vehicle dependency, especially in sprawling suburbia, urban fringe and rural areas where public transport is virtually non-existent and people commute long distances to meet basic needs. I've been there myself, living for six years on a large property 36 km from the nearest small town and over 50 km from a regional centre. The realities of socio-economic isolation can be debilitating, not just for individual households but for many intentional communities.

A hallmark of a village as a form of human settlement is that it is *human* scale, within walking distance. I know of several self-titled ecovillages where residents need to commute several kilometres to the community centre and for up to five km within the community to visit friends who live at the opposite end of the property. Unfortunately, topography often doesn't make for easy cycling, and walking can be a challenge with large loads or toddlers in tow. So we find intentional communities where residents depend on vehicular transport to move around and function *within* the community, and then to access needs *beyond* the community can involve commutes of 20 to 50 km or more to a town or significant service centre.

I conducted a workshop once for an intentional rural community of 23 adults and numerous children. The community had been going for 15 years yet had only three completed houses. Most residents were living in caravans and sheds and surviving on social security payments. The atmosphere of poverty and powerlessness was debilitating. Half of their meager incomes were being used to keep their motor vehicles on the road so they could drive 50 km to the nearest supermarket mall to buy cheap food with the other half of their income. They couldn't afford fencing materials to protect gardens from wildlife so very little food was actually grown in the community. Over $55,000 a year was being spent on motor vehicles for fuel, oil, registration and essential repairs (Note: this amount does not include the initial cost of the vehicles or replacement value, just annual operating costs). At the time, early 1990s, $55,000 could build a modest house for an owner-builder. The equivalent value of a house a year was effectively going into greenhouse gas emissions and petrochemical company profits.

In the late 1980s, I began to seriously address these bigger-picture issues and developed a planning process for evaluating a property or settlement and its location in terms of access to human needs – bringing the principles of zonation (proximity, access and schedules) into bio-regional planning and community design. I later coined this process the Eco-Social Matrix (ESM).

ESM is a process of analysing the interplay of natural, social and services catchments of an area to explore the impact of land-use use decisions not only on the environment but on people's lives, how they access and meet their needs. The matrix can be applied to an individual

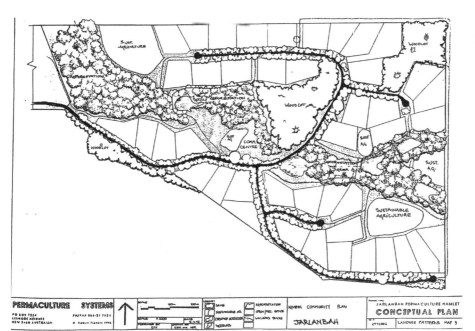

Jarlanbah concept plan.

property, neighbourhood, bioregion or larger scale. An ESM for a property is incomplete without the neighbourhood and bioregional context, so these scales of application nest within each other and interact with each other. It has proven to be an exceptionally useful tool for assessing the suitability of a location for a project, for local and regional strategic planning, human settlement design and bioregional development and has much to contribute to strategic approaches for re-localisation and Transition Town initiatives.

I employed this framework for designing Jarlanbah and for selecting land for my Permaculture Training Centre. My dream was to create a permaculture education centre with a living classroom of working systems – not in isolation, but somehow integrated with an ecovillage or hamlet development within close proximity (walking/cycling distance) from a well-serviced village or town centre, and with opportunities for interacting on a wider community level. The approach was also adopted by the New South Wales Department of Planning in the guidelines for Rural Residential Development where it was presented as a 'Catchment Planning Framework'.

The ESM Framework

The essence of the matrix is a series of overlays exploring the interplay of natural, social and servicing catchments. Of these, the Social catchment overlay is particularly significant as it most directly reveals the opportunities and challenges for people to meet their needs on a neighbourhood and bioregional level. The Social catchment analysis can also be useful for defining the physical boundaries of neighbourhoods and their relationship to different orders of human settlement in the immediate region or sub-catchment area.

Natural Catchment Overlay

This explores the biophysical characteristics and natural resources of the study area, including climate, geology, rock and soil types, mineral resources, water catchments and riparian systems, ecosystems, nature reserves, sensitive environments, biodiversity, wildlife corridors, land-use systems and capability, agricultural land, forestry, industries based on value-adding of local primary resources and production, and risk of natural hazards (fire, flood, etc.). This analysis also identifies regulatory bodies (local, regional, state and national), as well as professional and community organisations pertaining to the natural environment and resources.

This analysis is more than a simple inventory; it also evaluates the health of these systems, the sustainability and impacts of land use and management, threats and challenges, opportunities and thresholds. An example of thresholds might be water resources, including quality and availability, supply and demand, and relationship to factors identified in the Social and Services catchment overlays. It can support evaluating the potential for local food production and food security.

Social Catchment Overlay

Social catchments explore how people move around and congregate to satisfy material, social and cultural needs within an identifiable sense of community. Included are the historical context of settlement patterns and land-use, the relationship of people to their living environment and what contributes to their sense of place. Also included are demographics and demographic trends, socio-economic profiles and cultural and human diversity – including minority and special needs groups.

Material needs include access and proximity to shopping, commerce, education, employment, enterprise opportunities, specialist and professional services. Social and cultural elements include social meeting nodes, parks, open space, recreation facilities, entertainment, cultural events and facilities, community halls, community centres, as well as community groups and organisations.

The Social catchments overlay is useful in identifying the patterns and hierarchies of social nodes and settlement forms in the landscape and the layers of Social catchments for key functions, activities and themes. For example, to explore the theme of education in a bioregion, there will be all the primary school catchments, then the secondary school catchments which will encompass a number of primary schools, then local polytechnic/technical colleges which will have a much larger catchment than that encompassed by the catchments of a number of secondary schools.

Exploring the theme of shopping is a revealing activity, how far people need to travel to access essential needs and their commerce-related commuting habits. For example, my local village has a great little commercial centre of small local businesses: baker, butcher, organic shop, independent small supermarket with bulk foods, hardware, newsagent, bookstore, laundry,

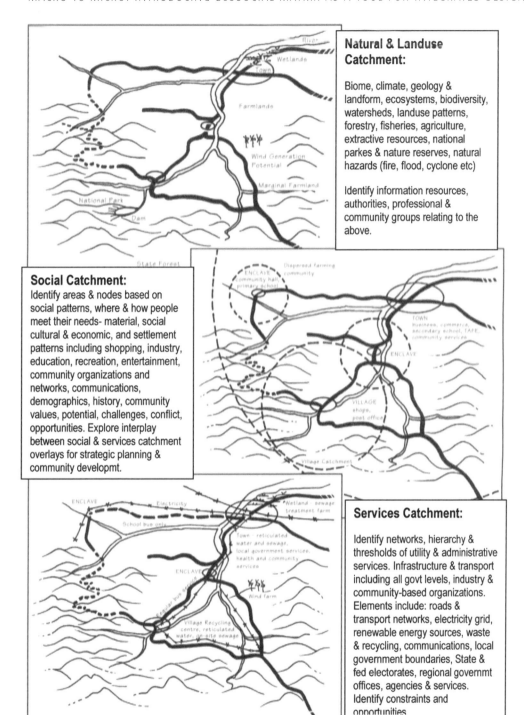

Natural & Landuse Catchment:

Biome, climate, geology & landform, ecosystems, biodiversity, watersheds, landuse patterns, forestry, fisheries, agriculture, extractive resources, national parkes & nature reserves, natural hazards (fire, flood, cyclone etc)

Identify information resources, authorities, professional & community groups relating to the above.

Social Catchment:

Identify areas & nodes based on social patterns, where & how people meet their needs- material, social cultural & economic, and settlement patterns including shopping, industry, education, recreation, entertainment, community organizations and networks, communications, demographics, history, community values, potential, challenges, conflict, opportunities. Explore interplay between social & services catchment overlays for strategic planning & community developmt.

Services Catchment:

Identify networks, hierarchy & thresholds of utility & administrative services. Infrastructure & transport including all govt levels, industry & community-based organizations. Elements include: roads & transport networks, electricity grid, renewable energy sources, waste & recycling, communications, local government boundaries, State & fed electorates, regional governmt offices, agencies & services. Identify constraints and opportunities.

ESM Catchment Overlays

Based on original diagram by Robyn Francis published in Permaculture Education PDC Handbook (Francis) and 'Rural Settlement Guidelines' – NSW Dept of Urban Affairs and Planning pharmacy, herbal apothecary, post office, local credit union banking facility – and lots of cafes! Nimbin also has a doctor's surgery, small hospital and other health services. I can comfortably cycle to meet most of my needs locally and need only do the 30 km commute to Lismore, my local provincial city, when I require specialist and higher order goods and services.

Friends living in the next valley, where there is only a small hamlet with a very small general store stocked mainly with junk food, a pub and a café, constantly need to commute over 20 km to Lismore to meet most of their basic needs. These are important things to consider when choosing where to live or to develop ecovillages or cohousing with their increased populations – what pressures will that increased population put on roads, on vehicular carbon footprints, on the economics of survival? On the other hand, the increased population of a community can present opportunities for viable small enterprise and provision of services. Is there sufficient population to support a bakery, a hairdresser, a food coop? Note that enterprise efforts often fail in intentional community and ecovillage developments due to insufficient Social catchment to support the business or service.

Social catchment analysis and community consultation processes can also reveal what circumstances take people out of the community. In 1983, Nimbin's village laundry burnt down. This had a major impact on the village economy as a whole as people commuted to Lismore to do their washing and consequently did their other shopping in Lismore. This resulted in an average 40% drop in trade turnover for most businesses in Nimbin village. When the new village laundry opened ten years later, local trade picked up substantially.

Services Catchment

Services catchments involve identifiable networks of utility, infrastructure, transport and administrative services from the community to the regional level, together with their hierarchies and thresholds. Examples of elements in a services catchment analysis include transport and mobility networks (pedestrian, cycle-ways, road, rail, air, sea/river, etc.); electrical grid and distribution, potential for co-generation, renewable energy resources and sites; waste management and recycling for solid waste, sewage and water; local government boundaries and precincts, higher government services and administration catchments; and other regulatory bodies and services.

An example of Services catchment in my own village is electricity. Most electricity for this region comes from dirty coal generators some 500 kilometers away. The substation that services this sub-catchment area provides data to monitor energy usage in the Nimbin Valley district. There are over 100 households on stand-alone solar or micro-hydro systems. Within the past two years, over 55 households have installed solar grid-feed, and now the community has received funding for a Community Solar Station which is currently installing solar arrays on the roofs of ten community-owned buildings in the village. When the community system is completed, our local Rainbow Power Company experts have calculated that on a sunny day over 75% of the sub-catchments' electricity will come from the sun.

Conclusion

Of course there are many further insights, perspectives and examples of ways the ESM analysis can be applied to integrated designs for individual properties, communities, villages and whole bioregions. Hopefully this short introduction will encourage designers to play with the ESM catchment overlays and use them as tools for integrated design to keep in mind the details in context with the bigger picture.

References

Rural Residential Development – A New Approach by Sustainable Futures Australia. Peter Cuming, Robyn Francis, etc al. NSW Department of Planning,1993.
Rural Settlement – Guidelines on Rural Settlement for the North Coast. [Based on the above study Rural Residential Development.] NSW Department of Urban Affairs and Planning, 1995. ISBN 0 7310 6223 X , 1995.
Ecovillage and Sustainable Settlement Design Course Handbook by Robyn Francis 1995, Revised 2002, 2006-7.
From Aquarius Dreaming to Nineties Reality – Nimbin's Coming of Age. Robyn Francis, 1996, IPC6 Conference Paper.
Jarlanbah Permaculture Hamlet was designed using a range of methodologies, including ESM, McHarg's exclusion process and insights gained from over 20 years involvement with the intentional community movement.

Robyn Francis, permaculture pioneer, educator, designer and innovator has been passionate about permaculture for over three decades. Founder of Permaculture International, Permaculture College Australia, editor of the *Permaculture International Journal*, designer of NSW's first ecovillage (Jarlanbah), and co-initiator of the Accredited Permaculture Training Center, she balances international work with direct action in her local community and bioregion. Since 1994 she is based at Djanbung Gardens, purpose-designed Permaculture Training Centre in the lush subtropics of NSW, Australia. Robyn is also a passionate gardener, gourd crafter, songwriter and composes luscious ambient music.
www.permaculture.com.au

Agroecology is yet another integrated way of looking at the Ecological dimension of ecovillage design. In this essay, Brasilian ecologist Diogo Alvim, after introducing the basic principles, defines agroecology as 'the investigation of the complex web of ecological interactions in any agricultural system, including those interactions between its economic, socio-political and cultural dimensions'. Once again, we witness that integrated ecological design is necessarily trans-disciplinary; the essence of ecovillage design itself is a strident moving-away from the reductionist paradigm. After reading this article, I'm sure you'll agree that Diogo's Terra Una project is an evolutionary interface between planned ecological diversity and spontaneous cultural regeneration.

Agroecology and Ecovillages

Diogo Alvim – Terra Una, Brasil

Presentation

In this article, we intend to reflect on what could be called the 'ecology of agriculture' and its relationship to an ecovillage approach to food production. The purpose of using ecology as the basis of agriculture is to demonstrate clearly that the process of food production and consumption is fundamentally an interface between species and their surrounding environment; or, in the case of the ecovillage, an interface between culture and nature.

The point here is to recollect that from a long-term evolutionary perspective, the process of producing and consuming food has always considered the necessary balance between energy stored and energy spent; not only that, each species has developed its own interface contact strategy for the purposes of maintaining life – and agriculture is one of our species' strategies for doing so.

From that perspective, we could say that each interface contact strategy is species-dependent, but that's not enough: No individual species can survive in isolation – its success ultimately depends on the beneficial interconnections it can make with other species. When we begin to understand the absolute necessity of these beneficial interconnections, then we start seeing the Web.

We are invited to realise that this Web is a pattern that supports life cycles, and energy cycling is a method that the evolutionary process has found to maintain itself and its constituent populations over time. That maintenance is a dynamic process; there are fluctuations, pulsing, ebbs and flows, discontinuous leaps, etc. However, just by the act of living, each individual of a species is taking part in the maintenance of the system as a whole – they cannot be considered in isolation. That is the Web we were born into, and these are the conditions where we experience being most alive.

This precedent was set on our planet Earth a long time ago.

The more we understand its 'mystery', the more we will be able to surrender ourselves to the emerging flows always moving through the system. The more we open our eyes to these flows, the more we will be able to see the underlying dysfunctions in the mechanical production of agriculture.

Our approach pays special attention to the evolutionary aspects of the ecology in productive agro-ecosystems. Any mode of agriculture will have its ecology, by definition, considering that ecology means

Having fun with a heliotrope.

essentially relationship and strategies of interaction. But those interactions take place on different scales: there are time, space and species-dependent considerations. As mentioned before, all these interactions are dynamic and no species can survive apart from a community. 'Community' here is understood as a group of populations interacting, and that is a useful metaphor for the 'ecovillage'.

Within an agro-ecological system we, as human beings, are always an active part of the total ecology, and our presence should be considered systemically. What this means is that we should be very conscious of the connections we are creating, judging whether each decision we make is enhancing or diminishing the long-term health of the system as a whole.

One could ask, "But from an evolutionary perspective, do we really have that much power? After all, life has been on planet Earth for 3.5 billion years". We wish to share the idea that the evolutionary process is taking place right here and now. From that perspective, each decision we make becomes vitally important; our persistence in either making or breaking beneficial connections can certainly influence planetary evolution.

Now, in order to understand how these principles may be applied, we want to present our experience of promoting resilience in agroecosystems at Terra UNA, our ecovillage project based in Minas Gerais State, Brasil.

Agroecology

What is agroecology? In this paper we share two definitions: agroecology can be defined as the study of the interactions between plants, animals, humans and the environment within agricultural systems. Agroecology can be seen as a discipline, therefore, which covers integrative studies within agronomy, ecology, sociology and economics.

We would combine these two definitions into a single conception, where agroecology can be seen as 'the investigation of the complex web of ecological interactions in any agricultural system, including those interactions between its economic, socio-political and cultural dimensions'.

Ecosystems and Agroecosystems

First of all, we could ask, "What is the difference between an ecosystem and an agro- ecosystem?" The main difference is our presence! An agroecosystem is a *managed* biological system created with human energy input – especially intelligence – with relationships selected to maximize food production over the long term. The Net Primary Production (NPP) of the original ecological base is then enhanced by the careful design of systems where high capacity photosynthetic conversion is possible, cyclically, by the plants selected and grown.

We shall understand that this 'photosynthesis' is a mysterious, seemingly magical, natural ability whereby sunlight-energy is transformed into edible living matter. There is a Chinese proverb which says, "Agriculture is the art of harvesting the Sun". That is why in an agroecosystem we tend to emphasize diverse poly-cultures, mixing together native species with domesticated varieties in an exuberant ecology.

The bio-technologists know that when we select a single characteristic and start to focus on its development, as the size or colour of a corn yield for example, we 'make' some other characteristic weaker. In other words, the evolutionary process generalizes across a broad spectrum; it has no place to perfect one characteristic at the expense of another. As we try to create a perfect species for our needs, by selecting a specific characteristic, we create vulnerability in another aspect. The sweeter the apple, for example, the more fragile it is to the herbivore; the larger the apple, the weaker it becomes in the immunology response.

So the difference between an ecosystem and an agroecosystem is, primarily, the human energy introduced to influence and focus direction – *by design*. Every ecosystem has its metabolism, which includes two main processes: 1) Energy Flow and 2) Nutrient Cycling. In operation, both processes are inextricably interconnected, so our dividing them here is for didactic purposes only. Both processes occur through the fundamental interaction between the biological community and its environment. In the first case we are talking about the food web and in the second case about the biogeochemical cycles.

These basic metabolic processes, and their consequences, can be considered as 'emerging properties' in the system. Emerging properties can be understood as the results of the interaction of existing properties in the system (agroecosystem in this case) that produce something not evident or possible in the initial properties alone. The energy flow, biogeochemical cycling, the resilience, the diversity, the ecological succession process – all are examples of emerging properties.

So, restoring and improving the ecology of agriculture, by reframing it as a process of working *with* nature rather than against, will result in enhanced metabolism within and among the elements we want to grow (plants) and raise (animals), thus resulting in healthier and more productive yields.

Applying Ecology in Agriculture

We've been trying to show that to restore the ecology of our agroecosystems, understanding their long-term evolutionary processes will be an inter-connecting and re-connecting

Steps of agroecosystem management.

priority. By selecting and utilizing the spoken-of 'emergent properties' from each interaction, the evolution can become consciously creative. The idea is that while growing our food and raising our animals, we first learn from and then direct the flow of evolution. The result of evolutionary creativity is diversity; therefore, as we promote diversity we improve resilience, energy flow and nutrient cycling.

This regenerative process can utilize a 'scale' approach to facilitate its understanding. Shown below are the classic examples of the levels in interacting scales within natural or agricultural systems (according to Odum, 1971) where: the lower levels of organization or complexity are to the left, and the higher levels to the right. Each scale could be further extended for each individual species, and from that investigation we could begin understanding the ecology of the system's inherent metabolism.

The boundaries between hierarchical levels may be visible, such as the skin of an organism or the shoreline of a lake, or intangible, as in the case between populations and species. We could say that the best seed, the best soil, and the most knowledgeable intention come together in a unified whole, inseparable. Each has evolved with the other – which means that the whole system had many either designed or natural bridges of connection. The less we disturb and the more we strengthen those bridges, the more we discover the source of resilience as our way of life.

Agroecology and Ecovillage

At Terra UNA Ecovillage we have been enhancing the emerging properties by designing our agroecosystems as resilient food webs. We are an active part of these food webs: we want to improve their metabolism and productivity so we never forget to prioritize the *relations* between species.

Agroecology is the introduction of agriculture into an existing ecological system.

In the actual practice of managing an agroecosystem, the flowers and the green manure are included to feed ants, bees, birds and micro-organisms. By doing that, we promote resilience due to a strengthened web that diminishes the inevitable herbivore and predation pressure on the yields of which we are concerned (in this case corn, beans, amaranto and manioc).

Here, the ecovillage meets the agroecology. As we design the agroecosystem to enhance diversity, we also invite the multicultural aspects present in the community to contribute to the flourishing. Flowers, animals, food, colours, smells and recipes are all included in the design strategy. The visual aspects are also considered: at Terra UNA we are working with more traditional cultural imagery, shapes, and geometries.

As an ecovillage, we don't ever want to miss the opportunity to celebrate and have fun while working with our agroecosystems. Somehow, Nature responds to our invitation by sending unforeseen and unimaginable 'gifts'. We have been learning that the power of diversity in community creates a strong bridge of mutual identification between the 'agroecology' and the 'ecovillage' approaches. Nature works with the power of diversity so deeply that we stand mesmerized, positioning ourselves as wide-eyed children exploring the world's mystery as if for the first time.

Diogo Alvim is a biologist, B.S. in Ecology and M.S. in Ecology in Agroecosystems. He is certified in permaculture by IPAB in Brasil and a beekeeper and the president and founder of Terra UNA Ecovillage project. A member of the Brasilian Ecovillage Network, he has served as coordinator and educator in the National Program of Education in Agrarian Reform in SC State for two years and coordinated an education project at the Registry of Green and the Environment of São Paulo. Now is part of the coordinating team of Gaia Education in Brasil as a member and as an educator, running the EDE in Rio de Janeiro with Terra UNA's team.

World-renowned speaker and entrepreneur Gunter Pauli takes us on a tour of what life would be like if we recognized the flows in our lives. Gunter shows quite clearly that recognizing flows is fundamental to designing healthy human systems. Modern buildings, especially, suppress natural flows, and this is the cause of many of our troubles. The author mentions six flows that need to be considered: air, light, sound, energy, matter, and people. I'm sure that after reading this article you will not only pay more attention to the flows in your designs, you also will understand 'design with the flow' as part of the larger science of 'making connections'.

Design with the Flow

Gunter Pauli – Zero Emissions Reduction Institute

Mirroring the macrocosmic connections of the earth in the universe, we focus on the immediate connections at the microcosm of our bodies. Whereas we have to be aware of what we eat and drink, and know how to manage our heath, it is also important to reflect on the structures in which we live. These have undergone major transformations; and even though we believe we are living in an age of 'modernity', it seems that quite a few realities about the way we live are missing quite a few basic connections.

Where do we spend most of our time? At home, at work, and at school. Remember that about eight hours a day are spent in bed. Perhaps another eight are spent in the office or in the classroom, so does it not seem logical that we reflect for a moment about all the connections that should be made when designing these places where we live our lives? What should be the first question we ask about the places where we will spend so many hours? Similarly, what is the most important question we should ask about our bodies?

Indeed, what is the pH of the air you breathe? Has it ever occurred to you that because you should eat as alkaline as possible, you should also *breathe* as alkaline as possible? And just as our food has turned acid over the years, the air we breathe has turned very acid as well. There is no escape possible. Due to our excessive use of fossil fuels and the massive amount of carbon dioxide that is pumped into the atmosphere every day, the air is acid, very acid indeed. If you live in a city, the pH is guaranteed to be below 6.

However, we each have the opportunity to create our own little cosmos at home, at school, or at work. The next time you talk to an architect, ask about the projected pH level this masterpiece of design will offer the people using the building. I am convinced that even the greenest of architects will never have thought about this key fact of life. It is part of our compartmentalization of life: acidity is for the chemists and not for the architects.

If you take the time to check the pH of the air in your house, you will quickly realize that the air from the outside is acid, compounded by the fact that just about everything in your home or office will be off-gassing more acids. So what is the use of making certain you drink and eat alkaline when in the end you need to also breathe alkaline? It is possible, actually quite easy, to achieve alkalinity in buildings on the condition that physical structures are not thought of as static but rather as areas that have multiple flows. If we understand the flows and how to design out what generates acidity and design in what offers alkalinity, within a general context of beauty and functionality, then we will see the emergence of completely new comfort and health levels.

There are seven major flows through a building: air, water, light, sound, people, energy, and matter. It is interesting that vernacular designs of dwellings accommodated the intensive flows of all. Over the years, architects have aimed at reducing the flow of air, in particular, such that lately, in order to save energy, many buildings have become so insulated that hardly any air gets in or out. The walls do not breathe anymore; the roofs do not seep. Whereas the aim of saving energy is to be applauded, shutting out the flow of air is not healthy. Is it possible to have airflow and at the same time save energy? Of course it is!

Airflow through the building has multiple benefits. Dust and increasing amounts of minute toxic substances vacate the building. Yet, the mere flow is not enough; there is a need to *cleanse* the air, and to bring more oxygen into the building. In natural systems, there are always plants and micro-algae involved, and it is not difficult to recreate this kind of environment. A small company has pioneered the concept of "living filters", a collection of 300 different plants strategically located throughout buildings, with a permanently lit environment that cleanses the air – and, if choices are well-made, will enrich the air, leaving it nice and…alkaline.

When the building is closed up and insulated, humidity gets trapped inside. This is the main reason fungus appears, especially in basements where there is no flow of light either. How do we 'fight' fungus? Expert companies treat the walls with metal oxides, which off-gas for a couple years, freeing you of the worry of fungus. However, this makes the air full of particles that should not be inhaled at all. Actually, we create conditions for the fungus to thrive; and in our 'cause and effect' simple way of thinking, without realizing the barriers to the flow of air we've created, decide that the best solution is to call the expert with the chemicals. If, on the other hand, we designed buildings to have airflow through the basement, then we'd eliminate the conditions for fungus, thus reducing spores in the air which cause respiratory diseases.

The next flow that needs consideration is water. What is the use of water in any building? Whereas we like to think that the main purpose of water is drinking, without exception the biggest use of water in houses – and definitely in schools and office building – is actually for toilets. It seems that whereas we are blocking the flow of light and air in modern buildings, we are exaggerating the flow of water. Why?

Imagine that it took our bodies, yes our human bodies, millions of years to design a digestive system whereby at the end of a lengthy and delicate process we excrete the solids through one channel and the liquids are discharged through another. And to think, in modern buildings, the first thing we do is mix them with… drinking water! If our method of acquiring nutrients were to blend solid and liquid waste, then why do we have this complex system of kidneys, liver and intestines? And if drinking water can be thought of as a 'commons', for which everyone should have ample access, how can we dump these waste products into the drinking water? It seems that we are not seeing the connections (again).

Water is the most precious substance on Earth. Drinking-water is expensive and not easily available to the whole population, so why do we spoil water by mixing feces and urine in it? Urine is a wonderful liquid. It is very rich in potassium, one of the core components for making our hearts pump. Urine should not be wasted but should be ploughed back into the nutrient cycle. Did we forget that the Roman emperor had the royal privilege of collecting urine from his citizens? Today, urine and feces are simply discharged and imagined 'gone and vanished'. In reality, they end up in expensive water treatment systems where the organic matter is chemically treated through the expense of massive energy.

The feces are a different matter. After all, that is the reason why they are separated from the urine in the first place. If you combine feces and urine, you get a typical smell, one that we really do not like around us. If you keep feces and urine separate, as was intended, then there is no smell on the condition that there is a flow of air that dries out the feces rather quickly. That is the function of the dry separation toilet that has been designed and operated for many years, while fine-tuned in recent history by Dr. Matts Wolgast, the Swedish scientist from Uppsala University.

If we reduce the flow of water by eliminating the need to use water as the transporter of feces and urine to central water treatment plants where E. Coli and Salmonella thrive, then we save a lot of risks that are linked to dealing with these potential carriers of illness. We are, of course, aware of the danger and therefore pour harsh chemicals into the system so that we can control the potential bacterial infections. Whereas bactericides eliminate the risk of diseases, they also render the water totally useless. There is no reason to deal with the health consequences of mixing feces and urine by adding chemicals – simply do not mix the two as was originally intended!

We think of water as the liquid that flows through pipes from somewhere where it is in abundance to wherever it is needed. Cities have established a vast network of water redistribution. Imagine the thousands of miles of pipe that bring water from the Colorado River to distribute throughout Los Angeles. Imagine the huge investments upstate New York is making to install septic tanks in order to preserve its catchment area. And now imagine what happens to all that rainwater? It is simply drained away! How can this be possible? The state of Colorado even prohibits residents from capturing rainwater; yet at a time when water is increasingly costly, how could it ever be permitted to simply flow into a sewage system when it could generate electricity or offer irrigation to farmers?

Time has come to think of water as the most precious resource on Earth. Our body is over 80% water. If you do not drink at least one liter of water per day you simply will not survive. So how come we treat water the way we do? We simply do not see the flows. Rainfall is the most natural way of capturing water. Every building and every street has large catchment areas that could be used to capture and channel water towards its immediate uses – without the need for pumps or treatments.

The rain falls on the roof and on the parking lot and there is no reason to let it all go down the drain. But a lot of moisture in the air is simply not recognized. We need to learn from the Namibian desert beetle or the *Welwitschia mirabilis*, the desert plant that shares the know-how with the beetle on how to condense water from the air. Have you ever observed your aircon? It drips water all the time. Have you ever asked yourself how much water flows from "the air"? Have you ever seen the cooling towers on top of office buildings? These towers are known to sweat. If the air expelled from the top of the building were to glide along a combined hydrophobic and hydrophilic surface, it would be the equivalent of a river channeling hundreds of cubic meters of water per day from the roof ... to the basement. Interestingly, when we study the flow of air from the cooling towers we are discovering flows of water from the top of the building down. That is reducing energy consumption and cutting down on water needs at the same time since water on top does not need to be pumped. Is this reality, or simply a dream?

Our understanding of how the flows of air, light, people, sound, energy, water, and matter shape the structures that we inhabit brings new insights into how Nature creates structures that accommodate these flows. On the other hand it gives us some very practical insights on how to build our homes, offices and schools beyond cost and functionality. Let us look at the flow of sound. The groundbreaking work of Alexander Lautenwasser offers a glimpse of something scientists will struggle with for decades to come. Lautenwasser took a drop of water, put it on a metal plate and turned on the sound machine. Sound is a wave, and these waves come at different levels or frequencies. The water starts moving around when the sound waves hit the metal plate, and different waves generate different patterns of movement. The movements are predictable, in that at specific frequencies there are associated types of movement. A minimal change in the wave causes a corresponding change in the movement, which can be quite complex.

So the flow of sound is causing the shape of the structure that emerges around this body of water. How does that apply to our bodies? Remember how some pediatricians suggest that expecting moms should listen to music, should chant like Gregorian and Tibetan monks? New insights are born; and of course this is only a hypothesis but we can see how new and creative ideas emerge when we start making connections. The hypothesis is that the sound causes water to flow and so the heart is shaped interactively according to the flows of specific types of water (blood). Interesting thought, the effect of sound on the fluids in our body.

Another observation is related to the most vulnerable in society: young children. Children are exposed to multiple flows which shape and form them.

Some of these flows we cannot do anything about; others we can. Once we start seeing the connections, we have the responsibility to channel these flows for the best of health and mind for the next generation. Two areas come to my mind: the bedroom and the school. Little babies spend more than half of their early life in a cradle sleeping their time away, building up those unique systems that will give personality and body. It is absolutely necessary that we start thinking in terms of the flows through these rooms where the infants are growing, so that we can give them the best possible start in life. If the room is full of formaldehyde (glue in the particle-board, carpet flooring, wall paper), heavy metals (bright colors, bactericides and fungicides), brominated fire retardants (mattress, bedding), and heavily chlorinated water, then we know the flows in the room will not permit the healthiest evolution for the child. Katherina Tiddens, the pioneer founder of the Terra Verde store in Soho, New York, gave up her store of healthy ecological products to dedicate all her time and energy to the design of cribs and interiors that are free of chemicals, where the air is fresh and the children can build up their immune systems without the risk of allergies and respiratory ailments which affect today up to 30 percent of the children in cities.

Imagine a school building where over 100 core concepts of physics, biology and chemistry are visibly included in the layout and structure of the place. This is not a demo in a lab; this is actually using the laws of physics in good design. One law states that hot air-rises and cold air-drops; this understanding can be used to maintain a comfortable temperature in a room, especially if it is combined with wind flow in the case of low and high pressure zones being equalized. Basically, the building combines meteorology with the basic principles of airflows to maintain constant temperature and humidity amid changing pressures. Imagine a school building where the highly efficient light bulbs shine day and night onto 100 varieties of plants (what a lesson in biodiversity of plants!) which are automatically sprinkled every 15 minutes with evaporated rainwater that was collected off the roof. The level of dust particles and air pollutants flowing in from outside, or generated inside, is kept very low. The inner walls, which are usually just filled with air and some insulation material, are now filled with shredded seashells and dried seaweed. This not only serves as a wonderful sound barrier, dried seaweed absorbs up to ten times its own weight in moisture while being highly alkaline. There is no risk of fungus attacking this building, and no need to have chemicals sprayed to chase mites from the carpets. Why? Because the air flows in the building combined with the materials turn the humidity stable and the pH alkaline.

Imagine human habitation systems of structures that accommodate and encourage flows of air, light, sound, energy, matter, and people! That is designing with the flow!

Gunter Pauli is an entrepreneur whose initiatives span business, science, culture and education. He is the founder of ZERI and the author of numerous books, including: *The Blue Economy: 100 Innovations*. At present, he publishes a series of one hundred innovative business models at a rate of one per week on **www.blueeconomy.de**

"Imagine: you've assembled a group of people who will form the nucleus of your new ecovillage, you've bought the land. There you stand, blank sheet in front of you. What do you do?" So begins experienced permaculture teacher and author Patrick Whitefield in this summation essay to the Ecological Key. Patrick answers his question in characteristic permaculture fashion: by focusing on the design! According to the author, the most important concept is that of listening, including 'listening to the land'. An overview of the four basic design strategies – zone, sector, network, and elevation – is then provided. This is no-nonsense permaculture, the very basis of the Ecological dimension of ecovillage designing.

A Design Framework

Patrick Whitefield – Patrick Whitefield Associates, Glastonbury, England

There can be no better illustration than these Four Keys of the wide array of skills and techniques which can contribute to a sustainable future. The question remains, how can they be put together in a coherent whole? Imagine: you've assembled a group of people who will form the nucleus of your new ecovillage, you've bought the land. There you stand, blank sheet in front of you. What do you do?

This is where permaculture comes in. Many people have an image of permaculture as being somewhat wild and woolly, and to some extent it is. Its essential idea is to take natural ecosystems as the model for our own farms, gardens, buildings and settlements. Natural ecosystems are not only more sustainable than anything we currently do, they also have a higher overall yield of biomass and, of course, a much lower need for external inputs. The catch is that very little of that biomass is edible to humans. The aim of permaculture is to create systems which have all the advantages of natural ecosystems combined with a high level of output which is useful to humans, in a phrase, 'edible ecosystems'.

In its original form permaculture focused on imitating natural ecosystems in a fairly direct way. Its key characteristics included, amongst others, a high level of plant diversity, growing perennial food crops rather than annuals, and not disturbing the soil by digging or ploughing. These are typical characteristics of natural ecosystems which can be observed and reproduced empirically in food-growing systems. An example of this approach is the forest garden, which mimics the structure of a natural woodland but replaces native plants with edible equivalents: fruit and nut trees, fruit bushes and perennial vegetables. This kind of permaculture can indeed look a bit wild and woolly. I call it 'original' permaculture.

But before long permaculturists began to look beyond the visible characteristics of ecosystems and ask what is the basic principle which enables them to be so high-yielding and self-reliant. The answer lies in diversity, but not so much in the diversity of the component species themselves as in the diversity of beneficial relationships between them. One example of this kind of relationship is that between the flowering plants and the pollinating insects, in which one gets its food need met and the other its reproductive needs. An ecosystem consists of a whole network of relationships of this kind, both between living organisms and between the living and non-living components of the ecosystem such as soil, water and climate.

An example of how beneficial relationships can be created in a human system can be seen in a productive conservatory – a greenhouse attached to the wall of a house. The conservatory collects solar energy and passes some of it on to the house in the form of space heating. Energy is also stored in the wall of the house and re-radiated at night, keeping the conservatory frost-free and warmer than a free-standing greenhouse. Thus each helps to warm the other. The greenhouse is relatively narrow from front to back, but wide, running all the way along the most southerly-facing wall of the house (in the northern hemisphere). This ensures maximum gain of heat and minimum loss. The conservatory is also used for raising vegetable plants in the spring, and the ease of visiting what is in effect another room of your house, compared to going to an outside greenhouse in inclement weather, means that the seedlings get more attention. This means they get off to a better start in life, which is a very important factor in the final performance of the crop.

A house with conservatory attached doesn't look like an ecosystem but it shares its most important characteristic: a network of beneficial relationships. The relationships include those between people and plants; people are an integral part of the system, not something which stands outside of it. This kind of permaculture isn't dependent on direct imitations of nature; it depends on placing things in relation to each other so that beneficial relationships can be formed between them. In short it's a matter of functional design. I call this approach 'design' permaculture. It can be practiced with or without the characteristics of original permaculture, though in practice most permaculture contains elements of both.

So how can design permaculture benefit the group of ecovillage pioneers with their newly-acquired land? The most important concept is that of listening. The main function of the permaculture designer is to listen to the people and observe the land. In fact, in my teaching I use the metaphor 'listening to the land', which suggests a degree of intimacy and humility in our approach to the landscape. It's from a deep understanding of the needs of the unique set of people who are to inhabit that piece of land and the unique characteristics of the land itself that a successful design can flow. The less the ego of the designer comes into it the better. In fact the best designer is the group themselves, working together, though a design consultant can be invaluable to guide them through the process.

In fact, the design process really needs to start before acquiring the land.

The aim of permaculture is to design productive, multifunctional landscapes within human systems.

It has been known for people to buy land and only afterwards discover that it's unsuitable for their aims. I'm thinking in particular of a group who bought a farm with the idea of planting a lot of trees only to discover that it was a rare repository of those sun-loving meadow wildflowers which have so nearly become extinct here in Britain. To plant trees over them would have been to kill them. It was a dilemma they never resolved as far as I know.

The listening part of the process comes first and foremost. Then comes the stage of evaluation and analysis of the information received and later the formulation of the design itself. Many methods can be used in these stages but prominent among them is what we call the key planning tools. These comprise the concepts of zone, sector, network and elevation.

By zone, we mean the amount of human attention which a piece of land receives. Crops and activities which need the most attention are placed where they will receive it with the least effort. In our ecovillage example, faced with a choice between a small back garden or an allotment some distance away, the wise permaculturist may forgo the allotment and grow their fruit and vegetables in the garden. The constant presence of the gardener means that production can be many times more intensive and the garden may outyield an allotment several times its size. In addition, more frequent harvesting means that a greater proportion of what's grown actually gets eaten. Although simple, this is a wonderfully powerful design tool for use on any scale, whether a single household, a farm or a whole settlement.

While the concept of zone deals with the human energy centred on the site, sector is about off-site factors which affect it. These include wind, light and shade, water, views, neighbours, and pollution. Many of these are climatic factors and the concept of microclimate – the characteristic climate of a small area – is important in permaculture design. Whilst creating a totally new microclimate, such as a conservatory, can be worthwhile it's not the first priority. The first step is to observe the site carefully through all the seasons and then match the planting to the various microclimates the site contains. For example, a tough fruiting tree such as a damson will yield as well in a windy or shady spot as it will in a south-facing sun trap. Not so a peach. Matching the plants to the microclimates available means that a wider range of plants can be grown, including more demanding ones, and the overall yield of the system will be higher than if they were placed at random.

Network is similar to zone but it comes to bear when there is more than one centre of human activity, so it's not relevant in the design of a single household but very much so on the scale of an ecovillage. It's concerned with access and links between different nodes of activity. All the elements, such as houses, communal buildings, gardens, orchards, fields and ponds, need to be placed in such a way that movement between one and another flows easily and effortlessly. Analysis of each link needs to include: frequency of movement; the kind of movement – from parents with push-chairs to farm animals to vehicles; and the acceptable distance – in the case of housing, for example, to avoid both extremes of crowding and isolation. One way of carrying out network analysis is to make a basic map of the terrain and card cut-outs of all the elements which need to go in it. Then it's rather like an enormous game of chess, though with a practical view in end.

Elevation is concerned with altitude, both relative and absolute, and with degree of slope. It's particularly relevant when dealing with water, both in domestic and broadscale situations. For example, the conventional approach to siting a pond for farmland irrigation is to place it on flat ground at the bottom of the slope and use fuel to pump the water to wherever it's needed. The permaculture approach is to find a spot which combines three characteristics: low enough in the landscape to be able to collect water; high enough so that it's above the area to be irrigated; and on a relatively flat piece of land for economy of construction – you need a taller dam to make a pond of given size on a steep slope than on a more gradual one. A pond in such a position may have to be a little smaller or may be a little more difficult to construct than one sited on the flat land at the bottom. But throughout the fuel-hungry ages which stretch before us it will irrigate the land entirely by gravity.

When they're used together as a set, the synergistic effect of these planning tools is powerful. They're far from being the only design methods used by permaculturists but they are perhaps the most effective. A frequent theme which runs through them is the reduction of energy expenditure, both human and fossil fuel. In the examples I've chosen here, more food is produced per unit of energy invested; tender fruit can be grown without the need for glasshouses or imports; journeys can be made by foot instead of powered transport; and water is available where it's needed without any

Polycropping as a study of interspecies communication and co-evolutionary genetic fitness.

pumping. In the past, human needs were met largely by muscle power, which meant unremitting drudgery for the majority of the population. In the present, our needs are met by throwing unlimited quantities of under-priced fossil fuel at any problem. People often assume that these are the only two options but permaculture seeks to provide a third, one which is based on design.

Most of the elements of permaculture design, from conservatories to irrigation ponds, are not unique to it. Even the less familiar elements which are associated with original permaculture, such as the forest garden, have their equivalents in other parts of the world or in other times. The contribution which permaculture brings to the practice of sustainability is less to do with the elements it contains than the connections between them. The network of beneficial relationships which characterises a permaculture system is an alternative to the excessive use of energy which is characteristic of present-day systems. Although I'm focusing here on energy use, permaculture is about much more than energy, just as the challenges which face us in the 21st century are not confined to climate change and peak oil. But these are certainly the biggest and most urgent of those challenges and permaculture has an important role to play in confronting them.

Whatever design methods are used, a great emphasis is placed on the early stages of observing and listening. The temptation to rush into making design decisions early on is always there, but a good, workable design is unlikely to result if the receptive part of the process is rushed. Listening rather than speaking, valuing the passive above the active, is the antithesis of our contemporary culture. We find it very hard to do. Yet it's a cultural change we need to make if we are to learn to live with nature rather than in spite of her.

Patrick Whitefield originally trained in agriculture and worked on farms in various parts of the world before returning to his home country in Somerset, England. Here he has grown vegetables, practised country crafts, planted trees, lived close to nature and was for a while a prominent member of the British Green Party. He finds permaculture makes use of all his skills and experiences and puts them in a coherent whole. He is a leading permaculture teacher and has written a number of books on the subject including the standard work for temperate countries, *The Earth Care Manual*. For more, see: **www.patrickwhitefield.co.uk**

*During a recent study called 'Consciousness and Human Development', I was introduced to many new interesting terms, concepts, and theories. One notion I recognized as a continuous thread that wound its way through many of my previous favorite writings. This notion is simple enough to say yet so very profound in its implications: the environments in which we live affect our consciousness. If this is so, then it must be possible to design environments that actually **enhance** consciousness. Could this not be the ultimate goal of an ecovillage designer? This article is one of my first attempts at elucidating this new potential.*

Ecology of Consciousness

E. Christopher Mare – Village Design Institute, Cascadia

What is an 'ecology of consciousness?' Let's begin like Socrates by defining our terms: "The word ecology is derived from the Greek *oikos*, meaning 'house' or 'place to live'. Literally, ecology is the study of organisms 'at home'. Usually ecology is defined as the study of the relations of organisms or groups of organisms to their environment, or the science of interrelations between living organisms and their environment." (Odum, 1959, p. 3) The key word here is *relations*; for ecology can be considered much more than a 'science'. In a broader sense, ecology can be viewed as a way of perceiving the world, a world literally teeming with relationships. This perspective has serious implications for a socio-economic order founded on the sanctity of the individual, so much so that Paul Shepard, during the 'consciousness revolution' of the '60s, was moved to describe ecology as 'the subversive science'. Ecology can be 'subversive' because with ecological understanding there is less meaning to be gained from looking at individuals in isolation than knowing how these individuals exist and interact *in relationship*.

Consciousness is a slipperier term: One study (Baruss, 1987) found that the word 'consciousness' can assume 29 different definitions! As ecovillage designers, which definition are we to align with? Well, for the purpose of this article, why don't we align with the definition formed by an ecologist? According to Cotterill (2000), consciousness is "intimately connected to self-paced probing of the environment... present even in the simplest monocellular organisms" (p. 283). "Consciousness lies at the operational interface between body movement and the body's surroundings" (p. 285). I like this image very much, for it means that consciousness is not a 'thing' that one 'possesses', as an isolated individual, but rather is an 'operational interface', a relationship. Consciousness is not contained simply 'in the head' but rather is a product of relationship – the inherent, mutually-defining relationship between a body and its environment. Does this mean that the quality of the environment could influence the quality of consciousness?

I think the eminent Chilean biologists Humberto Maturana and Francisco Varela would answer with a resounding '**yes**'. They developed a concept called 'structural coupling', an iteration of the 'interface' theme as defined by Cotterill. According to this concept, "the organism both initiates and is shaped by the environment... we must see the organism and environment as bound together in reciprocal specification and selection" (Varela, et al., 1991, p. 174). What this means is that the quality of consciousness is not a 'pre-given' – that is, already formed and determined at birth – but rather is the result of an ongoing history of 'structural coupling', or 'operational interface', between an organism and its environment. "As humans shape the systems in and through which they live, they are in turn shaped by their human systems" (Jantsch, 1975, p. 61). Or, in the stately words of Winston Churchill: "We shape our buildings, and afterward our buildings shape us" (quoted in Dubos, 1968, p. 190). Apparently, after World War II there was a proposal to build an entirely new House of Commons to replace the one that had been damaged in the war. Churchill strongly rejected this proposal on the grounds that conducting government in a new building would irretrievably alter the nature of the dialogue that had proceeded for centuries. The House of Commons was repaired instead.

Now that we have defined our terms, it is possible to move forward with a synthesis: 'ecology of consciousness' is the understanding that states of awareness (consciousness) are facilitated – even defined – by the nature of the ecology through which the perceiving body must move. But what exactly does this mean in real life?

Think about the Greek root for 'ecology' – *oikos*, meaning 'home' or 'place to live'. Now imagine two persons living in two very different kinds of places: The first person lives in the core of a large crowded city, and the second person lives in a dispersed suburb at the fringe of a metropolitan area. What will consciousness be like for these two people?

For the first person – let's call her Maria – there is an overload of discordant vibrations: intrusive traffic sounds, jackhammers, sirens, glares, helicopters, strange smells, unwelcome stares, and all sorts of electro-magnetic radiation. There is such an overload that Maria gradually becomes de-sensitized: her nervous system begins to shut down to protect itself. Perhaps Maria is living in a square room up on the 12th floor from where she is never able to step out onto the grass and smell the flowers. As soon as she goes down to street level and steps outside the door, she is surrounded by strangers, so she must put up a psychological defense barrier. There is great danger moving through this urban ecology, so Maria must remain hyper-vigilant, always scanning her surroundings to be on guard for a possible threat. As a result of living in these conditions day after day, Maria's body begins to become rigid, her posture slightly bent over to protect the heart area, her *chi* or life-force no longer flowing freely.

For the second person – shall we say John – there is adequate open space with plenty of trees, yet a conspicuous lack of people. The only people

John sees are encapsulated in the shells of their little automobiles. John has neighbors but he rarely gets a chance to interact with them because as soon as they return home they drive into their garage and disappear into the house. If John needs food, or medicine, or a job, he too must get into his little automobile and drive all over the metropolitan area. This means that his experience of the suburban ecology is always mitigated or deafened by the steel enclosure in which he must move; thus John's nervous system also becomes de-sensitized, his body posture accustomed to an unnatural sitting position with legs forward and hands on the wheel. Lacking meaningful stimulation with people or environment, John, like many of his neighbors, starts to feel isolated. He, like they, increasingly turn to artificial stimuli – electronic media, drugs and alcohol, consumerism, dysfunctional nuclear-family dynamics – in an attempt to fill the empty niche.

While these two examples may be situated at extremes, and while I may have dabbled in stereotyping (please excuse me if these portrayals represent people you know), the purpose was to highlight clearly the relationship that exists between states of awareness (consciousness) and the nature of the ecology through which the perceiving body must move. In both cases above, the nature of the ecology – the relationships that exist in the environment – compels the nervous system to de-sensitize. In the first case, a modern urban ecology, there are far too much stimuli, especially of an aggravating kind, so the nervous system begins to shut down. In the second case, a typical suburban ecology, there are not enough stimuli; the relationships existing in the environment do not enable satisfying interaction and so the nervous system begins looking for artificial stimulation. From this perspective, we could determine that the interface between ecology and a moving body is mediated and translated through a nervous system, and it is the activation or stimulation of this nervous system that produces states of awareness that we call consciousness. Obviously, then, if we want to expand or enhance consciousness we must learn how to create ecologies that activate or stimulate the nervous system in a most optimal, beneficial way.

In order to test this hypothesis, let's imagine a third person living in an 'ecovillage'. The ecovillage, by definition (Gilman, 1991), is symbiotically integrated into the local ecology, so there is an interesting interface between fractal Nature and the ordered built environment where the humans live. The ecovillage is compact, segregated into clusters of residential units which encourage 'variations on a theme' and a sense of inter-identity that complements the overall village identity. The ecovillage is arranged to have a well-defined boundary with a well-defined entrance, so there is a comforting sense of enclosure when one is 'in' the ecovillage and a sense of psychological transition as one exits 'out' into the greater unknown. The ecovillage also has a well-defined center which supports the possibility for feelings of common unity. As one moves away from the center towards a cluster, the feeling of unity transitions into a sense of subculture identity which then further evolves into a feeling of full individual identity as one enters a personal living space. So, in this case, we can see how the general

Perhaps the finest examples of ecovillages were built long ago.

morphology of the settlement ecology facilitates a variety of states of awareness: consciousness has multiple perspectives of 'parts within wholes' from which to view its experience: the nervous system is continually engaged in orienting itself in space and time with nested levels of differentiation, all contained within a complex yet coherent whole.

Now what would it look like to take this idea to finer levels of detail and, as designers, begin to imagine the interior circulation patterns of the ecovillage? Of course it is axiomatic that automobiles are left at the edge, so it is an interesting 'pedestrian environment' that we are creating for people walking or riding bicycles, maybe even horses and carts and electric shuttles. First off, avoid straight lines! The roads and pathways should conform to, even amplify, the existing features of the terrain. Pay special attention to 'view corridors' and existing landmarks such as special trees or rock outcroppings. The experience of moving through the space should be like a gentle massage for the nervous system: exceptional views or features should be approached with a sense of anticipation, gradually unfolding their splendor as the perceiving body moves around a curve, partly obscuring their approach behind some plantings, fencing, or buildings. In this kind of way, the nervous system always is actively involved with expectation, eagerness, possibly excitement; the awareness is continually drawn to the next level of experience, fulfillment, or understanding. This is an example of organizing the ecology so as to enhance consciousness.

We can then take the design to even deeper degrees of refinement. What does it take to optimally stimulate a nervous system? We can knowingly choose and work with the full palette of design enhancements, activating awareness at ever more subtle levels: colors, hues, textures, scents, sounds, shapes, harmonies and rhythms and reiterations on a theme, depth perception, the characteristics of various plants and the rotation of blooms through a season, the skilled placement of various water features and artwork, etc. We can become familiar with what are called 'sacred geometries', incorporating proportions according to the Golden Mean and the Fibonacci spiral. We can explore disciplines such as Feng Shui and Geomancy, learning how to perceive and work with the unseen energies of a site, designing around vortexes and ley lines and accumulated past histories. We can assume a fourth-dimensional perspective and realize that all is in flux, in evolution, and every act of the present becomes the seedbed for future potentialities. In short, there are infinite design possibilities for managing a site to achieve its optimal potential.

The 'ecology of consciousness' is truly a multi-faceted, multi-dimensional, multi-disciplinary perspective that assumes that our potentials as human beings are intimately connected to the quality of the environments in which we live. Once we have integrated this understanding, it becomes clear that the most important thing we can do, as a species, is to design holistic environments that actually *enhance consciousness* – places where the people moving through them experience a sudden flash of their latent possibilities, a palpable intuition that they are part of a larger and more perfect whole. The ecovillages of the world have taken the first step in grounding this ideal into reality. We, as students of Ecovillage Design in the 21st century, have the opportunity to advance their precedent to the next level by educating ourselves to be proficient designers of human habitation systems, systems that can bring out the very best in human potential. This kind of yoga would be an expression of the 'ecology of consciousness' that was introduced as subject matter in this essay. What kind of work could be more, shall we say, regenerative?

Further exploration of this theme could include a review of Bateson's *Steps to an Ecology of Mind* (1972), seeking to understand the 'difference that makes a difference' between an 'ecology of consciousness' and an 'ecology of mind', and Goonatilake's more recent "Knowledge as an Ecology" (2006). Also vitally important would be understanding the effects of 'wilderness' – a theoretically undisturbed ecology – on consciousness.

References

Baruss, I. (1987) "Meta-analysis of definitions of consciousness." *Imagination, Cognition and Personality,* Vol. 6, pp. 321-329

Bateson, G. (1972) *Steps to an Ecology of Mind.* Ballantine Books; New York

Cotterill, R.M.J. (2000) "Did consciousness evolve from self-paced probing of the environment and not from reflexes?" *Brain and Mind,* Vol. 1, pp. 283-298, Kluwer Academic Publishers; Netherlands

Dubos, R. (1968) *So Human an Animal.* Charles Scribner's Sons; New York

Gilman, R., et al. (1991) *Ecovillages and Sustainable Communities.* A Report for Gaia Trust by Context Institute; Bainbridge Island, WA

Goonatilake, S. (2006) "Knowledge as an ecology". *Theory, Culture & Society,* Vol. 23, pp. 170-172

Jantsch, E. (1975) *Design for Evolution: Self-Organization and Planning in the Life of Human Systems.* George Braziller; New York

Odum, E. (1959) *Fundamentals of Ecology.* W.B. Saunders Company; Philadelphia and London

Shepard, P. and D. McKinley, editors (1969) *The Subversive Science: Essays Toward an Ecology of Man.* Houghton Mifflin Company; Boston

Varela, et al. (1991) *The Embodied Mind: Cognitive Science and Human Experience.* MIT Press; Cambridge, MA

E. Christopher Mare has been a full-time student since 1994. He has been given the luxury of self-designed programs in which he gets to organize his own studies. The general progression of interest over the years has been: Permaculture to Ecovillage to Urban Village to Traditional Village to Design for Consciousness. In 2002, Mare founded an educational non-profit – Village Design Institute – which will one day secure a land-base for the purpose of setting up a combination 1) research, training, and demonstration site; 2) Academy of Village Design; and 3) community of contemplative scholars. This project most likely will be called an 'ecovillage'.

More books from Permanent Publications

   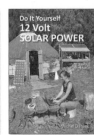 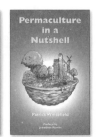

  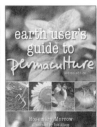 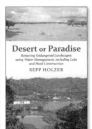 

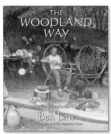   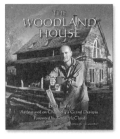

ALL THESE & MORE AVAILABLE FROM:

www.permanentpublications.co.uk

AVAILABLE IN THE U.S.A. FROM:

www.chelseagreen.com